Pursuing Practical Change

Pursuing Practical Change

Lesson Designs That Promote Culturally Responsive Teaching

Heather Dean and Amber E. Wagnon

ROWMAN & LITTLEFIELD
Lanham • Boulder • New York • London

Published by Rowman & Littlefield
An imprint of The Rowman & Littlefield Publishing Group, Inc.
4501 Forbes Boulevard, Suite 200, Lanham, Maryland 20706
www.rowman.com
86-90 Paul Street, London EC2A 4NE

Copyright © 2024 by Heather Dean and Amber E. Wagnon

All rights reserved. No part of this book may be reproduced in any form or by any electronic or mechanical means, including information storage and retrieval systems, without written permission from the publisher, except by a reviewer who may quote passages in a review.

British Library Cataloguing in Publication Information Available

Library of Congress Cataloging-in-Publication Data

Names: Dean, Heather, 1973- author. | Wagnon, Amber E., 1981- author.
Title: Pursuing practical change : lesson designs that promote culturally responsive teaching / Heather Dean and Amber E. Wagnon.
Description: Lanham, Maryland : Rowman & Littlefield, [2024] | Includes bibliographical references.
Identifiers: LCCN 2023055646 (print) | LCCN 2023055647 (ebook) | ISBN 9781475862805 (cloth) | ISBN 9781475862812 (paperback) | ISBN 9781475862829 (epub)
Subjects: LCSH: Culturally relevant pedagogy. | Multicultural education.
Classification: LCC LC1099.515.C85 D43 2024 (print) | LCC LC1099.515.C85 (ebook) | DDC 370.117--dc23/eng/20231213
LC record available at https://lccn.loc.gov/2023055646
LC ebook record available at https://lccn.loc.gov/2023055647

*To my past and current students at California State University,
Stanislaus. You have courageously chosen the path of education
in an era when education is often under attack.
With persistence, you meet the requirements
set before you to become a teacher.
With sacrifice, you give up both sleep and time with family to craft
lesson plans, attend classes, and dedicate yourself to your students.
With love, you invest in the future of the Central
Valley, and our community is better for it.
Thank you for being a continual reminder to me of the hope and joy
within the profession of teaching! I wish the world could see what I see!*

*With my admiration and appreciation,
Heather Dean*

*To Sherri, my cherished friend who brought joy and laughter to
many lives. This dedication is a tribute to your incredible spirit
and the impact you made as a teacher, mother, and friend. I will
always remember your quick wit and dry sense of humor that
brightened our days. Though you may have lost your battle with
cancer, your spirit remains eternally vibrant in our hearts.*

Amber

Contents

Acknowledgments ix

Introduction xi
    Amber E. Wagnon

Chapter 1: Caring for All Students as the Foundation for Language Arts Instruction 1
    Jennifer Rumsey

Chapter 2: History Is Not Static and Unchanging: Using Culturally Responsive Teaching to Develop Critical Social Science Thinking Skills and Active Citizenship 19
    Leona Calkins

Chapter 3: Culturally Responsive Mathematics Instruction 41
    Dana Mayhall

Chapter 4: Empowering Scientific Minds: Integrating Cultural Perspectives in an Inclusive Classroom 57
    Harleen Singh and Jose Pavez

Chapter 5: Caring for Body *and Soul* in Physical Education 95
    Derek R. Riddle

Chapter 6: Culturally Responsive Teaching in Music and Theater Classrooms 113
    Daniel Bryan and Lindsay Bryan

Chapter 7: Culturally Responsive Teaching with the Visual Arts 125
    Lauren Burrow

Chapter 8: Cultural Inclusivity and Gamification: Addressing Diversity in the Twenty-First-Century World Language Classroom   151
Jon McFarland

Chapter 9: Culturally Responsive Teaching in a Virtual Classroom   177
Heather Dean

About the Authors   199

Acknowledgments

We would like to thank all of the contributing authors within this book. They love this profession and are dedicated to both the science and the art of teaching. Most importantly, they love and care deeply for the students that come and go through the years.

Thank you for sharing with other educators your heart and the lessons you are learning and perfecting! We are thankful to share this journey with you!

With much appreciation,
Heather Dean and Amber E. Wagnon

Introduction

Amber E. Wagnon

Education either functions as an instrument which is used to facilitate integration of the younger generation into the logic of the present system and bring about conformity or it becomes the practice of freedom, the means by which men and women deal critically and creatively with reality and discover how to participate in the transformation of their world.

—Paulo Freire, *Pedagogy of the Oppressed*

WHAT YOU CAN EXPECT FROM THE TEXT

- Each chapter in this text is written by classroom teachers and education professionals with preservice and in-service educators in mind.
- Each chapter examines how the authors have implemented culturally responsive teaching in their content area.
- Each chapter includes a personal narrative from an educator, lesson plans that incorporate elements of culturally responsive teaching, and a reflection on the lesson plan.

THEORETICAL FRAMEWORK

Culturally Relevant Pedagogy (CRP) and Culturally Responsive Teaching (CRT)

While you will see many of our chapter authors cite both Ladson-Billings's and Gay's theoretical framework, it is important to understand the differences between culturally relevant pedagogy (CRP) and culturally responsive teaching (CRT).

Culturally Relevant Pedagogy

While in graduate school in the 1970s Gloria Ladson-Billings began to observe teachers and found that the exceptional teachers did not share pedagogical strategies but "a set of underlying beliefs that drove their teaching" (Ladson-Billings, 2021, p. 3). Through these observations, Ladson-Billings formulated the theory of culturally relevant pedagogy (CRP). Ladson-Billings defined CRP as a "theoretical model that not only addresses student achievement but also helps students to accept and affirm their cultural identity while developing critical perspectives that challenge inequities that schools perpetuate" (1995, p. 469).

In her most recent publication, Ladson-Billings explained that while she finds schools and teachers speaking about CRP, she often finds they "interchange it with terms like culturally responsive teaching" (2021, p. 4). She goes on to explain that "while each of these notions has merit, they do not all do the same thing or seek to produce the same outcomes" (Ladson-Billings, 2021, p. 4). Ladson-Billings continues by defining CRP as a "pedagogy that empowers students intellectually, socially, emotionally, and politically by using cultural referents to impart knowledge, skills, and attitudes" (Ladson-Billings, 2009, p. 20).

Culturally Responsive Teaching

Ladson-Billings's work was imperative in the formation of the culturally responsive teaching (CRT) theory by Geneva Gay in 2018. Gay argued that there must be a "paradigmatic shift in the pedagogy used with non-middle-class, non-European American students in U.S. schools" (p. 25). Gay argues that a different pedagogical model is necessary to support underachieving students from multiple ethnic groups.

CRT is a pedagogy that uses "the cultural knowledge, prior experiences, frames of reference, and performance styles of ethnically diverse students to make learning encounters more relevant and effective for them" (Gay, 2018, p. 36).

Gay (2018) reminded us that "all our children deserve to be empowered on multiple levels" and that "their achievement needs to be academic, social, emotional, psychological, cultural, moral, and political" (p. 215). As educators, we can work to empower all of our students through the implementation of culturally responsive work.

Cultural Competence

Educators seeking to engage in culturally responsive work must develop their own cultural competence. Cultural competence "is the ability to successfully teach students who come from cultures other than your own. It entails mastering complex awarenesses and sensitivities, various bodies of knowledge, and a set of skills that, taken together, underline effective cross-cultural teaching" (Moule, 2012, p. 12).

Moule (2012) and Cross et al. (1989) also explains that there are five essential skills and competencies for educators to have cultural competence:

1. Awareness and Acceptance of Differences
2. Self-Awareness
3. Dynamics of Difference
4. Knowledge of Other Cultures
5. Adaption of Skills

It is important to note that becoming a culturally competent educator is a continuous process. We believe that the narratives, examples, and reflections in this text will be a tool for that ongoing process!

REFERENCES

Cross, T., Bazron, B., Dennis, K., and Isaacs, M. (1989). *Towards a culturally competent system of care*, Volume I. Washington, DC: Georgetown University Child Development Center, CASSP Technical Assistance Center.

Gay, G. 2018. *Culturally responsive teaching: Theory, research, and practice.* New York: Teachers College Press.

Ladson-Billings, G. (1995). But that's just good teaching! The case for culturally relevant pedagogy. *Theory into Practice, 34*(3), 159–65.

Ladson-Billings, G. (2009). *The dreamkeepers: Successful teachers of African American children.* Second edition. Jossey Bass.

Ladson-Billings, G. (2021). *Culturally relevant pedagogy: Asking a different question.* Teachers College Press.

Moule, J. (2012). *Cultural competence: A primer for educators.* Second edition. Wad[1]sworth Cengage Learning.

Chapter 1

Caring for All Students as the Foundation for Language Arts Instruction

Jennifer Rumsey

A climate in which caring relations can flourish should be a goal for all teachers and educational policymakers. In such a climate, we can best meet individual needs, impart knowledge, and encourage the development of moral people.

—Nel Noddings

EXPECTED LEARNING OUTCOMES

- The reader will learn what it means to teach with an ethic of care.
- The reader will learn ways to begin building positive relationships with students on the first day of school.
- The reader will learn strategies for using care when dealing with challenging students.
- The reader will learn effective methods for teaching language arts with care.

Care is at the heart of successful teaching. I taught language arts to students in grades six through eleven for seventeen years, and caring for all my students was the foundation of the work that I did as a teacher. Although all teacher candidates have heard that the key to successful teaching is building a relationship with students, how to effectively create and maintain a positive teacher-student relationship is less clear.

Noddings (2005) describes caring as relational, consisting of mindful listening and a desire to respond positively to the cared for. However, a caring relationship does not exist unless the cared for recognizes that he or she is being cared for. Thus, if teachers want to successfully build a positive relationship with students, based on care, then the teacher must be an attentive listener (to her students) and work diligently to maintain a positive response and reaction to her students. Meanwhile, the students must be able to discern and believe that they are cared for (Noddings, 2012).

Interacting with students all day can be both rewarding and challenging. In this chapter, I am going to discuss best practices for using care to create and build positive student-teacher relationships. The importance of building positive relationships cannot be overstated, and without doing this effectively, most efforts at teaching language arts or any other subject will be in vain.

POSITIVE TEACHER-STUDENT RELATIONSHIPS BEGIN ON DAY ONE

An effective teacher must begin building relationships with students on the first day of school. The power of greeting students at the door on the first day of school as well as on every day thereafter is well known. Effective teaching is a balancing act between structure and kindness, and it is essential that all students are introduced to both sides of you on that first day.

The best teachers approach their work with an ethic of care. When we open our hearts each year to a new group of students, they can feel that warmth and care. It takes courage and some vulnerability to care deeply for all students, but ultimately, the caring relationship benefits the teacher and the students tremendously. Students will feel safe to ask for help and are more motivated to do the work when they believe that their teacher cares about them. Discipline problems diminish or disappear when students believe their teacher cares about their well-being.

In addition, students of all ages need structure and a sense of constancy in the classroom as well as care from their teacher. After all, creating a structured, consistent classroom environment where all students feel safe is another aspect of teacher care. If the teacher allows the classroom to degenerate into a chaotic environment, no learning takes place, and that teacher is not successfully doing her job. Effective teaching truly is a balancing act of authority and love.

SUGGESTIONS FOR THE FIRST DAY

Be Genuine and Be Prepared

The toughest audience a person can face is a room full of preteens or teenagers at the end of the first day of school. By the end of the first day, they have heard several versions of the first day introductions, rules, and classroom procedures; they are likely extremely tired (having become accustomed to staying up all night during the summer and sleeping until noon); and they could be entering their rebellious phase where they see adults as the enemy, or at least as people who are totally out of touch with reality.

Knowing that they will be dealing with a tough audience, probably from the first period of the day, on the first day of school, new teachers need to be prepared and have their caring armor on. Start with a smile, interact genuinely with your students as they enter your classroom, and make sure that you have a seating chart (yes, even with upper high school students). A seating chart is a lifesaver. It will help you learn all your students' names quickly, and it asserts your authority as the leader of the classroom.

Students want to be seen and known and acknowledged as individuals, and the fastest way for you to accomplish this is to use a seating chart to learn their names quickly. Students may groan or overtly complain about it, even on the first day, but stand firm and tell them that a seating chart is going to help you get to know them more quickly, and it is the way that you run your classroom. Do not apologize for it. You must be the authority, a warm, caring authority, but the authority in your classroom, nonetheless.

First Day Speech, Rules, Expectations, Freedoms, and Rewards

You should be prepared to capture your students' attention by sharing information about yourself, so they can begin to get to know you. You could share a video you made about yourself or use some other engaging method to introduce yourself. After everyone is settled and you have done the introductory piece, the key to building those positive relationships begins with the first "speech" you make to your students.

During this talk, you will share the classroom rules and expectations. I always had the rules posted (no more than five), written in positive language. For example: "All students will treat everyone in this classroom with respect, everyday." You will go over the syllabus, grading policy, supplies needed, etc. But the most important thing you will do is to tell them something like what I told all my classes, every year.

I wanted my students to know what I stood for and that I believed that the most important element in education is positive relationships with my students. What follows is what I would tell them:

Teaching is more than a job for me. Teaching is something that I believe I have been called to do with my life. I have always wanted to make a difference in this world, and since I was a little girl, I knew that I was supposed to help children. And so, I want you to understand that ensuring that all of you learn and succeed to the best of your ability in my classroom is very important to me.

But more importantly, I want you to feel safe and always cared for when you are in my classroom. I care about all of you, and I take your health and safety very seriously. When you are one of my students, I will care about you like you are my child. If you need someone to talk to, you can talk to me. If you need help with your work and feel embarrassed to ask for help, know that it is my job to help you learn, and every one of us needs some help sometimes.

When you are in my classroom, I will do my very best to ensure that you are always treated with care and respect, and I will not tolerate anyone picking on you or making fun of you. Because I care about all of you, any attempt to make one of you feel badly about himself or herself is something that I will not tolerate, and I will address it and assign consequences, just as I would take up for and protect my own children.

And I know that some of you have had tough times before in school and maybe you got into a lot of trouble and got a reputation for that. I want you to know that with me, you are starting fresh. I do not listen to any negative talk about my students, and anything that you have done in the past does not matter because all of us have the right and ability to change for the better. I promise you that I will look for and see the best in you, and I will do my best to encourage you, even when times are challenging.

From there, I would talk to my students about the classroom rules and expectations as well as the supplies they would need and the procedures for class (briefly). The rules, expectations, and procedures are not one and done on the first day of class. Teachers must repeat these daily for the first couple of weeks, and a good teacher recognizes when a refresher on the classroom rules, expectations, and procedures needs to happen throughout the year.

I want my students to understand that while I am the authority in the classroom, they are valuable members of the classroom and would be privy to some freedoms. Going over the rules and expectations and procedures would be balanced by my talking about how I would allow them to chew gum (if they didn't make noise with it and threw it away in the garbage can). I would allow snacks and drinks, if those fit certain criteria, and I would also disclose the rewards that classes and individual students would earn for working hard and meeting expectations.

The most important thing I can share with you is that if you tell your students that you care about all of them, you better mean it. Students can tell when a teacher really cares or when she is going through the motions. Many, many children come to school from very difficult, heartbreaking situations at home. These students are less likely to trust an authority figure and more likely to have built a protective wall (of behaviors) that they use while at school and in the world.

So how do teachers who really care about their students handle the students who, to put it mildly, are challenging?

USING CARE IN DEALING WITH CHALLENGING STUDENTS

The reality is that every teacher, every year, will likely encounter at least one really challenging student in her classroom, or perhaps there will be several.

Most of your students will respond positively to your ethic of care, and having built a safe and caring classroom environment, you will find that you have few disturbances. However, there are times when students act out; sometimes, these occurrences are because of the school environment, and sometimes these misbehaviors are not at all about school.

One-on-One Conversations Can Resolve Almost Anything

When my students were being disruptive or defiant, depending on the student and the situation, I would try talking to them quietly at their desk. Knowing your students is key in these situations, as some students cannot stand being redirected by their teachers with others looking on, feeling embarrassed in front of their peers. If this goes wrong, it can lead to an escalation of misbehavior. The other way to do this is to ask the student to meet you outside for a moment. It is natural that students who are asked to step into the hallway will be on the defensive.

Being a caring teacher means that you do your very best to understand how your student is feeling at that moment, and this means that the student's feelings are more important than your own feelings (possibly of annoyance, frustration, or even anger). Teachers who care about all their students do not show or express any feelings beyond patience and care during these hallway discussions. A one-on-one discussion, even if begun due to a student acting out, is an amazing chance to build the teacher-student relationship.

I would usually start by asking the student what is going on with them; is there something that they need to talk to me about? A lot of times, students would open up about different situations that were impacting how they were feeling: a breakup with a partner, an argument with a parent, or a failing grade on a test in another class. Being a caring teacher means that you listen attentively to what the student has to say, and you try your best to respond in a positive manner (Noddings, 2005).

After listening attentively, I would reassure the student that I care about how they are doing, and I would thank them for telling me. Then, I would ask the student if he could try to focus and do a better job of meeting my classroom expectations. Usually, the student would tell me yes, we would return to the classroom, and things would be smooth for the remainder of the period. I know that my calm demeanor, my attentive listening, and my reassurance of care for the student made the difference.

In fact, sometimes students will believe that you do not like them. If they tell you something like this, or if you get the feeling that they may think this, it is your responsibility to change this belief.

For example, one year when I was teaching middle school, I had a young lady in my class who went from being a quiet student to being a defiant one, rolling her eyes, making comments under her breath, etc. I had redirected her when she had made a negative comment about an assignment, and afterward, she shut down, refusing to participate or engage with the work for the period.

The next day, I could feel that she was very unhappy being in my class. I waited until the right moment (this is key), when students were doing independent practice, and I asked her to meet me in the hallway. When we were outside, she refused to look at me, but I know that this can be due to trauma or cultural practices at home, so I did not make the huge mistake of insisting that she look at me. Instead, I told her that I had noticed that she seemed to be unhappy in my class.

Through this conversation, she shared that she believed that I did not like her, and she told me about a previous incident where I had redirected her when she was talking to a friend during guided practice. I was able to explain to her why I would have done that, and I assured her that I did, in fact, like her. And because I had been paying attention and actively working to know my students, I was able to compliment her on multiple things I had noticed about her, including being a great writer and a caring friend.

I also reassured her that if I redirect any of my students' behavior, it is not because I dislike them but because I want to make sure that all my students are able to learn and succeed. This one-on-one conversation made a huge difference. She began excelling in class, and I made sure to show her a little extra care and praise. By the end of the year, she cried about moving on to ninth grade and not having me as her teacher. It is a success story because I approached this student with an attentive, caring heart.

This is not to say that I did not encounter more difficult situations, because I did experience plenty of these. There are times when being a caring teacher means that you have exhausted your best strategies to redirect the student, and the intervention of an assistant principal or the assigning of behavior consequences is necessary. Caring about all your students means that you can balance authority with care in order to create a safe, orderly environment where all students will learn.

EFFECTIVE PRACTICES FOR TEACHING LANGUAGE ARTS WITH CARE

When teaching language arts, especially writing, a teacher has a wonderful opportunity to allow her students to express themselves in creative, genuine ways. Although students of all ages are subjected to multiple standardized tests, teaching language arts should never be standardized. Our students are not standardized. They come to us from many different backgrounds and ethnicities, with multiple talents and abilities, and with ranges of skills and struggles. Therefore, the best teaching is not standardized. Instead, a good teacher provides her students with many creative outlets.

Student Choice Can Be a Motivator (Or Not)

Allowing students to have the freedom to choose what to write about is one way to help students feel engaged and empowered in the classroom. When our students are empowered, they take ownership of the work, and they are much more motivated. Compare a student-chosen writing activity to a standardized test writing prompt, and you can observe much more student investment in the activity and the learning. However, not all students like to be the one choosing what to write about. In fact, a caring teacher needs to listen to these students when they tell her that they don't know what to write about.

Noddings (2012) emphasizes that the foundation of teacher care is attentive listening. Teachers can make the mistake of thinking that they "know what is best" for students, ignoring what the student is really telling them. When a student is sitting, doing nothing during a writing activity, and she shares that she does not know what to write about in a self-directed activity, the caring teacher hears what the student is telling her, and she acknowledges that the activity is a struggle for this student currently.

The "not knowing what to write about" can kill student motivation just as quickly as a boring prompt can, so a caring teacher listens to her students and is able to provide them with ideas or even give some students a prompt to help them get past this hurdle, despite knowing that self-directed learning is beneficial for many. Balance is key in teaching.

Student Projects

When I assigned students projects over a unit that we completed or a book we studied, I always had multiple possibilities for the students to choose from. Also, I let them know that I am open to their imaginings for a project that they wanted to do.

Giving students this freedom and opportunity to create is an essential way to improve student engagement and intrinsic motivation in a language arts classroom. Our students have so many different talents, skills, and interests that it is a gift to see what they can come up with, and it is a means for the teacher to learn something new!

READING ALOUD MAKES A DIFFERENCE

Even when I taught juniors, I read aloud to my students. The way it worked is this: every student had a copy of what we were reading, and they knew that the expectation was that while I was reading the book, article, or short story aloud, they were to be following along silently. Being a caring teacher, I knew that some of my students would want to read ahead, and I was fine with that. The benefits of reading aloud while students read along silently are many.

First, all classes (even honors classes) consist of students with many different reading levels and abilities to comprehend what they read. In most of my classes, I would have inclusion special education students working alongside students who were at grade level, those that struggled, as well as gifted students.

When the teacher reads the assigned material aloud while students read along silently, students are learning and improving their reading fluency. Listening to an excellent reader helps students understand how good reading should sound, and it improves their ability to pronounce unknown and known words.

Students that read along with the teacher are more likely to stay focused on the material, stay engaged, and comprehend it. Many times, if a student is struggling with the reading material, she will lose focus and interest and engage in the act of looking at the words on the page rather than reading them. When the material is read aloud, the teacher can read dramatically to engage the students' interest. I loved doing this, somewhat acting out the characters' parts.

Another benefit to reading aloud while the students follow along silently is you can stop and have student-led discussions about what has just happened in the book or short story. I loved it when my students were so excited by what they had read that they could barely contain their questions or comments. This is an amazing opportunity to let them make inferences, draw conclusions, point out figurative language, and discuss the author's purpose, theme, sentence structure, and style.

Finally, reading aloud while students follow along ensures that everyone reads what is assigned. Unfortunately, a lot of the time, if silent, individual reading is assigned (especially for homework), the reading just does not get done, and some students wind up behind and lost. We do not know what our students go home to every day, and as a caring teacher, I was aware of this reality and willing to ensure that my students had every opportunity to learn the material.

TEACH THE ELEMENTS OF WRITING AND FIGURATIVE LANGUAGE USING WHAT YOU'RE READING

The idea of teaching the elements of writing using a book or short story or article that your class is reading makes a lot of sense, but many language arts teachers teach grammar, punctuation, and sentence structure separately from what is being read in class.

Some schools use online grammar and punctuation games/practice to teach these things, but I do not think this is an effective method. At one high school where I worked, my students would groan and complain when they had to do these grammar activities online. I groaned also because I did not choose to use this method but was told to use it. Luckily, I was able to supplement this online method by using what we were reading in class to teach my students these skills.

Students can delve more deeply into an author's craft when they study his writing to learn the elements of writing. Doing so adds another level of meaning and understanding to the written work being studied, and it engages the students more deeply.

The first lesson plan I am including in this chapter is an example of using one of my favorite books, *The Great Gatsby*, to study F. Scott Fitzgerald's syntax and use of figurative language. I used Fitzgerald's work to teach students how to write compound, complex, and compound-complex sentences, integrating figurative language.

In this lesson, I put students into partner groups. Being a caring teacher, I knew which of my students would be able to work together well, before creating partner groups. In addition, there are some students who just prefer to work independently, and rather than fight this inclination, I would allow them to do so. Knowing your students, taking their choices into consideration, and choosing your battles wisely are elements of teaching with care.

The lesson plan over *The Great Gatsby* is shown in textbox 1.1.

Title of Lesson:	Exploring Sentence Structure and Use of Figurative Language in *The Great Gatsby*
Grade Level:	11

Content Standard(s):

E2.7 Reading/Comprehension of Literary Text/Sensory Language. Students understand, make inferences, and draw conclusions about how an author's sensory language creates imagery in literary text and provide evidence from the text to support their understanding.

E2.17 Oral and Written Conventions. Students understand the function of and use the conventions of academic language when speaking and writing. Students will continue to apply earlier standards with greater complexity.

E2.18 Oral and Written Convention/Handwriting, Capitalization, and Punctuation. Students write legibly and use appropriate capitalization and punctuation conventions in their compositions.

Social Justice Standard: https://www.learningforjustice.org/frameworks/social-justice-standards

Students will develop language and knowledge to accurately and respectfully describe how people (including themselves) are both similar to and different from each other and others in their identity group.

Objectives: *Students will be able to*

identify figurative language within a literary text and explain how the figurative language creates imagery and contributes to the tone of the text;
identify the structure and punctuation of a compound sentence;
identify the structure and punctuation of a complex sentence;
identify the structure and punctuation of a compound-complex sentence;
create compound, complex, and compound-complex sentences using correct punctuation and structure; and
create sentences including figurative language.

Anticipatory Set: *(How will student interest be sparked to engage in the lesson of the day?)*

The teacher shares a mentor text of a couple of paragraphs in length that is written entirely in simple sentences and without any figurative language. These paragraphs will be projected on the Clear Touch. The teacher reads the paragraphs aloud and asks the students what they notice about the mentor text. Student-led discussion about how the writing seems "boring" and "basic." Students suggest different ways to improve the paragraphs.

Relevancy: *(How will the content be made relevant to the students in the context you are teaching? What connections can be made to their experiences and cultures?)*

Students will be given the opportunity to craft their own compound sentences, complex sentences, and compound-complex sentences over a topic of their choice, and they will include figurative language.

Academic Vocabulary: *(What academic vocabulary will be addressed in this lesson? How will it be taught and made comprehensible to ALL learners?)*

simile, metaphor, onomatopoeia, personification, imagery, compound sentence, complex sentence, compound-complex sentence

The literary terms have been taught previously and are being reinforced and reviewed through the literary scavenger hunt.

Students have previously learned compound and complex sentence structures, but compound-complex sentences are new. Students will learn the structures and punctuation for these types of sentences by reviewing mentor text sentences like these in the book the class is currently studying, *The Great Gatsby*. They will practice what they have learned by composing their own compound, complex, and compound-complex sentences, including figurative language.

Lesson Overview: *(Please describe the steps for each part of the lesson. Also, in parentheses, put a time estimate for each segment of the lesson.)*

Warmup: Teacher shares a mentor text of a couple of paragraphs in length that is written entirely in simple sentences and without any figurative language. These paragraphs will be projected on the Clear Touch. The teacher reads the paragraphs aloud and asks the students what they notice about the mentor text. Student-led discussion about how the writing seems "boring" and "basic." Students suggest different ways to improve the paragraphs. (6 minutes)

Guided Practice: Teacher gives students page numbers from *The Great Gatsby* (pages 9, 12, 21), and they work with partners to locate at least one sentence from each page containing figurative language or imagery. Students either write the sentences down or type them on their Chromebook.

The teacher asks student pairs to share the sentences they found. Teacher types them on a document projected on the Clear Touch.

Class discussion about the types of figurative language located in these sentences and the images that the language creates and how the figurative language adds to the appeal of the writing.

The teacher shares three sentences: one compound and two compound-complex sentences that she located in *The Great Gatsby*. All three also include figurative language. She asks students to share what they notice about the structure and punctuation of the sentences. The teacher highlights the complex sentences and circles the punctuation that indicates the sentence structures. She labels the sentences as compound or compound complex. (24 minutes)

Independent Practice: Students craft a compound sentence, a complex sentence, and a compound-complex sentence over a topic of their choice, as a rough draft. Final draft of sentences will include figurative language. (15 minutes)

Closure: Teacher again projects the warmup on the Clear Touch and asks the students which would they rather read: the warm up paragraphs, or the sentences from *The Great Gatsby*? Students respond and explain why. (5 minutes)

Materials Needed: *(Please list the materials that will be needed for this lesson.)*

Each student will have a copy of *The Great Gatsby*
Chromebook or paper and pen/pencil, Clear Touch
List of book pages (from pages previously read in class) that students will be using in their literary terms scavenger hunt
p. 9 simile, imagery, metaphor, onomatopoeia
p. 12 simile
p. 21 personification

Universal Design for Learning: *(How will the principles of UDL be utilized throughout this lesson to give students voice and choice?)*

Students will have a choice on what to write when they write their own sentences. They also can choose whether to handwrite the sentences or type them. Students who need copies of the literary terms notes will have those.

Access: *(What strategies will be used throughout the lesson to allow students multiple entry points into understanding the concepts taught?)*

The teacher provides a mentor text to stimulate student thinking.
The teacher reads the mentor text aloud.
Students work in pairs to identify one sentence from each page that includes figurative language.
Page numbers where these examples are located are shared with the students.
Student-led discussion of figurative language identified in partner groups and its meaning, as well as the imagery created.
Students needing assistance with writing their own sentences will be given a handout with examples and a written roadmap of how to write each type.

Higher-Order Thinking: *(In what ways will this lesson require students to utilize higher-order thinking? Please describe.)*

Students will need to apply their knowledge of figurative language to identify it in *The Great Gatsby*.
Students will apply what they have learned about compound sentence structure, complex sentence structure, and compound-complex sentence structure to create their own sentences of these types, using figurative language.
Students will evaluate how sentences of varying types and the inclusion of figurative language improves writing.

Assessments: *(How will each learning objective be assessed? What activities do you have planned to check for understanding approximately every 5 minutes of the lesson?)*

Checking for understanding will take place throughout the lesson as the teacher calls on students (some cold calling) to get their perspectives.
During guided practice figurative language scavenger hunt, the teacher will walk around the room to listen to students' discussions and view their responses.
During independent practice, the teacher will walk the room to monitor if any of the students are struggling, needing additional support.
The completed sentences will count as a formative assessment.

> **Closure:** *(What activity will you use to close this lesson and to assess students' understanding at the end of the period?)*
>
> Teacher again projects the warmup on the Clear Touch and asks the students which would they rather read: the warm up paragraphs, or the sentences from *The Great Gatsby*? Students respond and explain why. (5 minutes)

Lesson 1 Reflection

F. Scott Fitzgerald's masterpiece is filled with elaborately constructed sentences and images beautifully drawn with the use of figurative language. My copy of the novel is highlighted and annotated, and I recommend that you do the same to your copy in preparation for this or any other lesson drawn from the novel. When having students work together in a scavenger hunt for sentence types, it is good to prepare by having hints for any pairs who are struggling to locate sentence examples. Make sure to walk around and monitor each duo's progress, as sometimes students appear to know what they are doing when, in reality, they will need more of your assistance.

USE MENTOR TEXTS TO TEACH WRITING

Using mentor texts to teach writing is another valuable activity that connects to teaching language arts through what you are reading in class. A key element of this is that the students should see you writing also. Many times, I would share something I had written as a mentor text for my students to review and learn from.

An important point in using mentor texts is to teach students what is acceptable and what is not. They can use a mentor text as a model to inspire their own work, but they cannot copy it using word substitutions and call it done. This is an important lesson to review with students, with the added benefit of teaching them about plagiarism, which happens much too often.

A mentor text can teach students paragraph formatting, flow, and transitions. Mentor texts can help students see and comprehend the structure necessary to craft a persuasive argument, or they can teach them how to organize a research paper.

Mentor texts can also inspire imagination in our students and help their thinking processes have a starting off point from which to create. I loved using mentor texts during our poetry unit. I would first teach students how to comprehend poetry, then I would teach them the elements of poetry and the many forms that it can take. Finally, I would ask my students to create their own poems. The first activity always involved a mentor text.

I am including a lesson plan using a mentor text of the wonderful free verse poem by Lucille Clifton, "Miss Rosie." The poem's theme is about the speaker watching a woman who has made bad choices in her life, resulting in her becoming homeless. As a result, the speaker proclaims that she will do the opposite of Miss Rosie, learning from her mistakes.

After reading the poem aloud, my classes had a student-led discussion covering the imagery and figurative language used by the author, the tone of the poem, and the poem's theme. When using this poem as a mentor text, I asked that my students write a free verse poem from the perspective of someone who has learned something about life by watching someone else. I told them that the message could be like the one in "Miss Rosie," doing the opposite of the watched person, or it could be where the student learns something positive from a role model.

Title of Lesson:	*Writing a Poem Inspired by a Mentor Text: "Miss Rosie" by Lucille Clifton*
Grade Level:	10

Content Standard(s):

TEKS E2.3 Reading/Comprehension of Literary Text/Poetry. Students understand, make inferences, and draw conclusions about the structure and elements of poetry and provide evidence from the text to support their understanding.

E2.14 Writing/Literary Texts. Students write literary texts to express their ideas and feelings about real or imagined people, events and ideas.

Social Justice Standard: https://www.learningforjustice.org/frameworks/social-justice-standards

Students will respectfully express curiosity about the history and lived experiences of others and will exchange ideas and beliefs in an open-minded way.

Objectives: *Students will be able to*

draw conclusions about the theme of the poem "Miss Rosie" by Lucille Clifton through identifying the author's purpose, tone, and use of figurative language to relay her message; and

write a free verse poem expressing their ideas and feelings about a life lesson they learned by watching someone else.

Anticipatory Set: *(How will student interest be sparked to engage in the lesson of the day?)*

Warmup: Students will engage in freewriting in response to the question: Have you learned something about life from watching someone else? If so, write a paragraph or more about what you learned and explain how watching this person taught you this lesson. Teacher engages in a think aloud to model what is meant by "watching" someone else.

Caring for All Students as the Foundation for Language Arts Instruction 15

Relevancy: *(How will the content be made relevant to the students in the context you are teaching? What connections can be made to their experiences and cultures?)*

This content is relevant because a poem is connected to the students' lived experiences. The theme of the poem will be revealed, and the warmup will act as a starting point for students to plan their own poem based on the theme identified.

Academic Vocabulary: *(What academic vocabulary will be addressed in this lesson? How will it be taught and made comprehensible to ALL learners?)*

theme, metaphor, simile, author's purpose, tone, symbolism
These terms have been taught previously and are being reinforced and reviewed through the poetry analysis. Students will be applying their learning of these terms by crafting their own poem using some of these literary terms.

Lesson Overview: *(Please describe the steps for each part of the lesson. Also, in parentheses, put a time estimate for each segment of the lesson.)*

Warmup: Students will engage in freewriting in response to the question: Have you learned something about life from watching someone else? If so, write a paragraph or more about what you learned and explain how watching this person taught you this lesson. Teacher engages in a think aloud to model what is meant by "watching" someone else. (8 minutes)

Guided Practice: Teacher reads "Miss Rosie" by Lucille Clifton aloud while students follow along silently.
Students work in pairs to identify figurative language in the poem.
Student-led discussion of the figurative language located in the poem and what it means. Student-led discussion of the author's purpose, tone, and the theme of the poem.
Teacher models (using a think aloud) how to brainstorm/plan for writing her own poem using the theme from "Miss Rosie" as a mentor text. (20 minutes)

Independent Practice: Students begin the writing process, brainstorming/planning their own free verse poem with a theme of learning a life lesson by watching someone. (17 minutes)

***NOTE:** The creation of the student-written poem will likely take two days, so this part of the independent practice will continue the following day.

Closure: Students share what they like about "Miss Rosie" and who they are writing their own poem about. (5 minutes)

Materials Needed: *(Please list the materials that will be needed for this lesson.)*

Copies of the poem "Miss Rosie" by Lucille Clifton. Students will access the poem through a link to the poetry website poets.org, https://poets.org/poem/miss-rosie, using their Chromebooks. The poem will be displayed on the teacher's Clear Touch.
Students may use paper and pen/pencil to create their own poem, or they may write using their Chromebook.

Universal Design for Learning: *(How will the principles of UDL be utilized throughout this lesson to give students voice and choice?)*

Students will have a choice on what to write when they write their poems. They also can choose whether to handwrite the poem or type it. Students who need copies of the literary terms notes will have those.

Access: *(What strategies will be used throughout the lesson to allow students multiple entry points into understanding the concepts taught?)*

Teacher uses a think aloud to start the warmup activity and engage the students.
The teacher will read the poem aloud while the students follow along silently.
Student-led discussion about the author's tone, purpose, and the theme of the poem.
Students will work with partners to identify figurative language used in the poem.
Student-led discussion of figurative language identified in partner groups and its meaning.
Teacher will use a think aloud to model how to begin the rough draft of her free verse poem.

Higher-Order Thinking: *(In what ways will this lesson require students to utilize higher-order thinking? Please describe.)*

Students will apply their prior learning of literary terms to analyze the content and meaning of the poem.
Students will connect the theme of the poem to their own experiences.
Students will craft their own free verse poem over a shared theme, with student choice leading the writing.

Assessments: *(How will each learning objective be assessed? What activities do you have planned to check for understanding approximately every 5 minutes of the lesson?)*

During the warmup, the teacher will walk around and check that the students are understanding the task and see if any students need more assistance.
The teacher will travel the classroom, checking in on the student pairs to ensure they are locating the figurative language in the poem.
During independent practice, the teacher continues to walk the classroom, asking students how they are doing with their poem rough draft.

Closure: *(What activity will you use to close this lesson and to assess students' understanding at the end of the period?)*

Closure: Students share what they like about "Miss Rosie" and who they are writing their own poem about. (5 minutes)

Lesson 2 Reflection

The speaker in "Miss Rosie" reflects on lessons she has learned from "watching" Miss Rosie destroy her life. The poem is an excellent example of free verse with powerful figurative language used to draw mental images of Miss Rosie. The discussion about the poem's message can be very engaging for students, and I suggest that if your students are excited to talk about it and connect the poem to their own lived experiences or examples, you allow this to go on longer than the allotted time. Additionally, planning for and crafting their own poems may take some students extra time. Teaching language arts requires flexibility and adaptability on the teacher's part.

CONCLUSION

The best teachers approach their work from an ethic of care. They are genuine, listen attentively to their students, and work to build positive relationships with *all* their students from the first day of school. Allowing student choice and opportunities to be creative, reading aloud to students while they follow along silently, teaching the elements of writing through what you are reading in class, and using mentor texts are effective strategies in language arts classes that help motivate and engage students.

READER TAKEAWAYS

- The reader understands what it means to be a caring teacher and some of the actions necessary to maintain an ethic of care.
- The reader has learned strategies and ideas to promote student choice, creativity, motivation, and engagement in the language arts classroom.

REFERENCES

Fitzgerald, F. S. (1925). *The Great Gatsby.* New York: C. Scribner's Sons.
Noddings, N. (2012) The caring relation in teaching. *Oxford Review of Education, 38*(6), 771–81. https://doi-org.postu.idm.oclc.org/10.1080/03054985.2012.745047.
Noddings, N. (2005). *The challenge to care in schools: An alternative approach to education.* Teachers College Press.

Chapter 2

History Is Not Static and Unchanging

Using Culturally Responsive Teaching to Develop Critical Social Science Thinking Skills and Active Citizenship

Leona Calkins

Social Studies . . . is where students learn to see and interpret the world-its people, places, cultures, systems, and problems; its dreams and calamities-now and long ago. In social studies lessons and units of study, students don't simply experience the world but are helped deliberately to understand it, to care for it, to think deeply and critically about it, and to take their place on the public stage.

—Parker, 2015, p. 3

EXPECTED LEARNING OUTCOMES

- Readers will gain perspective via one teacher's experience (the author) teaching high school social science.
- Readers will gain an understanding of culturally responsive teaching in social science classrooms.
- Readers will gain insight into the instructional strategies of inquiry design model and structured academic controversy, which both align with culturally responsive teaching.
- Readers will have access to two secondary social science lesson plans rooted in culturally responsive teaching.

TEACHER NARRATIVE

I (Leona) have taught high school for fourteen years; for ten years I was a social science teacher and for four years I was a high school librarian in which I had the privilege of working with every single one of our students on campus. Throughout my career, I have only worked at urban high schools that were linguistically, culturally, and socioeconomically diverse.

As I reflect back on my high school teaching career, having recently transitioned to an assistant professor of teacher education, I am left with a sense of pride and a feeling of accomplishment. Not because I was a perfect teacher, in fact it is quite the opposite, but because I look back and I can see the growth I had as a teacher and the changes I made to become a better teacher for all of my students.

One moment that stands out to me was in my fourth year of teaching. After having taught US government for my first three years, I had moved school sites and was assigned to teach tenth-grade world history. This was an exciting time for me because I have a degree in history and have a genuine passion for the subject matter, especially world history. Early into that school year, I was struggling. My students lacked interest in the subject matter and I was overwhelmed by the amount of content, as I interpreted it, my standards dictated needed to be covered. Of the four world history class periods, not a single student was truly engaged with the material.

They were compliant; they came to class, they listened, and they completed their assignments. But true engagement was missing. I understood that when my students left my classroom, they were not still pondering the day's lesson or wrestling with multiple interpretations of a single event or person. The very essence of the subject I loved was missing in my classroom.

I decided to ask my students for feedback. What could I do to make my class more engaging? How could I change my instruction? I was looking for any insight into how I could develop more passion for history and help my students understand why learning history was important. Overall, there was a consensus that history was boring because all students learned were facts about dead, old men. This was eye opening!

First, my students viewed history as a static, unchanging subject; they saw remembering facts—dates, events, names—as the end goal of the class, despite this being far from the true goal of history and any social science. They lacked the understanding that history, though rooted in facts and evidence, is fluid and changes each time new information is discovered and with each interpretation of even previously available information.

Second, I learned that my students viewed history as a place for only men. And though not outwardly spoken, there was a sense that my students felt that history was a place for white men and that they did not see themselves in the stories told. There was clearly a missed opportunity, as their teacher, to highlight and incorporate more diverse and varied viewpoints and perspectives within the class. With this information, I knew I needed to do better for my students.

Almost a quarter into the school year, I decided to start over with my world history classes. I modified a wonderful lesson one of my professors, Dr. Graham Peck, used in an undergraduate course he taught in which he challenged us, his college students, with the question, "What Is Truth?" I posed that same question to my tenth-grade students. And with the use of guiding questions, I helped my students begin to understand the difference between facts, "a thing that is known to be true" (Oxford Learner's Dictionary, 2023), and how facts are interpreted to create the narratives of history.

By doing so, my students began to see that multiple perspectives can exist surrounding the same person or event both in history and current events. After we wrestled with the concept of truth, I then asked students to think about those things that impact how individuals interpret facts and create these differing narratives, essentially directing my students to think about point of view.

Throughout both of these activities, I used examples from common events in students' lives. For example, we discussed how students talking during a test can be viewed differently by students and teachers and why this might be the case. I also used examples of school dress codes and cell phone policies. Students brought up examples from home, including parental rules and disagreements with and between siblings.

As we continued to discuss point of view, I asked students whether any of the differing/varying perspectives were wrong. So long as the perspective was based on facts and used accurate evidence, was one perspective any more truthful than another? The discussion that followed helped students begin to see that there is no single, correct "truth," and though there can be a wrong representation of an event, if the facts are wrong, there can still be multiple correct views of the same situation. Students began to recognize and evaluate the complexity of multiple perspectives.

To close the lesson, I asked students why some states, including the state we lived in, did not celebrate Columbus Day while other states did. Why was Columbus and Columbus Day controversial? Though based on our course pacing guide, we were far from discussing the Age of Exploration, I knew my students were familiar with Christopher Columbus and we were relatively close to the holiday.

Students quickly came to the conclusion that some people viewed Columbus as a hero and brave explorer who should continue to be celebrated—he sparked the many changes coming to the Americas. They also recognized that some people, like Indigenous people, viewed Columbus as a murderer and sparked the decimation of longstanding, highly advanced cultures and peoples in the Americas. Furthermore, students understood that neither of these perspectives were wrong, in a factual sense. All of a sudden, my students were engaged.

The "What Is Truth?" lesson became a stepping stone for other activities—for the remainder of that year and throughout the rest of my high school teaching career—that helped students navigate and develop the complex social science thinking skills necessary to challenge the historical narratives students encountered and begin to develop their own interpretations of historical events. I would refer back to it when students were asked to analyze sources. I would ask them questions like: Whose truth is being told? Do other sources corroborate/challenge that interpretation? What is the goal of or who is the audience of the source? Is there a missing perspective of the event, if so, whose (or what group's) perspective is missing and how might it differ from the sources students were reading?

Furthermore, the "What Is Truth?" lesson helped create a classroom culture in which students felt safe to share family histories and experiences, to suggest different perspectives of historical events, and to make suggestions on course information. For example, I had students ask if the class could cover imperialism in Hawaii during our unit on imperialism because they were Hawaiian and had oral histories they wanted to share with the class. The sources I used became more diverse and more representative of my students, when possible, as well as more culturally uplifting. For units I could better tailor to students and their families' lived experiences, I did so.

There are many other times in my teaching career in which I have failed, evaluated, and revamped my teaching to do better for my students. However, it is this initial failure at teaching world history that helped me grow the most and learn new ways to better engage my students in a subject that I love!

CULTURALLY RESPONSIVE TEACHING IN SOCIAL SCIENCE/HISTORY

Defining Culturally Responsive Teaching

Though there is a great deal of literature by multiple researchers dedicated to culturally responsive teaching and pedagogy, the work of Geneva Gay and Gloria Ladson-Billings have been foundational in the field (Aronson and Laughter, 2016).

Culturally responsive teaching, as defined by Geneva Gay (2018, p. 31), is "using the cultural knowledge, prior experiences, frames of reference, and performance styles of ethnically diverse students to make learning encounters more relevant to and effective for them. It teaches *to and through* the strengths of these students." Gay (2018) establishes six characteristics on which culturally responsive teaching rests:

- Culturally responsive teaching is *validating and affirming* because it legitimizes cultural heritages and positions these heritages as worthy of being taught in school; it connects experiences of home and school life; it uses varying instructional strategies and incorporates multicultural curriculum; it also "teaches students to know and praise their own and one another's cultural heritages" (Gay, 2018, p. 31).
- Culturally responsive teaching is socially, emotionally, intellectually, and politically *comprehensive* as it aims to teach the whole child.
- Culturally responsive teaching is *multidimensional* because it incorporates cultural perspectives, knowledge, and contributions.
- Culturally responsive teaching is *empowering* because it sets high expectations for all students with emphasis not just on academic success but developing the belief in students that they can and will be successful.
- Culturally responsive teaching is *transformative* because it explicitly respects marginalized cultures and experiences of those within these cultures as well as uses strengths and assets of students to drive instruction.
- Culturally responsive teaching is *emancipatory and liberating* because it "helps students realize that no single version of 'truth' is total and permanent" (Gay, 201, p. 38). Students are taught to critically analyze mainstream curriculum and develop their own voices and become more active in shaping their learning.

Gloria Ladson-Billings (1995, 2014) highlights three major aspects of culturally relevant pedagogy: academic success of students from experiences within the classroom, cultural competence in which students embrace their own cultures and learn of other cultures, and sociopolitical consciousness in which students transfer what has been learned in the classroom to the real world. In her more recent work, Ladson-Billings (2014) emphasizes the importance of recognizing the fluidity of culture, as opposed to presenting a static view of culture.

Culturally Responsive Teaching in Social Science: What Is It?

When thinking about culturally responsive teaching in the social sciences, including history, we must first recognize the current status of social science education in the country. First, although the social science curriculum has seen a growth in diverse perspectives, especially since the 1970s, much of the social science curriculum still focuses on Westernized, Eurocentric perspectives (Fitchett and Heafner, 2012; Thornton, 2017). Furthermore, the inclusion of diverse perspectives are far from being equally presented (McBean and Feinberg, 2020; Thornton, 2017). For instance, LGBTQ+ perspectives are extremely limited in social science curriculum, including in California, which is the leading state for inclusivity of LGBTQ+ perspectives within state curriculum with the passing of the FAIR Act (Berman, 2022).

Additionally, when marginalized groups are included in curriculum they are most often simply mentioned without being presented as having an active role in shaping history (McBean and Fienberg, 2020). Social science teachers, also, tend to utilize more teacher-centric instructional strategies that emphasize acquisition of knowledge as opposed to student-centered ones that focus on skill and concept development (Knowles et al., 2020; Thacker et al., 2017; Wiens et al., 2022). Because the social science curriculum continues to stem from Eurocentric perspectives, teachers often continue to marginalize minority groups (Fitchett and Heafner, 2012; Thornton, 2017).

Students who identify with these marginalized groups thus struggle to connect with the curriculum and become either disconnected or form a misguided understanding of where they belong in society (Aronson and Laughter, 2016; Fitchett and Heafner, 2012). The very subject that is explicitly designed to develop active democratic citizenship and efficacy (National Council for the Social Studies, 2013) is, as pointed out by Fitchett and Heafner (2012), creating alienation and discouraging political participation.

In challenging the current status of the social science curriculum and teaching, culturally relevant teaching can help bridge the gap between what the subject is meant to do for students and what it is currently perpetuating onto students. Culturally responsive teaching in social science must move beyond superficial cultural inclusiveness and mere mentioning of marginalized groups of people (Ladson-Billings, 2014) and instead help develop students' social science disciplinary skills and inquiry-based skills so they may develop "an authentic, critical understanding of the past" (Fitchett and Heafner, 2012, p. 198).

Marginalized peoples must be treated with dignity and not just viewed as victims of their circumstances throughout history; rather, both instances of struggles and inspirations should be presented. Furthermore, considering social science classrooms ideally provide students the space to discuss, deliberate, and inquire about problems in the world and then learn how they can work to solve these problems (NCSS, 2013; Parker, 2008), culturally responsive teaching must have students transfer what they are learning in class to then consider policies that may have a direct impact on them and their communities, which is most missing in classrooms according to Ladson-Billings (2014).

FRAMEWORK FOR CULTURALLY RESPONSIVE TEACHING IN SOCIAL SCIENCE/HISTORY

In a world in which social science education has become more prescribed (Fitchett et al., 2012) and yet classrooms have become more diverse with students of color accounting for over 50 percent of all public school students (National Center for Education Statistics, 2023), it can feel overwhelming to determine how culturally responsive teaching can be thoroughly incorporated into each classroom. In order to provide a scaffold for just this, Fitchett and Heafner (2012) created a framework for social science teachers to use, in conjunction with their state curriculums, to provide culturally responsive teaching in their classrooms. The framework consists of three stages: review, reflect, react.

Review

In reviewing, teachers should critically review their course standards and prescribed curriculum materials and determine whose values, norms, and beliefs are presented and validated. Critiquing the curriculum allows teachers to determine how it addresses or fails to address the diverse needs of students.

Reflect

After reviewing, teachers must then reflect on how they can transform their curriculum to meet the needs of their students. In order to successfully reflect, teachers need to know their students: What are their strengths and assets? What are students' lived experiences and how can these experiences and students' prior knowledge be utilized to bridge home and school life? "Getting to Know You" activities can help address this stage of the process.

React

Last, teachers must then react by using students' funds of knowledge to guide planning and instructional implementation that addresses the strengths of their students. Lessons are developed that move away from textbooks and prescribed materials that affirm "historical positionality" of students (Fitchett et al., 2012, p. 592). Furthermore, this step requires more than supplementing the curriculum with readings and resources from diverse groups but, rather, in teaching students how to think historically, encourage discourse around race and identity, and challenge students' views of history by presenting multiple interpretations. Additionally, teachers need to move away from teacher-centered, didactic instruction and incorporate more student-centered lessons.

Instructional Strategies Further Promoting Culturally Responsive Teaching in Social Sciences

In further consideration of the "react" portion of the previous framework, the inquiry design model (IDM) from the College, Career, and Civic Life (C3) Framework and Structured Academic Controversy (SAC) instructional strategies, among others, align well with culturally responsive teaching. Both strategies shift toward student-centered instruction as well as building upon students' experiences and prior knowledge while also developing social sciences skills and deeper interpretation of social science content (Jaffee and

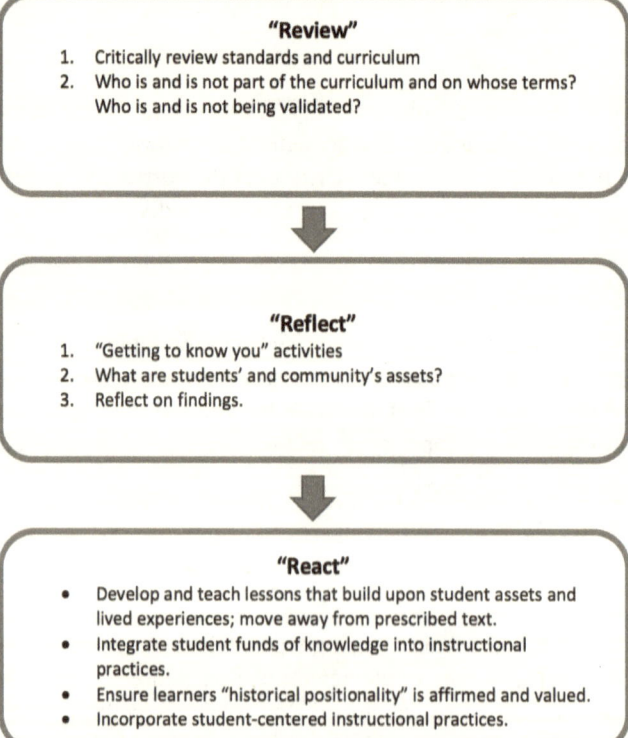

Figure 2.1. A Framework for Culturally Responsive Teaching.
Source: Fitchett and Haefner, 2012; Fitchett et al., 2012.

Yoder, 2019). Throughout both IDM and SAC, teachers take on the role of facilitator, guiding students and helping them elaborate on what they are learning.

Furthermore, because both of these strategies incorporate the analysis of multiple perspectives, these strategies can be helpful when working with emergent bilingual students who may have had social studies education in a different country, allowing them to navigate the changes to this part of their education and the different interpretations of social science content taught (Jaffee and Yoder, 2019).

IDM is at the heart of the inquiry arc of the C3 Framework (NCSS, 2013) and provides a practical way to employ inquiry in social studies classrooms (C3Teachers, n.d.; Swan et al., 2015). The inquiry arc incorporates four main steps: (1) creating compelling and guiding questions and developing inquiries, (2) applying disciplinary concepts and skills, (3) evaluating sources and using evidence, and (4) sharing conclusions through activities that align with the goals of college and career readiness and taking informed action through civic engagement (NCSS, 2013). IDM offers a blueprint for teachers to develop lessons that incorporate these multiple facets of inquiry, allowing students to interact with multiple sources and perspectives, analyze and critique sources, and enhance their own understandings of social science content that builds upon their funds of knowledge.

The instructional strategy of SAC focuses on discourse surrounding controversial topics, both in history and current events (Bruen et al., 2016; Jaffee and Yoder, 2019). Through this strategy students are required to analyze at least two different sides of a controversial topic and deliberate, or compromise, how to move forward with this topic through small group and partner discourse. The main elements of SAC include the use of groups, usually four, in which students are then paired down within the groups. In the first step, Pair A presents an argument in favor of the topic/issue and Pair B presents an argument against the topic/issue. In the second step the pairs reverse sides and Pair A presents an argument against the topic/issue and Pair B presents an argument in favor of the topic/issue. In the final step, the entire group must deliberate and come to a consensus on the topic: What side do they, as a group, believe is the most compelling side of the argument (Bruen et al. 2016)? If students cannot agree upon this final step, then they must elaborate on why they could not agree and where exactly they find their differences. This strategy, however, is not about winning a debate but rather about "uncovering the various arguments around the issue in question" (Bruen et al., 2016, p. 19). Furthermore, SAC easily allows for teachers to develop extension activities that can be completed individually or in groups.

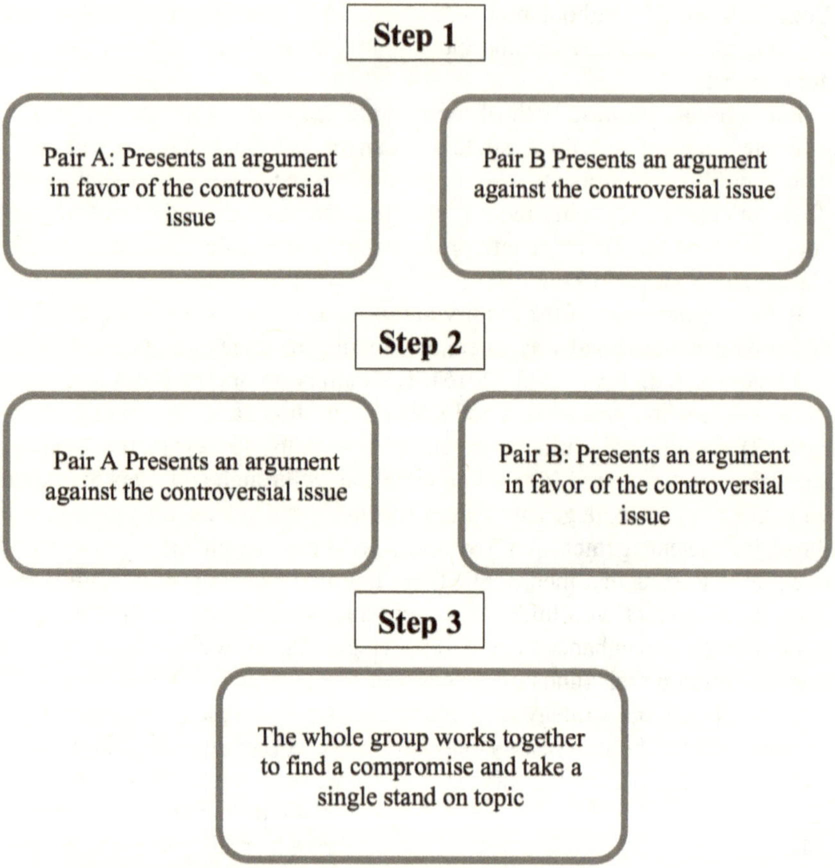

Step 1

Pair A: Presents an argument in favor of the controversial issue

Pair B Presents an argument against the controversial issue

Step 2

Pair A Presents an argument against the controversial issue

Pair B: Presents an argument in favor of the controversial issue

Step 3

The whole group works together to find a compromise and take a single stand on topic

Figure 2.2.   The Essential Elements of SAC.
Source: Bruen et al., 2016.

CULTURALLY RESPONSIVE LESSONS FOR SOCIAL SCIENCE

Lesson 1: "What Is Truth?" Developing Multiple Perspectives in the Social Science Classroom

The first lesson presented in this chapter is the "What Is Truth?" lesson described in the narrative. This lesson sets the stage for students to begin understanding the more critical analysis required of a high-level social science education and begins to paint a picture that history, geography, government, and economics are not static subjects that require simple, boring, rote memorization. They are, instead, fluid and ever changing and, though there can be wrong interpretations if facts are wrong or misused, there is no one right interpretation.

Again, this lesson is a building block for further development of historical and social science thinking skills that will allow students to more fully critique the sources they encounter, both primary and secondary, build an understanding and respect of multiple perspectives including their own, and empowers students to question the status quo presented in course curriculum, textbooks, and society, eventually, with continued teacher guidance, leading students to learn how to become active citizens, which is one of the main outcomes of the C3 Framework (NCSS, 2013), and begin making the societal changes they believe necessary to make the world a better place. Furthermore, this lesson can act as a foundational activity for the use of other instructional strategies that help foster culturally responsive teaching, like SAC and IDM (Jaffee and Yoder, 2019).

LESSON PLAN TEMPLATE 1

Title of Lesson:	*What Is Truth?: Developing Multiple Perspectives in the Social Science Classroom*
Grade Level:	6–12

Content Standard(s):

***This lesson is an introductory lesson designed to develop students' understanding of multiple perspectives and what factors may contribute to different perspectives. The exact standards can vary based on grade level and when the activity is completed during the school year. However, this activity directly connects to the following California Historical and Social Science Analysis Skill (in addition to multiple facets of the C3 Framework).

CA.6–12 Historical and Social Science Analysis Skills. Students detect the different historical points of view on historical events and determine the context in which the historical statements were made (the questions asked, sources used, author's perspectives).

Social Justice Standard: https://www.learningforjustice.org/frameworks/social-justice-standards

ID.6–8.3: I know that overlapping identities combine to make me who I am and that none of my group identities on their own fully defines me or any other person.

ID.9–12.3: I know that all my group identities and the intersection of those identities create unique aspects of who I am and that this is true for other people too.

DI.6–8.6: I interact with people who are similar to and different from me, and I show respect to all people.

DI.9–12.6: I interact comfortably and respectfully with all people, whether they are similar to or different from me.

Objectives: *Students will be able to*

differentiate between facts and perspectives/points of view and analyze how people's lived experiences can shape their perspectives of both current and past events.

Anticipatory Set: *(How will student interest be sparked to engage in the lesson of the day?)*

Students will complete a 5-minute write, in which they should free write for 5 minutes, answering the following question: What is truth?

Relevancy: *(How will the content be made relevant to the students in the context you are teaching? What connections can be made to their experiences and cultures?)*

This activity directly relates to students' lives as they are faced with differing perspectives and points of views every day, from events within their families and circle of friends to larger societal events. This activity helps students begin to analyze what constitutes "truth" in the social sciences and what factors may shape people's perspectives, including their own. Furthermore, students can begin to grapple with other critical thinking skills around sources like validity, reliability, audience, etc. through the use of instances in their own lives.

Academic Vocabulary: *(What academic vocabulary will be addressed in this lesson? How will it be taught and made comprehensible to ALL learners?)*

truth, fact, opinion, evidence, point of view/perspective
These terms will be introduced throughout the lesson and examples will be provided by the teacher, as well as peers, to ensure all students are gaining a deeper understanding of the terms. Because this is an introductory lesson with several overarching themes and social science skills being introduced, it will be beneficial to reintroduce each of these terms and continue to revisit them during later activities.

Lesson Overview: *(Please describe the steps for each part of the lesson. Also, in parentheses, put a time estimate for each segment of the lesson.)*

1. Anticipatory Set (5 minutes): Free write answering the question, "What is truth?"
2. Pair-share to class discussion answering the question, "What is truth?" (5 minutes)
   a. During the class discussion, the teacher should compile a list of words/phrases that students use to describe "truth."
      * During this time students usually begin recognizing the complexity of "truth" and that it is different than a fact.
3. Possible scenarios that can be used to help students navigate these concepts: students talking during a test (students talking, students not talking, teacher's interpretation of the event); use of school dress codes and/or cell phone policies; age laws around driving, joining the military, compulsory school; rules within students' families and homes (chores, allowance, dating, etc.). Be sure to choose topics students show interest in and can relate to as well as allow students to introduce topics that they know have differing perspectives and are age and school appropriate.
   a. By the end of this portion, students should begin understanding that facts are used as evidence to support a truth (or people's interpretation of the facts).
4. Direct Instruction (5 minutes): Introduce the terms "perspective" and "point of view." Work with students to define these terms and create a connection to their interpretations of "truth."
5. Think-Pair-Share (5 minutes): What things/factors can impact our perspectives of the world (specific situations, rules, laws, people, events, etc.)? What makes one person's point of view different from another?

6. "My Window to the World" Point of View Activity (15 minutes): Using the "I do, we do, you do" strategy students will work to add as many factors as they can that influence their point of view.
   a. The teacher should begin with adding two to three factors on their own personal "window" that impacts their point of view.
   b. The teacher should then ask the class for other factors that can influence point of view.
   c. Students work individually or in small groups to come up with other factors that influence their point of view
7. Reflection (5 minutes): Have students choose one topic that has been discussed in class or any controversial topic that is school appropriate and have them complete the following sentence stem: The factors on my "window" impact how I view _____ because . . .
8. Closure: Connecting It to History/Social Science small group to class discussion (5–10 minutes):
   a. Choose a controversial figure, holiday, law, etc. that students are familiar with and ask them to explain at least two points of view regarding it as well as what might influence peoples' perspectives/points of view.

Materials Needed: *(Please list the materials that will be needed for this lesson.)*

Presentation resources (computer, projector, and/or white board and markers)
Paper, writing utensils
"My Window to the World" Activity below (this can be done with the below handout or have students draw their own "window"

Universal Design for Learning: *(How will the principles of UDL be utilized throughout this lesson to give students voice and choice?)*

UDL principles are included through several different means:
- This lesson provides students with relevance, value, and authenticity and allows for the skills learned to be used within the course content and transferred to their personal lives.
- The lesson fosters collaboration and community through pair, small group, and class discussions.
- This lesson also acts as and includes scaffolds to help students develop a better understanding of perspective/point of view.

Access: *(What strategies will be used throughout the lesson to allow students multiple entry points into understanding the concepts taught?)*

Different instructional strategies will be used to allow students multiple entry points to the concept being taught. These include: responding to questions individually in written form, having small and larger group discourse, using the visual of a window to represent factors of point of view, and the ability to have students move about the room in search of new partners/groups for discussion.

Higher-Order Thinking: *(In what ways will this lesson require students to utilize higher-order thinking? Please describe.)*

Students are required to think analytically about the concepts of truth, evidence, and point of view. Furthermore, not only are students asked to identify factors that influence point of view but then examine how their own life experiences shape their point of view. Students are then required to transfer their understanding of these concepts from a more personal level to that of history/social sciences, synthesizing what they learned from the lesson and using it to conjecture two possible views of a controversial topic and explain how certain factors influence point of view.

Assessments: *(How will each learning objective be assessed? What activities do you have planned to check for understanding approximately every 5 minutes of the lesson?)*

Students will be assessed, predominantly, through their discussions. The teacher will walk around the room listening to students speak and facilitating deeper conversations through guiding questions. Students will also be assessed through their "My Window to the World" activity.

Closure: *(What activity will you use to close this lesson and to assess students' understanding at the end of the period?)*

9. Connecting It to History/Social Science small group to class discussion (5–10 minutes)
   a. Choose a controversial figure, holiday, law, etc. that students are familiar with and ask them to explain at least two points of view regarding it as well as what might influence peoples' perspectives/points of view.

My Window to the World

This is your window to the world. It is through this window that you see the entire world, and it shapes (or shades) how you view aspects of the world (that is, events, laws, rules, other people). There are multiple factors that shape how you see the world; some of those factors other people will share with you, others will feel more unique to your own lived experiences. It is all of these factors and experiences, though, that shape your view and understanding of the world around you.

Directions: List as many factors as you can think of that shape your view of the world. Make sure that you are as specific as you can be; for example, instead of writing "age," write your age (that is, fifteen). Write as much as you can and feel free to talk with other people in the room to help write as many things as you can.

Reflect: Choose one of the topics we discussed in class or any other topic, including controversial ones, and complete the following sentence stem:

The factors on my "window" impact how I view _____ because . . .

Figure 2.3. Reflection Window.

LESSON 2: "SHOULD THE ELECTORAL COLLEGE BE ABOLISHED?"

The second lesson presented in this chapter is titled "Should the Electoral College Be Abolished?" The lesson uses the SAC to have students collaboratively analyze the pros and cons of the Electoral College and come to a group consensus answering the essential question of whether it should or should not be abolished. As the lesson is currently designed, especially because it aligns with twelfth-grade standards, students must complete their own research on the Electoral College. It is suggested that students use the database Opposing Viewpoints, which is specially designed to help students navigate and find reliable resources on myriad controversial topics. One way this lesson can be scaffolded is by providing students with preselected sources covering the basic information about the Electoral College and as well as both sides of the argument.

In this lesson, students work collaboratively in groups to uncover as many arguments surrounding the pros and cons of the Electoral College. Students are first divided into groups of four and within these groups students are further separated into pairs. One pair of the group will begin researching and then presenting the pros of the Electoral College, while the other pair will research and present the cons of the Electoral College. The pairs then reverse the side of the argument in which they research and present.

Again, the goal of a SAC lesson is not about winning an argument or debate; instead it rests upon gaining as much knowledge as possible about the topic. After the second round of pair presentations, the whole group must come to a consensus, using the most compelling arguments, to argue one side of the essential question "Should the Electoral College Be Abolished?" If students cannot come to a consensus, then they must thoroughly explain why and where they continued to disagree with each other.

This lesson uses SAC because it builds upon the aspects of culturally responsive teaching because students are examining multiple perspectives in a supportive fashion. Using SAC allows and encourages students to consider varying perspectives and provides avenues for students to develop and express their own perspectives, in this case on the Electoral College, and learn to respect others' views as well. This lesson also directly connects with students' lives as they learn about the importance of voting and how their vote counts toward the election of the president. Last, through extension activities, students can also learn how to take informed action as a citizen living within a democracy by writing, calling, and/or emailing elected representatives regarding their perspective of the Electoral College.

LESSON PLAN TEMPLATE 2

Title of Lesson:	*Should the Electoral College Be Abolished?*
Grade Level:	12, US Government *This can be used as a lesson in a Survey of Social Studies Class as well.

Content Standard(s):

CA. 12.4.4. Discuss Article II of the Constitution as it relates to the executive branch, including eligibility for office and length of term, election to and removal from office, the oath of office, and the enumerated executive powers.

Social Justice Standard: https://www.learningforjustice.org/frameworks/social-justice-standards

DI.9–12.8: I respectfully express curiosity about the history and lived experiences of others and exchange ideas and beliefs in an open-minded way.
DI.9–12.9: I relate to and build connections with other people by showing them empathy, respect, and understanding, regardless of our similarities or differences.

Objectives: *Students will be able to*

use appropriate evidence to argue for and against the abolishment of the Electoral College and, collaboratively, reach a group compromise taking a stand using the most compelling evidence.

Anticipatory Set: *(How will student interest be sparked to engage in the lesson of the day?)*

Students will watch the short video "Does Your Vote Count? The Electoral College Explained" found at https://www.youtube.com/watch?v=W9H3gvnN468.
During the video, closed captions should be played.

Relevancy: *(How will the content be made relevant to the students in the context you are teaching? What connections can be made to their experiences and cultures?)*

As students turn eighteen they will be allowed to and are encouraged to vote in local, state, and federal elections. Through voting students are enacting one of their powers as a democratic citizen in the United States. One of the most important elections is that of the president; however, this is one position that is not won through popular vote but, instead, through the Electoral College, allowing some presidents to win an election after having lost the popular vote. This lesson helps students develop a deeper understanding of the process that impacts the election of the president, how this process impacts them as a voter as well as other citizens throughout the states, and develop their own perspective on this controversial process.

Academic Vocabulary: *(What academic vocabulary will be addressed in this lesson? How will it be taught and made comprehensible to ALL learners?)*

Electoral College, electors, direct popular vote, majority
These terms will be introduced toward the beginning of the lesson and examples will be provided by the instructor, as well as peers, to ensure all students are gaining a deeper understanding of the terms.

Lesson Overview: *(Please describe the steps for each part of the lesson. Also, in parentheses, put a time estimate for each segment of the lesson.)*

1. Anticipatory Set (6 minutes): Students will watch the short video "Does Your Vote Count? The Electoral College Explained" found at https://www.youtube.com/watch?v=W9H3gvnN468.
2. Think-Pair-Share (2 minutes): How does the Electoral College work in relation to the election of the president? Do you have any initial views/feelings toward this process? Explain.
3. Direct Instruction (5 minutes): Introduction and discussion of academic vocabulary.
4. Structured Academic Controversy Activity (70 minutes): Students will be preassigned to groups of four and then further paired with a student from the group (two pairs per group). Within these groups, students will use the database Opposing Viewpoints (or similar) to research the pros and cons of the Electoral College and present their findings to their fellow group members.
    Step 1 (30 minutes): Pair A researches and presents why the Electoral College should be abolished. Pair B researches and presents why the Electoral College should not be abolished.
    Step 2 (30 minutes): Pair A researches and presents why the Electoral College should not be abolished. Pair B researches and presents why the Electoral College should be abolished.

Step 3 (10 minutes): The entire group compromises and takes a stand, using appropriate and the most compelling evidence, to argue whether or not the Electoral College should be abolished.

***This strategy is not designed to have a pair "win the debate" but rather try to find all the various arguments surrounding the topic (pros and cons of the Electoral College).

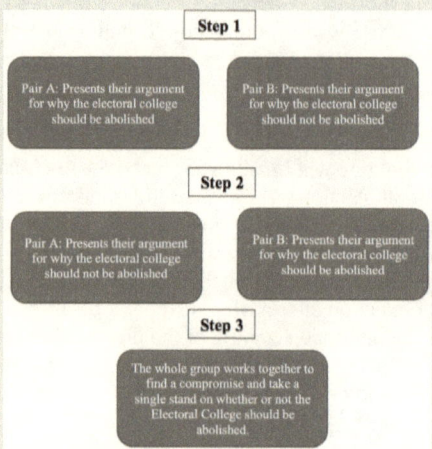

5. Closing (5–10 minutes): Exit Ticket
   a. Reflect: Did your group reach a consensus regarding whether or not the Electoral College should be abolished? If not, where did the difference(s) lie? Overall, do you fully agree with the stand your group compromised on? Why or why not?

***This lesson can be further scaffolded by providing students with the sources that present the pros and cons of the Electoral College, eliminating the research element of the lesson.

Materials Needed: *(Please list the materials that will be needed for this lesson.)*

Computers
Opposing Viewpoints Database
Presentation Software (Google Docs, PowerPoint, Canva, Prezi, etc.) or Poster Paper and markers

Universal Design for Learning: *(How will the principles of UDL be utilized throughout this lesson to give students voice and choice?)*

UDL principles are included through several different means:
- This lesson provides students with relevance, value, and authenticity and allows for the skills learned to be used within the course content and transferred to their personal lives.
- The lesson fosters collaboration and community through pair and small group discussion and collaboration.
- This lesson also acts as and includes scaffolds to help students develop a better understanding of the content as well as multiple access points for the content.

Access: *(What strategies will be used throughout the lesson to allow students multiple entry points into understanding the concepts taught?)*

Different instructional strategies will be used to allow students multiple entry points to the concept being taught. These include responding to questions individually in written form, having small and larger group discourse, use of a video, and choice in source type as they research the Electoral College.

Higher-Order Thinking: *(In what ways will this lesson require students to utilize higher-order thinking? Please describe.)*

Students are to think critically and analyze several sources pertaining to the Electoral College. They must also use appropriate evidence to argue both sides of the essential question, Should the Electoral College be Abolished?, and then further develop a group argument after critiquing all the presented evidence and determining which evidence is most compelling to them.

Assessments: *(How will each learning objective be assessed? What activities do you have planned to check for understanding approximately every 5 minutes of the lesson?)*

Students will be assessed, predominantly, through their discussions. The instructor will walk around the room listening to students speak and facilitating deeper conversations through guiding questions. Furthermore, students will be assessed on their pair presentations, group argument, and personal reflection exit ticket.

Closure: *(What activity will you use to close this lesson and to assess students' understanding at the end of the period?)*

Exit Ticket:
Reflect: Did your group reach a consensus regarding whether or not the Electoral College should be abolished? If not, where did the difference(s) lie? Overall, do you fully agree with the stand your group compromised on? Why or why not?

Possible Extension Activity:
Have students write, email, or call one or more of their elected representatives to express their stance regarding the Electoral College.

REFLECTION ON LESSONS

The lessons presented in this chapter barely touch the surface of how social science teachers can incorporate culturally responsive teaching into their classrooms; however, they offer a starting point and insight into how this can practically be done. Both lessons, though facilitated by the teacher, are student centered and encourage student participation and dialogue with the SAC lesson heavily focused on student collaboration.

These lessons also break away from the prescribed curriculum and provided textbooks to help students better understand that multiple, correct perspectives do exist and that no one "truth" exists. Instead, the social sciences are fluid and ever changing. Furthermore, these lessons help build a classroom culture in which all perspectives and experiences are respected, allowing students the freedom and safety to develop and share their own interpretations of topics being studied, current events, and/or school rules and regulations among others.

READER TAKEAWAYS

- The social sciences are explicitly designed to develop active democratic citizenship and efficacy; therefore, social science teachers have a responsibility to incorporate instructional strategies that align with culturally responsive teaching so students from marginalized communities feel empowered as citizens of a democracy and not further disregarded.
- Social science teachers must continue to move away from teacher-centered, didactic instructional approaches that present the social sciences as static and unchanging. Instead, teachers must incorporate more student-centered instructional practices to help students develop historical and social science thinking skills, including the analysis of multiple perspectives.
- The use of the "review, reflect, and react" framework can help social science teachers develop culturally responsive teaching practices. Using this framework teachers can identify whose perspective is and is not part of their curriculum as well as who is validated within the curriculum. Teachers can then use this to reflect and develop lessons that build upon concepts of culturally responsive teaching to better address the needs of and build upon the assets of their students.
- Instructional strategies like IDM and SAC provide social science teachers with practical ways to bring culturally responsive teaching into their classrooms.

REFERENCES

Aronson, B., and Laughter, J. (2016). The theory and practice of culturally relevant education: A synthesis of research across content areas. *Review of Educational Research, 86*(1), 163–206. https://doi.org/10.3102/0034654315582066.

Berman, S. B. (2022). *LGBTQ+ history in high school classes in the United States since 1990.* London: Bloomsbury Academic. http://dx.doi.org/10.5040/9781350177352.

Bruen, J., Crosbie, V., Kelly, N., Loftus, M., Maillot, A., McGillicuddy, A., and Pechenart, J. (2016). Teaching controversial topics in the humanities and social sciences in Ireland: Using structured academic controversy to develop multi-perspectivity in the learner. *Journal of Social Science Education, 3*, 18–25. https://doi.org/10.4119/UNIBI/jsse-v15-i3-1459.

C3Teachers. (n.d.). *The inquiry design model.* https://c3teachers.org/inquiry-design-model/.

Fitchett, P. G., and Heafner, T. L. (2012). Culturally responsive social studies teaching. In W. B. Russell (Ed.), *Contemporary social studies: An essential reader* (pp. 195–214). Information Age Pub.

Fitchett, P. G., Starker, T. V., and Salyers, B. (2012). Examining culturally responsive teaching self-efficacy in a preservice social studies education course. *Urban Education, 47*(3), 585–611. https://doi.org/10.1177/0042085912436568.

Gay, G. (2018). *Culturally responsive teaching: Theory, research, and practice.* Third edition. Teachers College Press.

Jaffee, A. T., and Yoder, P. J. (2019). Teaching social studies to English language learners. In deOliveira (Ed.), *The handbook of TESOL in K–12* (pp. 307–21). John Wiley & Sons, Ltd. https://doi.org/10.1002/9781119421702.ch20.

Knowles, R. T., Hawkman, A. M., and Nielsen, S. R. (2020). The social studies teacher-coach: A quantitative analysis comparing coaches and non-coaches across how/what they teach. *The Journal of Social Studies Research, 44*, 117–25. https://doi.org/10.1016/j.jssr.2019.04.001.

Ladson-Billings, G. (1995). Toward a theory of culturally relevant pedagogy. *American Educational Research Journal, 32*(3), 465–91. https://doi.org/10.3102/00028312032003465.

Ladson-Billings, G. (2014). Culturally relevant pedagogy 2.0: a.k.a. the remix. *Harvard Educational Review, 84*(1), 74–84. https://doi.org/10.17763/haer.84.1.p2rj131485484751.

McBean, T. R., and Feinberg, J. R. (2020). Critically examining virtual history curriculum. *The Journal of Social Studies Research, 44*(1), 61–76. https://doi.org/10.1016/j.jssr.2019.08.002.

National Center for Education Statistics. (2023, May). *Racial/ethnic enrollment in public schools. Condition of education.* US Department of Education, Institute of Education Sciences. https://nces.ed.gov/programs/coe/indicator/cge.

National Council for the Social Studies (NCSS). (2013). *The college, career, and civic life (C3) framework for social studies state standards: Guidance for enhancing the rigor of K–12 civics, economics, geography, and history.* NCSS. https://socialstudies.org/C3.

Oxford Learner's Dictionary. (2023). *Fact.* https://www.oxfordlearnersdictionaries.com/us/definition/english/fact.

Parker, W. (2008). Knowing and doing in democratic citizenship education. In L. S. Levstik and C. A. Tyson (Eds.), *Handbook of research in social studies education* (pp. 65–80). Routledge.

Parker, W. C. (2015). Social studies education eC21. In W. C. Parker (Ed.), *Social studies today: Research and practice* (pp. 3–13). Routledge.

Swan, K., Lee, J., and Grant, S. G. (2015). The New York state toolkit and the inquiry design model: Anatomy of an inquiry. *Social Education, 79*(5), 316–22.

Thacker, E. S., Lee, J. K, and Friedman, A. M. (2017). Teaching with the C3 Framework: Surveying teachers' beliefs and practices. *Journal of Social Studies Research, 41*(2), 89–100. https://doi.org/10.1016/j.jssr.2016.08.001.

Thornton, S. (2017). A concise historiography of the social studies. In M. M. Manfra and C. M. Bolick (Eds.), *The Wiley handbook of social studies research* (pp. 9–41). John Wiley & Sons, Inc. https://doi.org/10.1002/9781118768747.ch2.

Wiens, P. D., Calkins, L., Yoder, P. J., and Hightower, A. (2022). Examining the relationship between instructional practice and social studies teacher training: A TALIS study. *Journal of Social Studies Research, 46*(2). https://doi.org/10.1016/j.jssr.2021.05.006.

Chapter 3

Culturally Responsive Mathematics Instruction

Dana Mayhall

Educators have a moral and ethical responsibility to help all children reach their potential. No child should sit on the margins, feeling either physically or socially isolated from the rewards of learning and educational challenge.

—Donna Ford (University of Virginia)

EXPECTED LEARNING OUTCOMES

- Readers will gain perspective via one teacher's experience with middle school mathematics.
- Readers will understand culturally responsive pedagogy and instruction in the mathematics classroom.
- Readers will gain insights into practical suggestions for culturally responsive teaching in a mathematics classroom.

FROM THE AUTHOR

As I started writing this chapter about culturally responsive mathematics instruction, my brother-in-law (a retired college professor) asked me about my writing. When I told him it was about how teachers need to implement new strategies in math instruction to reach all students no matter their diversity, he was surprised. He said he thought there was only one way to teach math so that students get the right answer.

There it was, staring me in the face: the reason this chapter needed to be written. Many educators do not realize that students of diverse cultures need a different kind of instruction to successfully master mathematical concepts. The academic needs of those students and the instructional techniques educators require to meet those needs are the reasons for this work.

TEACHER NARRATIVE

From a Middle School Mathematics Teacher

When I began teaching math to eighth graders, I thought I'd be great at it because I love math. I found out very quickly, however, that just because I was a good math student didn't mean I'd be a good math teacher. I had never struggled to learn math concepts, so I didn't understand how to teach my students who were struggling to comprehend what I was trying to teach. When I tried to teach my students the way I had learned math, it just didn't work, and I didn't know what to do.

I talked to our math coach about what I could do to improve my instruction and really reach my students. He suggested I attend training about teaching mathematics to culturally diverse students. Wow! My eyes were opened to things I never had thought of before. I learned ways to make math fun and understandable to all learners. I learned to start with methods to present the concepts in concrete ways using hands-on materials. At first, I thought that using manipulatives was too elementary for my students, but I quickly found out they needed that support and scaffolding even being eighth graders.

Many of my learners also needed visuals to internalize their learning so the next step in my math class would be to use representational ways of instruction like using drawings and models. After students gained understanding through concrete and representational instruction, I'd move into the abstract equations and algorithms that required higher-order thinking skills. By implementing these procedures, I was able to help my students grasp the concept behind the math, which built their confidence because they had been presented with multiple ways to "figure it out."

I began to create a safe environment for my students to explore, risk, and learn math when they had struggled to do so in the past. I focused on helping my middle school students develop a growth mindset where mistakes are used to teach us, not shame us for failing to give the right answer. It takes time to develop the level of trust needed for students to risk and speak up, asking questions and giving solutions to math problems, but that is what I found helps me reach everyone no matter their level.

I learned that culturally responsive instruction isn't about dumbing down the curriculum. I had to establish a supportive environment and demonstrate to my students how math was relevant to them. Then I could challenge them with the rigor of higher-order thinking. By following what I had learned about culturally responsive instruction, I was able to get all my students engaged while meeting their various levels of math abilities in my eighth-grade classes.

I guess I'm one of those strange people who like both math and writing, so I decided to fuse them together in my class and use storytelling in eighth-grade math. After teaching a math unit, I had the students create their characters and write an adventure plot that included conflict and resolution. My students would take the math concepts from the unit and use them as events in the story. If we studied transformations (where objects are rotated, reflected, or translated), we would brainstorm ways characters could behave like they were transformed on a coordinate plane.

For example, if a character was rotating, it might be spinning. My students would write their stories and share them with their classmates. Students got very excited about their stories and began to illustrate them. Some of the best stories were shared with our sixth graders to help them better understand transformations. The students had fun while mastering the concept, and that's what math is all about.

In my culturally responsive math class, I use puzzles, games, music, and group problem solving. This helps my students develop a love for math because they see its relevance to their own world. Through cooperative learning groups, students see a problem from different perspectives, which can lead to creative thinking and solutions. We use oral and written (or drawn) reflections because students who can discuss their mathematical thinking can also demonstrate their understanding of the math concept. In our class, we also celebrate our achievements so that the students grow in math confidence and motivation to learn more.

I love teaching math and now, because I'm implementing culturally responsive strategies, my kids love math too!

CULTURALLY RESPONSIVE MATHEMATICS INSTRUCTION

Mathematics education is about understanding ideas and establishing authentic connections that create powerful learning through new ways of thinking (Boaler, 2022; Louie, 2017b). However, American mathematics practices historically have provided unequal learning opportunities for some students while affording challenging instruction for others (Louie, 2017a; Yeh, 2021). Some students have been denied access to exceptional mathematics learning experiences so they have developed a negative attitude toward math (Gutierrez, 2017).

Many educators believe this discrepancy is due to the more diverse student population in the United States (Bonner, 2021). Statistics from the Department of Education report that 45 percent of public school students were White while 55 percent were students of color (National Center for Educational Statistics, 2023). To meet the needs of these students, mathematics educators should consider the various cultures of their students when making decisions about curriculum as well as pedagogy (Yeh et al., 2020).

By utilizing inclusive mathematics instruction, students are encouraged to actively explore new strategies to understand math and begin to identify as mathematicians (Belsha, 2023). Many people believe that math is simply a set of formulas or procedures to be memorized, but that belief severely limits the learner (Bonner, 2021; Yeh et al., 2020). Mathematics education must strengthen all students' conceptual understanding while building on their strengths, which will lead to students developing identities as "good at math" (Gutierrez, 2017; Louie, 2017a). To provide rich learning experiences for all students, innovative mathematics instruction in student-centered classrooms where all learners are appreciated is necessary (Bonner, 2021).

1. Learn about culturally responsive mathematics pedagogy.

For teachers to successfully implement culturally responsive mathematics instruction, it is important that they educate themselves (Gay, 2002; Hammond, 2015; Ladson-Billings, 1995). Even though culturally relevant pedagogy is considered to be good teaching practice, many mathematics teachers do not understand how to implement it in their teaching to challenge the deficit views about how some students learn (Yeh, 2021).

The first step in educating oneself is to consider your background in terms of culture and view of mathematics and how that informs your practice as a math teacher, then read literature about culturally responsive instruction especially in the context of mathematics (Bonner, 2021). Teachers need to help their students see themselves in the curriculum (Yeh, 2021) and shift their thinking to see themselves as having mathematical competence and something important to contribute to the learning (Louie, 2017b; Yeh et al., 2020).

Educators should also study mathematicians of all cultures and learn about their struggles as well as their successes (Braun, 2017). Teachers can share the stories of mathematicians so that students can see themselves in the lives of these diverse thinkers. One way to do this is to introduce a new mathematician every week and put up a poster with their picture so students can see for themselves the diversity and recognize that they, too, can accomplish great things in mathematics. This is providing access to new opportunities that some students have never thought they could ever have (Bonner, 2021; Dunleavy, 2018).

2. Provide a safe and welcoming environment to create a community of learners.

To establish an inviting environment in a mathematics classroom, teachers must consider how to develop students' positive mathematical identity (Candela et al., 2020; Dunleavy, 2018; Boaler, 2022). Experts suggest that students need to learn to see math as a fun and accessible subject and see themselves as important participants in the learning process (Louie, 2017b). In an equitable mathematics classroom, teachers have time and autonomy to establish a creative, collaborative, and problem-solving environment (Belsha, 2023; Cohen, 1997), thus providing students the opportunities to engage with others and make connections with their ideas (Yeh et al., 2020). Students are recognized for their strengths, and their mathematical ideas of various solutions are welcomed (Dunleavy, 2018; Louie, 2017b).

In an inclusive mathematics learning environment, all students are validated as contributors and are encouraged to learn together with others (Louie, 2017a; Yeh, 2021). Teachers must actively work to provide an environment where taking risks is welcomed, learning is more public through cooperative groups, and students are active participants in their own learning (Belsha, 2023; Candela et al., 2020; Dunleavy, 2018). The class becomes a community where it is acceptable to work and help each other master difficult mathematics concepts together (Currell, 2021; Dunleavy, 2018; Packer, 2022). Working with diverse learners requires setting up a solid foundation of acceptance from which all students can be successful within their own cultural context (Bonner, 2021).

This can be accomplished by building positive and supportive relationships with students by spending time listening to them (Belsha, 2023; Ferlazzo, 2020). Teachers need to learn about their students' backgrounds and attitudes toward math. This can be done by simple surveys, essays, or drawings to understand students' culture and learning styles as well as their ideas about math (Bonner, 2021). Finding out students' strengths, needs, and motivations connects the teacher to the students (Belsha, 2023; Packer, 2022), therefore providing information that informs motivating and engaging instruction (Braun, 2017; Ferlazzo, 2020). With this support, students who feel that their teachers believe in them can become academically successful in math (Gutierrez, 2017).

3. Establish high expectations.

Excellence in mathematics education requires high expectations and the support to attain them so that "all students, regardless of their personal characteristics, backgrounds, or physical challenges, must have opportunities to study and support to learn mathematics" (National Council of Teachers of Mathematics, 2000, p. 12). Teachers must communicate their expectations to their students with more than words and show them with their body language and actions that they believe they can accomplish the goals (Bonner, 2021; Packer, 2022).

Teachers have to be honest with their students as to the challenge and rigor required while assuring them that they can do it by working together in community (Belsha, 2023; Louie, 2017b; Packer, 2022). By doing this, students who have struggled with math in the past will achieve success through the use of stimulating learning experiences in an integrated approach to the subject matter (Dunleavy, 2018). Working toward equity in the mathematics classroom is a continuous work of providing access as well as setting high expectations that all students can and will learn (Boaler, 2022; Yeh et al., 2020).

4. Engage students with authentic mathematics learning opportunities.

Effective mathematics teachers find ways to help their students understand how the course relates to their own lives. This is done by learning about your students and then using that information to inform instruction and tasks (Braun, 2017; Yurekli et al., 2020). Applying math skills to real-world situations is an excellent way to connect diverse cultural experiences so that the students become excited about math (Ferlazzo, 2020). Students need opportunities to learn beyond the classroom and textbooks, so teachers need to provide authentic learning activities using dialogue, games, hands-on projects, and other experiences (Boaler, 2022; Currell, 2021).

For example, students can role-play a real-world math scenario about budgeting for a week's groceries or ordering food at a restaurant and figuring out the cost of meals, tax, and tips. Teachers should use students' interests and apply math activities to real professions like business, medicine, baking, and others (Braun, 2017). Authentic mathematical instruction shifts from working on the problem for the answer toward representations of the concepts so that students use deeper thinking to get understanding (Dunleavy, 2018).

An inclusive mathematics classroom includes student-centered activities such as debate, experimentation, cooperative learning groups, and collaborative problem solving instead of worksheets and rote learning (Dunleavy, 2018; Louie, 2017b). We know that educational researchers Piaget and

Vygotsky believed that learning is constructed in social settings because we learn from others to make meaning of experiences (Piaget, 1926; Vygotsky, 1962). Learning in social settings is the most natural way for children to learn because they enjoy working with others (Currell, 2021; Dunleavy, 2018).

Achievement levels of students improve when they are learning through collaborative problem solving (Boaler, 2022; Premo et al., 2018) because of both interdependence and the personal accountability of the group members (Ferlazzo, 2020). This may look like students sitting in groups working together on whiteboards or sharing their math journals. Instead of selecting a few students as math experts and expecting them to help others, inclusive teachers create a classroom where students are both learners and contributors so that there is a mutual dependence on each other for success (Louie, 2017a).

Using collaborative groups goes beyond being the best or fastest at getting the right answer because the inclusive teacher focuses on more than speed and accuracy (Dunleavy, 2018). Mathematical learning is in the public space and a matter of discourse among the group members providing more time to process their learning so that the students internalize the knowledge (Candela et al., 2020; Currell, 2021).

Teachers who want to successfully teach math to a diverse population of students need to implement inclusive pedagogies and use a student-centered lens (Dunleavy, 2018; Gutierrez, 2017). Mathematics classrooms provide an atmosphere where teaching and learning is collective so that both the teacher and students learn and grow (Yeh et al., 2020). This can be done as students play an active part in their own learning and are given as much choice as possible from differentiated assignments (Bonner, 2021).

Mathematics instruction in early grades utilizes a hands-on approach where math manipulatives are provided as resources for student learning. However, these physical resources are not just for elementary math classes. Many secondary pupils can benefit from using concrete materials to help them secure their conceptual understanding (Packer, 2022).

Teachers can scaffold learning by providing the temporary support students may need to become independent learners. For example, if students are working on word problems, teachers can help them by using visual cues or reviewing important vocabulary for the class (Braun, 2017). Instead of giving a traditional test, inclusive teachers can have their students participate in a group assessment or a take-home assessment so that extra time and support can be provided (Packer, 2022).

Inclusive teachers anticipate the misconceptions some students may have due to cultural differences, so they use multimedia and visuals such as anchor charts to support student understanding and motivation (Yeh et al., 2020). Some secondary students believe visuals are too juvenile for them; however, some of the most important mathematicians use visuals in many ways

(Boaler, 2022). Teachers need to use developmentally and culturally appropriate language and encourage the students to do so as well (Bonner, 2021). Providing the time for students to use discourse to discuss their mathematical thinking and provide feedback for others' ideas allows for more successful participation and academic success (Candela et al., 2020; Yeh et al., 2020). Once students know that their ideas are welcomed and accepted, they will be encouraged to take on more challenging mathematics tasks (Bonner, 2021; Louie, 2017b).

5. Encourage a mathematical growth mindset.

Carol Dweck's work with mindsets demonstrates that students' ideas of their own intelligence can influence their motivation and academic success (2013). Much of what we think or understand about our personalities comes from our mindset. A student with a fixed mindset hates to make mistakes so much that sometimes this fear can completely shut them down in class.

However, a student with a growth mindset in math is willing to take risks, make a mistake, and learn from it (Boaler, 2022). When a student is willing to make a mistake in math and learn from it, their brain truly grows and new connections are made through this productive struggle (Braun, 2017). Learning from mistakes is essential as we provide specific feedback on students' thinking and ideas, not just on their answers. When students in a math class have growth mindsets, they accept the challenge of rigorous learning without the fear of failure (Boaler, 2022; Dweck, 2013). Teachers in inclusive classrooms must learn to praise the process and effort as students engage in learning. Assessments become opportunities for students to display their effort and understanding in a safe atmosphere of acceptance and success (Braun, 2017).

Here are two secondary mathematics lesson plans that incorporate culturally responsive strategies to meet the needs of all learners.

MATH CULTURALLY RESPONSIVE LESSON PLAN 1

Title of Lesson:	*Compound Probability*
Grade Level:	Seventh grade
Content Standard(s):	
7.SP.A.1 Common Core. Understand that statistics can be used to gain information about a population by examining a sample of the population; generalizations about a population from a sample are valid only if the sample is representative of that population. Understand that random sampling tends to produce representative samples and support valid inferences.	

7.SP.A.2 Common Core. Use data from a random sample to draw inferences about a population with an unknown characteristic of interest. Generate multiple samples (or simulated samples) of the same size to gauge the variation in estimates or predictions.

Social Justice Standard: https://www.learningforjustice.org/frameworks/social-justice-standards

DI.6–8.6: Interact with people different from me with respect.

Objectives: *Students will be able to*

determine the sample spaces of compound events, and
calculate compound probabilities.

Anticipatory Set: *(How will student interest be sparked to engage in the lesson of the day?)*

(During this introduction, flip a coin over and over.) Remember how we talked about probability yesterday? Who can tell me what it is? That is the definition of simple probability. If I flip this coin three times, what is the probability I'll get heads twice? How can I figure that out? (Have a student come to the board and show how they came up with the answer. If they don't show a tree diagram, remind students of that as well.)

Relevancy: *(How will the content be made relevant to the students in the context you are teaching? What connections can be made to their experiences and cultures?)*

Everyone uses probability every day because we are constantly making choices. You choose what to wear to school, what to eat for lunch, and even what song you like to listen to on the radio. When you are thinking about what to wear to school, do you ever consider the weather? The weatherman uses probabilities to report the chances of rain in the forecast. People use probabilities to see who might win a sports championship. We use probabilities every day. Today we are going to expand our learning to look at ways to figure compound probability: the probability of a combination of two or more simple events.

Academic Vocabulary: *(What academic vocabulary will be addressed in this lesson? How will it be taught and made comprehensible to ALL learners?)*

outcomes, events, sample space, dependent event, independent event
These words will be defined and placed on the Word Wall during this unit on probability. Students will add them to their math journals and come up with an illustration that helps define the word. This will be shared with their group.

Lesson Overview: *(Please describe the steps for each part of the lesson. Also, in parentheses, put a time estimate for each segment of the lesson.)*

Introduction (5 minutes):
- Let's review simple probabilities. In this jar, I have three different pieces of candy: apple, watermelon, and cherry flavored. With your shoulder partner, determine what the probability is of me selecting a cherry piece of candy. (Call on students to answer using a randomizer.) (Make sure manipulatives are available for those who need the extra support.)

Now try another one. Here is a simple die. What is the chance of me rolling a 5? Discuss it with your partner then put your marker down when you've got your answer. (Call on students to answer using a randomizer.)

Instruction (10 minutes):
- Good work on simple probabilities. Today we are going to be finding compound probabilities. Let's write that definition in our math journals. Compound probability is the probability of a combination of two or more simple events. This combination is called compound events. An example of a compound event is: randomly selecting a piece of candy from a container and rolling a die together are compound events.
- Remind me of the ratio we use to find simple probability. (random answer) The ratio is the number of favorable outcomes over the number of outcomes in the sample space. We will use this same process for finding probabilities of compound events.
- Turn to your shoulder partner and review these ratios.
- Let's look back at our sample space for selecting the candy and rolling a die we did earlier. Is there just one way to show the sample space? Of course not. We have seen students do this three ways: using a table, a tree diagram, and an organized list. When we look at this problem, we see that all three ways get to the same answer of eighteen possible outcomes.
- Explain that once you've listed the events in the sample space, you can find the probability of a specific outcome. Model how to find the probability of randomly selecting a specific piece of candy from the container and rolling a 5 on the die.
- Now working with your shoulder partner, let's find some more compound probabilities: randomly selecting a piece of candy and rolling a number greater than 4.
- Come back together and have students model how to find the probability.

Guided Practice (10 minutes):
- Hand out the compound events worksheet to students and have them work with their partners to complete it.
- Monitor students' progress as you move around the room.
- Encourage dialogue about their thinking processes.

Independent Practice (20 minutes):
- Pass out an independent practice sheet; students select to do eight out of the ten problems and work on their own while the teacher monitors progress.
- After fifteen minutes, ask students if there were any challenging problems. Go over answers for these problems with the class.

Materials Needed: *(Please list the materials that will be needed for this lesson.)*

Math journals, whiteboards and markers, dice, coins, and probability worksheets for groups and individuals, teacher-created guided practice and independent practice sheets. (Make sure to create probability word problems that use students' names and experiences from their cultures.)

Universal Design for Learning: *(How will the principles of UDL be utilized throughout this lesson to give students voice and choice?)*

Students work in pairs and independently. They have a choice in the assignment to do eight out of ten problems. Encouraging the dialogue about their thinking encourages students to use their voice in their partnership.

Access: *(What strategies will be used throughout the lesson to allow students multiple entry points into understanding the concepts taught?)*

Students have access to their learning with the stories to begin the lesson, through the written definitions, through the illustrations they create of the vocabulary words, and through the hands-on manipulatives to figure out the probabilities.

Higher-Order Thinking: *(In what ways will this lesson require students to utilize higher-order thinking? Please describe.)*

In explaining their thinking about the concept of compound probability, students have to use HOTS in their dialogue and demonstrations.

Assessments: *(How will each learning objective be assessed? What activities do you have planned to check for understanding approximately every 5 minutes of the lesson?)*

To meet the needs of diverse learners, make sure to use their names and experiences from their cultures when constructing the probability problems for both the guided practice sheet and the independent practice sheet. Throughout the lesson, formative assessment will be completed as shoulder partners work together to figure out the probabilities. The teacher will also assess the learning by monitoring students' work on both guided and independent practice.

Closure: *(What activity will you use to close this lesson and to assess students' understanding at the end of the period?)*

Students will complete an exit ticket before leaving class. The question will be: You have the choice of milk, soda, or horchata to drink and four snacks (Flamin' Hot Cheetos, Takis, Oreos, or M&Ms). What is the probability that you would pick horchata and Takis?

Lesson 1 Reflection

This lesson is a fun way to get students involved in probability when they may not have in the past. Sometimes middle school students have blocks when it comes to solving probabilities, but this lesson makes it more hands-on so that every student can be successful. Make sure to have plenty of manipulatives for those students who require that support.

MATH CULTURALLY RESPONSIVE LESSON PLAN 2

Title of Lesson:	*Systems of Linear Equations Review*
Grade Level:	Ninth-grade algebra
Content Standard(s):	

HSA.REI.C.6 Common Core. Solve systems of linear equations exactly and approximately (for example, with graphs), focusing on pairs of linear equations in two variables.

Social Justice Standard: https://www.learningforjustice.org/frameworks/social-justice-standards

DI.6–8.6: Interact with people different from me with respect.

Objectives: *Students will be able to*

use linSolve to correctly determine the solution set of two equations with 100 percent accuracy.

Anticipatory Set: *(How will student interest be sparked to engage in the lesson of the day?)*

Today we are going to review systems of equations. We will review how to solve them first then have fun participating in a unique activity.

Relevancy: *(How will the content be made relevant to the students in the context you are teaching? What connections can be made to their experiences and cultures?)*

Has anyone heard of speed dating? What do you know about it? (allow for responses) Speed dating is a way to help people meet potential dates in a short, effective way. Today we are going to do some speed dating with our equations to see how "compatible" we are with each other—in math terms, that is.

Academic Vocabulary: *(What academic vocabulary will be addressed in this lesson? How will it be taught and made comprehensible to ALL learners?)*

This is a review lesson, but a teacher may want to have students look in math journals for vocabulary about linear equations.

Lesson Overview: *(Please describe the steps for each part of the lesson. Also, in parentheses, put a time estimate for each segment of the lesson.)*

Introduction (5 minutes):
- Remember the poster over here (refer to anchor chart for visual learners) that said linSolve? That's what we will be reviewing today.
- This is an important skill especially for your future math work.
- Let's review how to use linSolve. On your calculator, how do you get to linSolve? (menu 3–2) From this screen, tell the calculator you have two equations and variables x and y. Those are the default settings, so you can just hit enter.
- Now type your first equation in the top box and the second equation in the bottom box. Hit enter and get a solution set of answers.
- In our calculators, we can type equations in standard form, which is nice because we don't have to change our equations into y=mx+b. But when we type our equations into Desmos, it's sometimes easier for us to see where the graphs intercept and what that ordered pair means. So if you would like to use Desmos, you can type your two equations in and see where they meet. You would just need to change them to y=mx+b first. Either way, a calculator or Desmos will get you to the right answer.

Guided Practice (5 minutes):
- Pass out the speed dating sheets.

Speed Dating Systems

Name: $2x+6y=18$

- Slope-intercept Form:

Your Slope is (circle one)
Positive   Negative   Zero   undefined

- Your rate of change is: _____
- Your y-intercept is: _____
- Your x-intercept is: _____

Date Card

Who your date is with	Where you met

- At the top of each one is an equation (each student's page will have a unique equation).
- Before the speed dating starts, students will need to fill out their "dating card." They need to write a little about themselves, like their slope, y- and x-intercepts, and their slope-intercept form equation. Students may consult their shoulder partners for help and clarification.
- Teacher will monitor to make sure all students are successfully completing their dating card.

Group/Partner Practice (30 minutes):
- Now students will move through the speed dating circle, finding the solution between their and their partners' equations. This will help them practice using linSolve.
- Using a timer, students will have
  4 minutes to work with their "date" to figure out their solution for the two equations.
- In the chart, students will write the equation of their "date" in the column about who their date is.
- Using their own creativity and thinking skills, students will determine where the date might take place. This can be done by thinking about if there was a good solution so the place probably would be a good place to meet. If there is not a good solution, students might put unlikely places to have a good date.
- As the timer sounds, the outside group of the circle moves one seat to the left and the process begins again.
- Continue the speed dating until time runs out.
- Make sure students put their real name on the paper and turn it in before leaving.

Materials Needed: *(Please list the materials that will be needed for this lesson.)*
Speed dating worksheet
Calculator
Chromebook for Desmos
Pencil
Desks need to be rearranged to face each other in pairs.

Universal Design for Learning: *(How will the principles of UDL be utilized throughout this lesson to give students voice and choice?)*

Students are in control of their learning and activity in this lesson. They are able to use their creativity as they complete their dating profile.

Access: *(What strategies will be used throughout the lesson to allow students multiple entry points into understanding the concepts taught?)*

This lesson involves a great deal of dialogue so students have multiple opportunities to engage with the concepts and each other.

Higher-Order Thinking: *(In what ways will this lesson require students to utilize higher-order thinking? Please describe.)*

Students will be demonstrating their mastery of solving linear equations using lin-Solve and working with partners throughout the lesson. They will have to use HOTS in their dialogue with dates as well as with the teacher.

Assessments: *(How will each learning objective be assessed? What activities do you have planned to check for understanding approximately every 5 minutes of the lesson?)*

During the speed dating, the teacher will monitor the activity to ensure the students have mastered the process. When a misunderstanding arises, the teacher can address it immediately to redirect learning.

Closure: *(What activity will you use to close this lesson and to assess students' understanding at the end of the period?)*

This is a fun activity where students aren't even aware of how much they are learning. It is informative to ask them before they leave: What did they learn. Listen! You will find out more about your students than you thought as they share their process.

Lesson from algebra teacher Raegan Palacio

Lesson 2 Reflection

I observed this lesson being taught in a ninth-grade algebra class. The students got so invested in the lesson, they groaned when the teacher said the time was up. The creative ways they responded to their partners were humorous and demonstrated their total engagement with the lesson. I believe these students will be very successful in the future when solving linear equations.

CONCLUSION

Teachers who care about their diverse student population will create an inclusive classroom where students participate in cooperative activities, working together to discover new ways of understanding mathematical concepts. When teachers use culturally responsive pedagogy in mathematics, they will welcome their students' diverse cultures and create an atmosphere of discovery and learning where new positive mathematical identities can be established and celebrated (Yeh, 2021; Yeh et al., 2020).

READER TAKEAWAYS

Culturally responsive mathematics instruction can be successfully implemented by a dedicated, passionate educator establishing a welcoming learning environment where students are free to learn from their mistakes as they grasp challenging math concepts.

- All students can become mathematicians when they are allowed to learn and grow in their own way and at their own rate.
- Culturally diverse students deserve to be taught using culturally responsive mathematics instruction.

REFERENCES

Belsha, K. (2023, April 19). Math can be intimidating. Here's how the 2023 National Teacher of the Year uses stories to connect. *Chalkbeat*. https://www.chalkbeat.org/2023/4/19/23690235/national-teacher-year-math-rebecka-peterson.

Boaler, J. (2022). *Mathematical mindsets: Unleashing students' potential through creative mathematics, inspiring messages and innovative teaching*. Second edition. Jossey-Bass.

Bonner, E. P. (2021). Practicing culturally responsive mathematics teaching. *Mathematics Teacher: Learning and Teaching PK–12, 114*(1), 6–15. https://doi.org/10.5951/MTLT.2020.0119.

Braun, B. (2017). Six ways mathematics instructors can support diversity and inclusion. *American Mathematical Society*. https://blogs.ams.org/matheducation/2017/03/06/six-ways-mathematics-instructors-can-support-diversity-and-inclusion/.

Candela, A. G., Boston, M. D., and Dixon, J. K. (2020). Discourse actions to promote student access. *Mathematics Teacher: Learning and Teaching PK–12, 113*(4), 266–77. https://doi.org/10.5951/MTLT.2019.0009.

Cohen, E. G. (1997). Equity in heterogeneous classrooms: A challenge for teachers and sociologists. In E. G., Cohen and R. A. Lotan (Eds.), *Working for equity in heterogeneous classrooms: Sociological theory in practice* (pp. 3–14). Teachers College Press.

Currell, J. (2021). Working together: How collaboration creates meaningful learning. *MATHS No Problem!* https://mathsnoproblem.com/blog/teaching-practice/collaboration-for-meaningful-learning.

Dunleavy, T. K. (2018). High school algebra students busting the myth about mathematical smartness: Counterstories to the dominant narrative "Get it quick and get it right." *Education Sciences, 8*. https://eric.ed.gov/?id=EJ1199595.

Dweck, C. S. (2013). *Mindset: New psychology of success*. Ballantine Books.

Ferlazzo, L. (2020, December 17). Twelve ways to make math more culturally responsive. *EducationWeek*. https://www.edweek.org/teaching-learning/opinion-twelve-ways-to-make-math-more-culturally-responsive/2020/12.

Gay, G. (2002). Preparing for culturally responsive teaching. *Journal of Teacher Education, 53*(2), 106–16.

Gutierrez, R. (2017). Why mathematics education was late to the backlash party: The need for a revolution. *Journal of Urban Mathematics Education, 10*(2), 8–24.

Hammond, Z. (2015). *Culturally responsive teaching and the brain: Promoting authentic engagement and rigor among culturally and linguistically diverse students* (2014-55978-000). Corwin Press.

Ladson-Billings, G. (1995). But that's just good teaching! The case for culturally relevant pedagogy. *Theory Into Practice, 34*(3), 159.

Louie, N. L. (2017a). The culture of exclusion in mathematics education and its persistence in equity-oriented teaching. *Journal for Research in Mathematics Education, 48*(5), 488–519. https://doi.org/10.5951/jresematheduc.48.5.0488.

Louie, N. L. (2017b). Supporting teachers' equity-oriented learning and identities: A resource-centered perspective. *Teachers College Record: The Voice of Scholarship in Education, 119*(2), 1–42. https://doi.org/10.1177/016146811711900203.

National Center for Educational Statistics (2023). *Racial/ethnic enrollment in public schools* (Condition of Education). US Department of Education, Institute of Educational Sciences. https://nces.ed.gov/programs/coe/indicator/cge/racial-ethnic-enrollment.

National Council of Teachers of Mathematics (2000). *Principles and standards for school mathematics*. National Council of Teachers of Mathematics.

Packer, N. (2022). SEND inclusion jigsaw: A teaching strategy for all learners. *MATHS No Problem!* https://mathsnoproblem.com/blog/learner-focus/send-inclusion-jigsaw-teaching-strategy.

Piaget, J. (1926). *The language and thought of the child*. Harcourt, Brace, and Co.

Premo, J., Cavagnetto, A., and Davis, W. B. (2018). Promoting collaborative classrooms: The impacts of interdependent cooperative learning on undergraduate interactions and achievement. *CBE Life Sciences Education, 17*(2), ar32. https://doi.org/10.1187/cbe.17-08-0176.

Vygotsky, L. (1962). *Thought and language* (E. Hanfmann & G. Vakar, Eds.). MIT Press.

Yeh, C. (2021). Responsive and relevant to whom? *Mathematics Teacher: Learning and Teaching PK–12, 114*(1), 83–84. https://doi.org/10.5951/MTLT.2020.0083.

Yeh, C., Sugita, T., and Tan, P. (2020). Reimagining inclusive spaces for mathematics learning. *Mathematics Teacher: Learning and Teaching PK–12, 113*(9), 708–14. https://doi.org/10.5951/MTLT.2019.0101.

Yurekli, B., Stein, M. K., Correnti, R., and Kisa, Z. (2020). Teaching mathematics for conceptual understanding: Teachers' beliefs and practices and the role of constraints. *Journal for Research in Mathematics Education, 51*(2), 234–47. https://doi.org/10.5951/jresematheduc-2020–0021.

Chapter 4

Empowering Scientific Minds
Integrating Cultural Perspectives in an Inclusive Classroom

Harleen Singh and Jose Pavez

EXPECTED LEARNING OUTCOMES

- Readers will develop an insight into teaching culturally relevant science that is connected to the lives and community of their students.
- Readers will be acquainted with instructional strategies and recommendations to teach science through a cultural lens.
- Readers will understand the importance of critical reflection and cultural competence as an important aspect of teaching and learning science.
- Readers will gain an insight into teaching science through the critique of discourse of power.

THE CASE OF MS. BENTLEY'S SCIENCE CLASSROOM

Ms. Alison Bentley is a science teacher teaching eighth-grade general science at Florence High School. This is her first year of teaching school. Ms. Bentley has a diverse classroom. She has students from different cultural backgrounds, and about half her students are English learners. Ms. Bentley has good knowledge of science content, is passionate about teaching science, and wants her students to learn and love science.

She believes in including a lot of hands-on activities in her lessons and spends a lot of time and effort preparing for her classes. However, Ms. Bentley has a dilemma and wonders what she is doing wrong. She notices that while doing hands-on activities, all her students are super engaged and excited. However, this engagement and excitement is not apparent at other times when she is teaching.

The other day, while teaching a lesson on friction, she demonstrated friction with two interleaved books. She interleaved the pages of the two large books by folding down one page of the first book, then a page from the second book, and then a page from the first book, and so on. Students took turns trying to pull the books apart but were not able to. There was a lot of laughter and excitement in the class as the students engaged in the activity. The activity was successful in terms of engagement and excitement produced, as well as clarifying the concept of friction between two objects.

Once the activity was over, Ms. Bentley had a problem getting the students back to learning, as she theoretically explained the concept of friction. While some of the students paid attention, others did not. She could make out that some students listened to her while she presented the information, some pretended to pay attention, and others did not disguise their disinterest. She was including hands-on activities in her science lessons, but not managing to engage all the students in the class. Ms. Bentley wondered if she was doing something wrong or was it that some of her students did not have an aptitude for science.

Back in the teachers' lounge, she brought up this topic during lunch. She hoped to gain some insight from the more experienced teachers. Some of the comments she received were, "My class has several low-motivated Black and Hispanic students as well. No matter what I do, they are simply not interested"; "You should try to plan two different lessons. One for the high achieving students and one for the rest of the class"; and "Give these students some busy work to keep them out of mischief."

Ms. Lee, the other science teacher at the school, saw the distressed look on Ms. Bentley's face. "Don't worry Alison," she said. "Start by getting to know your students. Get to know their strengths, interests, skills, etc. When you teach science which students cannot relate to, they will not deem it as meaningful. Think about teaching them in ways that can help students connect science with their home and communities. And most important, think about the conceptions and funds of knowledge that your students bring to the classroom. Think of the minority and diverse students in your classroom as an asset and not an obstacle."

In this chapter, we will try to help Ms. Bentley solve her problem and design instruction that is meaningful and relevant for *all* students in the classroom. Minority and diverse students are indispensable in the educational system because of the different views, experiences, and ways of knowing that they bring to the learning environment. There is increasing recognition that the diverse customs and orientations that members of different cultural communities bring to formal and informal science learning contexts are assets on which to build—both for the benefit of the student and ultimately of science itself (National Research Council, 2012). Diversity should be celebrated because it enriches our schools and society. It is important to not just build schools free of discrimination and prejudice but also a workplace and a society where there is awareness, dialogue, and action that helps people to recognize that diversity as an asset.

SCHOOL SCIENCE AND ITS RELEVANCE FOR STUDENTS

Traditional ways of teaching science no longer meet the needs of the diverse students in today's classrooms. Studies from all over the world have indicated a growing disenchantment of students with school science. Interest in science as a subject and in science-related careers has seen a downward trend. Despite recognizing science as an important subject, students often prefer not to take up science subjects in high school as they are perceived as boring, difficult, or simply due to the way they are taught.

Even high-achieving students often turn their back on science due to their negative experiences with school science. Students experience a tension between benefits of choosing a science-based career and the disadvantage of studying a subject that does not provide intrinsic satisfaction (Lyons, 2006). Lyons (2006) has compared narratives of students from Sweden, England, and Australia to highlight how students in different countries have remarkably similar experiences with school science.

We know that the classroom is a site for social change that provides a setting for new ideas. In John Dewey's (1910) paper "Science as Subject-Matter and as Method," he identified the importance of the social role of science in modern-day society. Dewey attributed the failure of science in schools to the way science was taught. He believed that science education should aim at inculcating a scientific attitude and a way of thinking in the students and drew attention to the fact that too much focus was laid on ready-made material for the teaching of science, which the students need to learn and be familiar with.

Learning of the numerous facts of nature would make science too far off and abstract and may not be the best method for teaching science to students whose lives and careers exist in the local context. Instead, Dewey recommended focusing on the method of science and envisioned the social role of science where science generates a reliable knowledge of the world around us and is used for the betterment of society. Dewey's recommendations are as relevant today as they were more than a century ago. More than a hundred years down the line, we continue to teach students in ways that alienate them from science, especially students from minority cultures.

IS CULTURALLY RELEVANT AND
RESPONSIVE SCIENCE THE ANSWER?

Gloria Ladson-Billings (1995) defines culturally relevant teaching as a pedagogy of opposition that is committed to collective and not individual empowerment. She proposed the theory of culturally focused pedagogy that could be considered in the reformation of teacher education. She suggests that the term "culturally responsive" as a way that would help students maintain their cultural identities, simultaneously succeed in academics, and help them recognize, understand, and critique the current social inequalities, that is, help them become sociopolitically critical.

She argued that culturally relevant teaching is distinguishable by three broad criteria. These include students experiencing academic success, students developing and maintaining cultural competence and a critical consciousness to challenge the status quo of the current social order. Culturally relevant teaching is recognized by propositions or conceptions regarding self and other, social relations, and knowledge. This theoretical perspective was originally suggested to educate teachers for success with African American students, but is equally relevant to all nonmainstreamed students who are marginalized from the mainstream in societies all over the world. Ladson-Billings (1995) describes an effective teacher as one who develops a knowledge base about the community, including its people, places, and events, things that may not be mentioned in the standardized curriculum.

Culturally responsive teaching connects what the students already know to their lived experiences and their funds of knowledge to academic knowledge and intellectual tools in ways that legitimize what students already know (Gay, 2013). Geneva Gay (2013) places the onus of responsibility of culturally responsive teaching on the teachers who need to understand the resistance to culturally responsive teaching and its critique, to become confident and competent in implementing it and making pedagogical connections within the context that they are teaching.

The classroom culture of a culturally responsive teacher reflects the community where the students come from. Teachers transcend their own cultural beliefs and preferences that engage and sustain student participation and achievement (Gay, 2013). The six dimensions identified by Geneva Gay that define culturally responsive teachers include teachers being socially and academically empowering by setting high expectations for students; engaging cultural knowledge, experiences, contributions, and perspectives; validating every student's culture and bridging the gap between school and home; being socially, emotionally, and politically comprehensive in order to educate the whole child; being transformative of schools and societies; and being emancipating and liberating from oppressive educational practices (Gay, 2010).

Geneva Gay's work focused on teacher practice and culturally responsive teaching, and Gloria Ladson-Billings's work focused on teacher posture and paradigm and culturally relevant pedagogy. Both recognized the classroom as a place of social change and strongly endorsed social justice. Aronson and Laughter (2016) combined the fundamental work of Geneva Gay and Gloria Ladson-Billings as representatives of the two strands as culturally responsive education (CRE): teaching and pedagogy.

Gay focuses on teaching by describing what a teacher needs to do in a classroom to be culturally responsive; Ladson-Billings focuses on pedagogy, describes the attitude and disposition a teacher must adopt in the class, that would determine planning, instruction, and assessment. The CRE framework combines the framework of Gay and Ladson-Billings with the four markers of CRE (Dover, 2013) to envision how to teach for social justice (Aronson and Laughter, 2016).

1. Culturally relevant educators use constructivist methods to develop bridges connecting students' cultural references to *academic skills and concepts*. Culturally relevant educators build on the knowledge and cultural assets students bring with them into the classroom; the culturally relevant classroom is inclusive of all students.
2. Culturally relevant educators engage students in *critical reflection* about their own lives and societies. In the classroom, culturally relevant educators use inclusive curricula and activities to support analysis of all the cultures represented.
3. Culturally relevant educators facilitate students' *cultural competence*. The culturally relevant classroom is a place where students both learn about their own and others' cultures and develop pride in their own and others' cultures.
4. Culturally relevant educators explicitly unmask and unmake oppressive systems through the *critique of discourses of power*. Culturally relevant educators work not only in the classroom but also in the active pursuit of social justice for all members of society.

In this chapter, we have used the four markers of culturally relevant education to teach culturally responsive science. The following section outlines teaching strategies and recommendations specific to each marker.

1. USE CONSTRUCTIVIST METHODS TO DEVELOP BRIDGES CONNECTING STUDENTS' CULTURAL REFERENCES TO ACADEMIC SKILLS AND CONCEPTS

Constructivism as a pedagogy focuses on active learning by the students, and not on instruction by the teacher. The basic premise of constructivism is that knowledge is not discovered but is constructed by the human mind (Richardson, 2003). Constructivism learning theory posits that students build their knowledge on a foundation of what they already know, or their prior knowledge. In other words, learning is a result of students' experiences and ideas.

In a traditional classroom, science was considered as a set of facts and principles independent of the learner. Here the goal was often to complete a task, do it right, or do it quickly. Such learning is procedural and may make little sense to the learners. On the other hand, in a constructivist classroom, knowledge is seen as a learner's activity, also called instruments of problem solving (Sinclair, 1990). The social aspect of science knowledge implies the presence of a learning environment where students have opportunities to share ideas with peers within small and large groups in the classroom. The teacher plays the role of a facilitator rather than that of an authority figure.

Four guiding principles of constructive pedagogy (Brooks and Brooks, 1999) include the following:

i. Pose problems of emerging relevance to students. Though relevance may not be preexisting for students, it can emerge through teacher mediation. A good problem-solving situation is one in which students make a testable prediction, use relatively inexpensive equipment for activities, tackle the problem through multiple problem-solving approaches, and benefit from working together in groups (Greenberg, 1990).
ii. Organize information around conceptual clusters where ideas and problems are presented holistically rather than as isolated parts. This helps students make meanings by breaking down the whole into smaller parts they can understand. Students institute making sense of the information and construct their own understanding. When activities cluster around broad concepts, students can choose their own problem-solving approaches and use them to construct their understanding. On the other hand, when students are presented with information that has been broken down into small parts, they may focus on memorizable aspects of the broader unit without being able to build skills and concepts from parts to whole.

For example, a unit on contact forces titled "Why do things sometimes get damaged when they hit each other?" (see Openscied.org) is designed around a common experience of a phone screen shattering when the phone falls to the floor. Students explore what happens to objects when they collide. This unit can be used to teach a number of concepts like forces and motion, collision, Newton's second law of motion, and Newton's third law of motion.

iii. Seek and value students' point of view. Eliciting students' point of view provides a teacher with a window into their reasoning. It can help teachers challenge students and make their learning contextual and meaningful. A teacher can maximize opportunities for students to express their point of view, reveal their conceptions, and to grow intellectually. Use probing questions and ask students to elaborate on their answers.

iv. Adapt curriculum tasks to address students' suppositions. The curriculum's cognitive demands should match students' cognitive abilities. The first three principles help teachers know what ideas are within the students' reach, and consequently guide them in adjusting curricular demands to student suppositions.

Use Phenomenon to Anchor Your Lessons

In the Next Generation Science Standards (NGSS), phenomena are central to science teaching and learning. A phenomenon can be an event or a specific example of something happening in the world that can be experienced or documented. We can use scientific knowledge to explain phenomena. For example, sunburn is an event that happens when skin is exposed to the direct sun for a prolonged period. On the other hand, Lisa getting a sunburn when she tanned in the sun without using sunscreen is a specific example of a phenomenon.

Traditional approaches to teaching science involve the teacher presenting science information as a body of static knowledge, followed by application of this knowledge. Teacher-centered strategies like lecturing and doing traditional prescriptive labs where students follow the set procedure are hallmarks of this pedagogy. This has been found to decontextualize science knowledge, which students are unable to apply to contexts in their real life (Achieve, 2016). On the other hand, phenomenon can be used as a hook or the starting point of a lesson. It can drive the lesson and learning by providing a context to the science learning and gives a purpose to the lesson beyond fun and engagement.

A phenomenon-based lesson helps students engage deeply with the material to explain the phenomenon using the science and engineering practices, disciplinary core ideas, and cross-cutting concepts (Lead States, 2013).

Traditionally, marginalized students in science may not see science as relevant to their lives or future careers. Phenomena based on students' real-life experiences in school, home, or community can make the learning of science meaningful and relevant for all students.

The NGSS does not specify phenomena that teachers can use for science instruction. This is because phenomena need to be authentic and relevant to students' lives (California Department of Education, 2016). Teachers should select phenomena based on local context and the ability, interest, and prior knowledge of students. While selecting a phenomenon to anchor a lesson, keep in mind that *all* students, including diverse students and English learners, are supported and engaged in the practices for science knowledge development. Selecting a phenomenon relevant to the lives and cultures of the students makes the lesson equitable. For an example of a lesson anchored in phenomenon, see the lesson plan titled "Why Do People Feel Direct Heat from the Sun Differently?" at the end of this chapter.

Integrate Students' Assets into your Science Lessons

Teachers can integrate students' assets into the science classroom in various ways. For example, students from rural communities possess intricate Indigenous knowledge about agricultural practices, local ecosystems, flora, fauna, and the environment. This knowledge, complex and encompassing sophisticated categorization, deep observation, experimental techniques, and cultural significance (Cajete, 1999), can be integrated into lessons on ecology, earth science, biology, and environmental science.

Students from coastal communities might possess insights and knowledge on marine conservation, which can be utilized to create resonating lessons. Moreover, cultures with strong oral traditions can benefit from storytelling as an effective strategy for teaching scientific concepts, incorporating stories that align with these traditions to explain scientific phenomena. Incorporating Indigenous knowledge systems passed down through generations can offer alternative perspectives and depth to topics such as plant biology, climate, and astronomy.

Identify and Use Students' Science Preconceptions

Another potent strategy involves leveraging students' prior knowledge and experiences. Understanding students' preconceptions is crucial for science teaching (Driver et al., 1994). A culturally relevant educator can encourage students to share their cultural practices or beliefs that relate to scientific topics. This strategy promotes student engagement and sets the stage for exploring scientific concepts through a culturally relevant lens.

In a unit on the properties of matter, an educator can employ this constructivist approach by initiating the lesson with a discussion on students' preconceptions about the states of matter. Students may bring forward everyday experiences and cultural insights related to changes in the state of matter, such as the melting of butter while cooking traditional dishes or freezing water into ice.

A unit on botany could involve students sharing the different plants used in their cultures and the purposes these plants serve. By eliciting and acknowledging this knowledge base of the students, the educator creates opportunities for students to actively construct and refine their understanding of the scientific principles underlying the changes in states of matter through experiments, collaborative learning, and reflection. Moreover, when students see the relevance of scientific concepts to their daily life and cultural practices, it fosters a sense of ownership and engagement in the learning process, which is a cornerstone of constructivist education (Windschitl, 2002).

2. CULTURALLY RELEVANT EDUCATORS ENGAGE STUDENTS IN CRITICAL REFLECTION ABOUT THEIR OWN LIVES AND SOCIETIES

Culturally relevant educators actively engage students in critical reflection and thinking about scientific concepts through the lens of culture and society (Warren et al., 2001). This involves acknowledging that science is not neutral, and that it is influenced by cultural, societal, and historical contexts. As posited by Gay (2010), culturally relevant pedagogy not only incorporates students' cultural references but also encourages them to critically analyze their cultural contexts. When teaching science, this approach invites students to scrutinize the socioscientific issues, ethics, and implications of science within their cultural spheres. Furthermore, it is crucial for teachers to engage in continuous dialogue with students and remain adaptive to diverse and evolving cultural expressions and identities within the classroom. These conversations are imperative for identifying the interests, values, and concerns that can be integrated into the science curriculum.

Engage Students in Place-Based Education to Foster Critical Reflection on Your Students' Communities

Think of some of the most memorable learning experiences from your school days. They are unlikely to be an essay, an assignment, or a laboratory experiment. It is most likely an exceptional or an extracurricular experience related to a place such as a trip to the museum or the zoo or a nature walk.

Place-based learning provides a context for learning and connects science to the community, city/town, and the world. Educators can use place-based education to connect scientific concepts to the local environment and community. This helps increase engagement, learning outcomes, and involvement in the community.

In a science classroom, students can study local ecosystems, geography, and environmental challenges, critically examining how science can address issues affecting their communities. For example, students can study environmental issues affecting their communities, such as air and water pollution, and explore scientific approaches to addressing these problems. Engaging students in classroom research and problem-solving activities with local relevance empowers students to be agents of change within their communities. This approach enables students to explore local ecosystems, understand how Indigenous knowledge can contribute to current science practices, and understand the environmental impacts of local industries (Semken, 2005).

Zoos and aquariums provide educational opportunities for students. They house animals from the local environment. Zoos or aquariums can be used to anchor science lessons. In addition to studying about the animals, students can explore ethical issues such as if zoos are an appropriate habitat for animals as well as issues like conservation and protection. When an actual field trip to the local zoo or aquarium is not possible, explore options for an online visit.

For example, the Yellowstone National Park offers the Expedition Yellowstone, which is a curriculum-based residential program for teachers and grade four through eight students. The Georgia Aquarium offers self-guided field trips, instructor led field trips, and virtual field trips. Other local places such as parks, gardens, ponds, lakes, creeks, and swimming pools are also a good resource for teachers.

Incorporating social action into science teaching can be instrumental in unmasking and unmaking of oppressive systems. By involving students in community-based projects that address societal issues through scientific inquiry, educators can cultivate students' sense of agency and their capacity to enact change (Bencze and Carter, 2011). Such projects might include environmental conservation efforts, community health initiatives, or citizen science projects that focus on social justice issues.

Design and Select Culturally Responsive Instructional Materials

Designing and selecting instructional resources and materials that reflect diversity in culture, race, ethnicity, and gender is crucial in a today's classroom. The selection of scientific texts, visuals, and examples should reflect the cultural diversity of the classroom. Educators might use texts that incorporate diverse scientists and cultural practices relevant to the science curriculum. For instance, Lee and Fradd (1998) demonstrated that the integration of instructional materials reflecting the cultural and linguistic diversity of students improved the scientific literacy among language-minority students. The inclusion of diverse materials fosters a sense of belonging and legitimizes the varied cultural perspectives within science.

Traditional narratives often portray science as a domain primarily influenced by White, male, cisgender figures. Curricular materials should also encompass contributions from non-Western cultures to science, such as explaining how ancient civilizations like the Chinese, Egyptians, or Mayans contributed to science (that is, Temple, 1998). Moreover, developing curricular materials that integrate indigenous science knowledge with contemporary Western science is particularly effective for Indigenous students and fosters cultural competence among non-Indigenous students (Aikenhead and Michell, 2011; Cajete, 1999). Including the history and nature of science with stories about the challenges and triumphs of scientists from diverse backgrounds can humanize science, making it more approachable and relatable for students (Clough, 2006).

Additionally, educators need to critically analyze curricular materials for any cultural biases or stereotypes, ensuring they do not perpetuate stereotypes or present a biased view of science (Banks, 1993). In cases where bias is present, educators can use it as a teaching moment to critically analyze the material with students, discussing the importance of cultural sensitivity in science. This critical examination not only helps in delivering unbiased education but also cultivates students' cultural competence.

Integrate Stories of Scientists That Resonate with Students' Cultural Background

Integrating stories of diverse scientists who share the same ethnicity, cultural background, or life experiences as the students can make learning more relatable and engaging (Barton, 2003; Schinske et al., 2016). For instance, including the works and achievements of female scientists, scientists of color, and scientists from different age groups and geographical locations is beneficial. Utilizing case studies that spotlight diverse scientists helps to create connections with students and empowers them to envision themselves as contributors to the field of science. By broadening representation in science through the inclusion of diverse scientists, educators facilitate the creation of a more inclusive science education that acknowledges contributions from diverse groups (Barton, 2003; Schinske et al., 2016).

For instance, in a lesson on environmental science, educators could weave in the story of Dr. Wangari Maathai, the first African woman to receive the

Nobel Peace Prize for her contribution to sustainable development, democracy, and peace through the Green Belt Movement in Kenya (Maathai, 2004). Incorporating her narrative into the class not only makes the environmental science concept tangible and contextually relevant, particularly for students of African descent, but also showcases the potential of science to create meaningful societal change (Brand and Moore, 2011).

As students discuss Dr. Maathai's scientific and environmental conservation work, they gain a sense of cultural pride and identity, seeing a role model who shares their cultural heritage, contributing significantly to global scientific discourses. Thus, these narratives not only contribute to scientific understanding but also foster critical reflection about students' own lives and other cultures.

3. CULTURALLY RELEVANT EDUCATORS FACILITATE STUDENTS' CULTURAL COMPETENCE

Facilitating students' cultural competence involves creating an inclusive classroom where students learn about and appreciate their own and others' cultures. Cultural competence involves understanding and appreciating one's own culture as well as the cultures of others (Gay, 2002). A culturally relevant classroom is a place where students learn about their own and others' cultures and develop pride in their cultural heritages.

Creating a safe and inclusive environment where students feel respected and valued for who they are is an essential component of this process. This can be achieved by employing inclusive language, highlighting the achievements of scientists from diverse backgrounds, and creating opportunities for students to share their own cultural experiences in relation to science. Establishing this supportive environment is foundational for students to actively engage in learning and in contributing their unique perspectives to the science classroom.

Encourage Cross-Cultural Collaboration and Communication between Students

Another critical strategy is encouraging cross-cultural collaboration and communication. Through group discussions, students can share their cultural perspectives on scientific concepts and practices. Engaging in cross-cultural collaboration and communication helps students acquire new skills, knowledge, and abilities. Students bring their diverse perspectives to the table, enriching the learning experience for everyone involved. These cross-cultural collaborations can be facilitated both within the classroom and globally through online platforms.

Cooperative learning strategies are an effective approach in facilitating these cross-cultural collaborations and, consequently, fostering students' cultural competence. Cooperative learning involves students working together in small groups to achieve common goals (Johnson and Johnson, 2009). In a diverse classroom, this promotes interaction among students from different cultural backgrounds, which not only enhances their understanding of the science content but also fosters intercultural understanding and collaboration.

Incorporate Scientific Achievements from Different Cultures

Incorporating scientific achievements from different cultures in science education is an essential component in developing culturally relevant pedagogy. This approach recognizes the universality of scientific discovery and acknowledges the contributions of diverse cultures in shaping modern scientific knowledge (Brandt, 2008). When students learn about the scientific achievements of cultures they identify with, they can develop a sense of pride and ownership over the material, which can be motivational (Sleeter, 2011). Students need to learn that scientific knowledge is not confined to a specific region or culture but rather is a shared human endeavor that transcends geographical boundaries and cultural differences (Nasir et al., 2014).

Historically, cultures worldwide have made significant contributions to science, and recognizing these diverse contributions fosters an inclusive science classroom environment. It allows students from various cultural backgrounds to see themselves as potential contributors to the field of science. This method not only motivates students but also encourages them to view science as a dynamic, evolving discipline with a rich, varied history, enhancing their understanding and appreciation of science (Hodson, 2011).

As a concrete example, a high school biology teacher can incorporate the work of renowned Mexican scientist Mario J. Molina, who was a Nobel laureate in chemistry, for his role in the discovery of how chlorofluorocarbons deplete the ozone layer. Additionally, the ancient practice of Ayurveda from the Indian subcontinent can be included in the curriculum to demonstrate early understanding of natural medicines and herbal treatments, contrasting it with modern pharmacology. This can be accompanied by hands-on activities, such as studying the medicinal properties of plants that are prevalent in the students' local cultures. The amalgamation of contemporary scientific achievements with historical knowledge from different cultures can be an effective way to engage students and foster a deeper understanding and appreciation for the subject (Rodriguez, 2015).

Use Culturally Inclusive Language

Finally, educators should be conscious of the language used in science teaching. Language holds cultural value, and utilizing culturally inclusive language is crucial in promoting cultural competence (Warren et al., 2001). This may include the thoughtful use of terminology that respects cultural diversity and, where possible, incorporates students' native languages in science instruction.

One tangible example of utilizing culturally inclusive language in science instruction can be observed in bilingual education programs where teachers interweave students' native language with the target language, thereby enriching their cognitive and cultural experiences (Cummins, 2007). For instance, in a chemistry class, a teacher may introduce a concept such as "acid-base reactions" in English but also share the translation in Spanish ("reacciones ácido-base"). This is especially impactful in classes with a significant number of Hispanic students.

Efforts such as these be instructors facilitates comprehension, acknowledges students' cultural and linguistic backgrounds, and fosters an environment of inclusivity (Lee et al., 2009). Moreover, employing culturally specific examples, such as Indigenous methods of fermentation or metallurgy, can bridge the gap between local cultures and scientific principles (Aikenhead, 2001). Such methods can augment students' understanding and application of science while validating their cultural heritage. This way, language becomes not just a medium for conveying scientific knowledge but a tool for cultural affirmation and empowerment (Moje et al., 2001).

4. CULTURALLY RELEVANT EDUCATORS EXPLICITLY UNMASK AND UNMAKE OPPRESSIVE SYSTEMS THROUGH THE CRITIQUE OF DISCOURSES OF POWER

The fourth marker emphasizes the role of culturally relevant educators in addressing and challenging oppressive systems through a critique of power structures. According to Giroux (2021), education should function as a form of cultural politics that critically engages with issues of power and inequality. Culturally relevant educators actively engage in unmasking and critiquing oppressive systems through inclusive curricula and critical discussions. They take responsibility to ensure that materials do not perpetuate stereotypes and present an unbiased view of science (Banks, 1993). This involves challenging and dissecting common misconceptions and oppressive narratives. For instance, science, often perceived as neutral and objective, is imbued with societal values and can either perpetuate or challenge oppressive systems.

Use Science Topics to Intentionally Address Common Oppressive Narratives

Culturally responsive teaching strategies in science can be used to address historical and contemporary social issues. For example, teaching genetics can debunk racial misconceptions by highlighting genetic diversity within populations. It is important to challenge and dissect common misconceptions, such as the belief that individuals within a racial group are genetically more similar compared to individuals from different racial groups (Donovan et al., 2019; Kampourakis, 2023).

When teaching ecology, instructors can address issues related to environmental racism and environmental justice. Discussions can explore how marginalized communities often bear the brunt of environmental degradation due to historical inequalities and systemic biases. Examining case studies such as the Flint water crisis (Neu et al., 2020) can shed light on how political negligence and systemic racism can lead to public health disasters. Similarly, when teaching immunology, educators can address the historical stigma of AIDS in the queer community and use this as a basis to discuss broader issues related to health disparities and discrimination.

Engage Your Students in Socioscientific Issues Discussions

Furthermore, engaging students in discussions of socioscientific issues relevant to their cultural contexts helps them to see real-world applications and implications of science (Bencze and Alsop, 2014). This engagement supports students in understanding the power dynamics and social justice implications of scientific developments. Incorporating socioscientific issues, such as climate change, genetic engineering, and health disparities, can also make science more pertinent and encourage students to see the value of science in understanding and addressing real-world problems (Sadler, 2011).

By ensuring that science education is grounded in social justice and is actively engaging in the critique of discourses of power, educators work not only within the classroom but also in the pursuit of social justice for all members of society. This inclusion of real-world issues in science teaching encourages students to think critically and to understand the complex interplay between science, society, and culture (Zeidler, 2014). By contextualizing science within the broader sociopolitical landscape, students can develop a more nuanced understanding of the content.

Explicitly Address Issues of Racisms Through Science

Science curricula can benefit from an antiracist pedagogical approach, which actively addresses and counters racism within scientific contexts (Leonardo, 2004). For example, teachers can facilitate discussions about the historical misuse of science to perpetuate racial hierarchies and critically examine how certain scientific fields might still harbor biases. Through this approach, students will be better prepared to recognize and challenge racist ideologies in science and in society.

In biology lessons, educators can incorporate the history and ethics of the Tuskegee Syphilis Study as a concrete example to address racism within science. The Tuskegee Study, conducted between 1932 and 1972, is an infamous clinical study in which African American men were intentionally left untreated for syphilis without their knowledge (Brandt, 1978). Teachers can use this study to spark discussions on the ethical violations and racism involved, and further explore the historical context in which the study was conducted. This critical examination of history exposes students to the oppressive ways in which science has been misused against marginalized communities (Scharff et al., 2010).

Furthermore, educators can facilitate discussions on the current disparities in health and medical treatment among different racial groups. For instance, analyzing recent studies that reveal racial biases in pain management and access to health care (Hoffman et al., 2016) can provide contemporary relevance. Through such analyses, students become aware of systemic biases and are empowered to critically evaluate information and advocate for ethical and just practices. As posited by Bang and Medin (2010), this not only brings cultural relevance to science education but also promotes social justice by empowering students with knowledge and tools necessary for civic engagement and advocacy.

Incorporate Feminist Perspectives and Highlight the Contributions of Women and Other Marginalized Groups in Science

Educators can also incorporate feminist science education as a means to critique traditional power structures and gender dynamics. This approach recognizes the ways in which science has historically been shaped by male-dominated perspectives and challenges the marginalization of women and other underrepresented groups in science (Hoffmann and Stake, 1998). By highlighting the contributions of female scientists and engaging in critiques of gender bias in scientific research, science educators can foster a more inclusive and socially just learning environment.

Social science and natural science have drawn from each other, mutually influencing each other. For example, cultural ideas of passive and weak females and heroic males are used in describing male and female gametes. Research has proved the active role of the cell in the fertilization process, showing both egg and sperm to be mutually active partners.

However, science textbooks stereotypically represent the fertilization of sperm and egg with the sperm highlighted in an active role, describing the sperm as penetrating the egg, while the egg is depicted as a passive entity penetrated by the egg. The egg is seen as feminine, passive, fragile, dependent, and waiting to be rescued, while the sperm is portrayed as energetic, powerful, and efficient. Such imagery keeps alive cultural stereotypes about women being weak and men being their strong saviors (Martin, 1991).

One practical example of incorporating feminist perspectives into a science class is through the analysis and discussion of case studies that center on the scientific contributions of women and highlight the impact of gender bias in research. For instance, educators could present the groundbreaking work of Rosalind Franklin in the discovery of the DNA double helix and foster discussions around how her contributions were historically marginalized (Sayre, 1975).

This example can be further enriched by introducing contemporary studies showing that gender bias in scientific publications and research funding still persists (Larivière et al., 2013; Witteman et al., 2019). Furthermore, engaging students in analyzing how bias affects scientific credibility and progress (Handelsman et al., 2005) prepares them for critical reflection on societal structures and their own positions within them. By incorporating these strategies, educators not only provide a more comprehensive view of scientific knowledge but also empower students to challenge traditional power structures and gender dynamics within the scientific community.

READER TAKEAWAYS

- Culturally relevant educators should employ constructivist methods that actively engage students in constructing knowledge through the integration of their cultural assets and prior experiences, thereby fostering deeper understanding and relevance in science learning.
- Implementing a curriculum grounded in real-world phenomena, particularly those that are culturally relevant, can empower students by situating science in context, facilitating meaningful connections, and promoting equity and inclusion in the science classroom.
- Culturally relevant educators must facilitate critical reflection among students to analyze and appreciate the diverse cultural perspectives

represented and to unpack the complex interplay between science and societal contexts. This approach, which includes place-based education and community engagement, empowers students to connect science with their lived experiences and to actively participate in the construction of knowledge.
- The selection and design of instructional materials that reflect cultural diversity, coupled with the integration of narratives about scientists from varied backgrounds, is pivotal in fostering an inclusive science education. This strategy not only engenders a sense of belonging among students but also cultivates cultural competence and broadens students' understanding of the historical and contemporary contributions of diverse cultures to science.
- Culturally relevant educators are instrumental in fostering cultural competence by curating an inclusive learning environment that not only incorporates but celebrates the diverse cultural heritages represented in the student body through cross-cultural collaborations and by integrating scientific contributions from diverse cultures.
- The utilization of culturally inclusive language and pedagogy helps affirm students' cultural identities while enriching their scientific learning experience through the amalgamation of contemporary and traditional knowledge bases from across the globe.
- Culturally relevant educators take a proactive role in deconstructing oppressive systems by critically examining power structures and biases inherent in scientific discourse and curricula, thereby cultivating a critical consciousness among students and enabling them to challenge societal inequities.
- The integration of antiracist pedagogy and feminist perspectives in science education, underscored by an examination of historical and contemporary social issues, equips students with the tools to critically evaluate scientific knowledge and its societal implications, thereby fostering advocacy for social justice.
- The role of self-reflection for educators is paramount. Educators should critically reflect on their own biases, privileges, and positions within power structures and consider how these affect their teaching. Engaging in critical self-reflection enables educators to align their teaching practices with the principles of social justice and equity, fundamental to culturally relevant education. Through this self-reflection, teachers can more effectively engage students in critical reflection, supporting a more culturally relevant science education.

LESSON PLANS

Lesson Plan 1: Why Do People Feel Direct Heat From the Sun Differently?

Next Generation Science Standards Performance Expectation: MS-PS3–4. Plan an investigation to determine the relationships among the energy transferred, the type of matter, the mass, and the change in the average kinetic energy of the particles as measured by the temperature of the sample.

Science and Engineering Practices

1. Planning and carrying out an investigation
2. Collecting and analyzing data
3. Creating and using models
4. Engaging in argument from evidence

Disciplinary Core Idea: Conservation of energy and energy transfer

Cross-Cutting Concept: Scale, proportion, and quantity

Nature of Science: Scientific knowledge is based on empirical evidence

Learning Objectives: Students will be able to

1. design an investigation to show that different colors absorb heat differently,
2. investigate how the amount of heat absorbed by a substance depends on its color,
3. collect and analyze data,
4. discuss the scientific principle that explains a phenomenon experienced differently by racially diverse people, and
5. apply their new knowledge to real-world situations.

Note: This lesson works best on a sunny day, near noon.

The phenomenon of two girls feeling the heat differently when playing in the sun is used as an anticipatory set. The discussion will help focus attention on the concept (transfer of heat energy) and connect it to everyday experiences in a culturally relevant way. This is a good opportunity to identify students' prior knowledge, and any misconceptions they may have.

This lesson plan uses the 5E model of instruction.

ENGAGE (Day 1)

Share figure 4.1 and the following scenario with the students.

Scenario: Finally, it was summer and time to enjoy the sun. Jenna and Maya were playing on the beach, in the direct sun. Around noon, the temperature rose to 95°F. Maya started to feel uncomfortable and wanted to be in the shade, away from the direct heat of the sun. Jenna was surprised that Maya, being from India, was feeling uncomfortable in the sun. "But you are from India! How can you feel the heat so much? Aren't you used to the heat?"

Figure 4.1. A preservice elementary education student in Dr. Burrow's Fine Arts for Elementary Education course creates a self-portrait that showcases how they personally connected to the identity-affirming themes throughout the shared children's books My Map Book by Sara Fanelli, Mommy's Khimar by Jamilah Thompkins-Bigelow, and When Sophie Gets Angry—Really, Really Angry by Molly Bang.

Maya was offended. Jenna had just negated her experience due to some preconceived notions.

Sample Discussion Questions

Have you ever had an experience like this?

How do you think Jenna should have responded to Maya's experience? Why?

Why do you think that Maya felt the heat more than Jenna?

Student Behavior
Students will engage in a discussion to answer the discussion questions. They will then work in small groups to identify a question they would like to investigate.

Teacher Behavior
The teacher acts as a facilitator and guide, scaffolding students' ideas and guiding the discussion to come up with a question like "Does the color of hair influence the amount of heat absorbed by the hair when exposed to the sun's radiations?"

EXPLORE (Day 2)
In this section, students will explore the science behind the phenomenon they discussed the previous day. The *explore* activity will provide a common, concrete experience for *all* students in the classroom. These experiences will help the students build their knowledge and understanding of the concept that heat absorbed by an object depends on its color.

Student Behavior

Small Group Work: Students will work in small groups to design an investigation to answer the question they have formulated earlier, that is, "Does the color of a material influence the amount of heat absorbed by the material, when exposed to the solar radiations?" Each group will do the following:

- Develop a hypothesis to answer the question.
- Identify variables to explore.
- Design an investigation to prove the hypothesis.
  - A tentative procedure for the investigation.

- Data to be collected.
- A table to record the data.
- Identify safety procedures to be followed while collecting data.
* Try different ways to solve a problem or answer the question

Large Group Work: Each group will share their design with the rest of the class. This is a good opportunity for the students to share their work, ask and answer questions, and justify their reasoning. The class as a whole will finalize the procedure for data collection and analysis.

Small Group Work: Within their small groups, students will conduct the investigation. They will record and analyze their observations, observe patterns in the data collected, and make causal relationships.

Teacher Behavior

The teacher acts as a consultant for the students. The teacher will walk around the class to

1. observe students and listen to student interactions,
2. ask probing questions that will help the students answer the phenomenon question and redirect the conversation when necessary,
3. answer student queries and clarify doubts,
4. encourage student-to-student interactions, and
5. provide adequate time for students to puzzle through the problem.

Sample Guiding Questions

1. Do you think the girls felt the heat differently?
2. Why do you think the girls felt the heat differently, or not?
3. What is different between the two girls that causes them to feel the same heat/radiation from the sun differently? (Introduce them to the term radiation at this time.)
4. In your groups, form a hypothesis for the phenomenon.
5. How will you test your hypothesis?

Materials Required Per Group

1. Four thermometers
2. Four sheets of construction paper (black, white, and any two other colors)
3. Graph paper

Procedure: Fold the construction paper along its length. Fold it again along the long and short ends to form a pocket. Place a thermometer in each pocket. The initial temperature of each thermometer should be the same. Now take the setup outside and place it in the sun. Note down the temperature of the thermometers after every 5 minutes. Continue noting the temperature until the temperature stops rising. Plot the temperature versus time graphs for all colors (temperature on the Y axis and time on the X axis).

Teacher Note: This procedure is one possible way of investigating the question. Allow the students to design their own investigation.

EXPLAIN (Day 3)

Student Behavior
In the explain phase, students explain and present their findings from the previous day's activity and demonstrate their conceptual understanding. They compare ideas with those of others. Students then apply their conceptual understanding to explain why the two girls playing in the sun felt the heat differently.

Teacher Behavior
Present additional questions to support the discussion. Introduce a formative assessment at this point, to determine if any additional instruction is needed, and check the readiness of the class to move on to the *elaborate* phase.

Teacher Notes: Bring the discussion back to the question asked at the beginning: "How do you think Jenna should have responded to Maya's experience? Why?" This discussion can also be used to highlight inequities among races. For example, notions like White people get sunburns and need sunscreen and darker people do not (because the burns do not show on dark skin). Medical research on a White population does not necessarily apply to people of color.

ELABORATE/EXTEND (Day 3)
In this phase, students continue to explore the implications of their new knowledge, connect this new knowledge to other related concepts, and apply it to a different setting in the world around them.

Student Behavior
Students will work individually to answer the following questions, and then discuss them in their small groups:

1. Ubrique is a picturesque *pueblo blanco* (white town) in southern Spain. All houses in this town are white. Why do you think houses in Ubrique are painted white?
2. What kind of clothes would you wear outside on a hot day in the summer? In the winter? Explain your reasoning?
3. What happens to the heat energy absorbed by the papers in the activity we performed?

Teacher Behavior
Answers to the third question can be used to assess students' prior knowledge on how kinetic energy of particles changes with change in temperature. This can also be used to connect this lesson to the next topic, that is, to investigate change in average kinetic energy of particles as measured by the temperature of the sample (MS-PS3–4).

EVALUATE (Day 3)
The *evaluate* stage helps both teacher and students ascertain how much learning and conceptual understanding has taken place. This is an ongoing process and can take place all times of the lesson. It will help the teacher assess conceptual understanding and knowledge gained by students.

Student Behavior
Students will demonstrate their new knowledge and mastery of concepts through presenting the final product created for the activity.

Teacher Behavior
Evaluation and assessment can occur at all points along the continuum of the instructional process. Both teachers and students can determine how much conceptual understanding and learning has taken place. The product of this investigation can be used for assessment purposes. Give the students a choice in their final product. For example, students can write a report, make a PowerPoint, design an infographic, make a video, or create a pamphlet, as well as many other possibilities.

Reflection for This Lesson Plan
This 5E lesson plan is based on an everyday phenomenon of how the color of a person's hair can make them feel the heat differently because the amount of heat absorbed by a substance depends on its color (among other things). Done traditionally, this lesson would have students do the investigation by following a prescribed procedure. Anchoring a lesson within a phenomenon provides a context to the science concept being taught and helps students see the relevance of science in their lived experiences.

Using the 5E model of instruction allows opportunities for effective inclusion of the science and engineering practices. As an extension of this lesson, students can bring different materials from home to test how they absorb solar radiation and change in temperature. Using materials from their homes will help students make connections between school science and culture. When asking students to bring items from home, give students options of what they can bring. It is a good idea to keep spare materials at hand, as some students may not bring material from home, due to various reasons. Like this lesson, traditional science lessons can be converted into phenomenon based and culturally responsive by anchoring them in a phenomenon.

Give students options to design and conduct their own investigation, which may be different from the procedure described in the lesson plan. This will make the lesson student centered and shift the power to the students, away from the teacher. It also makes the class less structured. Consequently, the teacher may feel a loss of control. This can be challenging for teachers, especially for early career teachers. The shift to a student-centered classroom may be difficult to make for some teachers, as it is against their lived experiences as students in a teacher-centered classroom. It is a good idea to start with structured investigation, and gradually move on to more student-centered and open-ended investigations where students have more autonomy. The role of the teacher in a student-centered classroom would be more of a facilitator and guide.

Lesson Plan 2: Understanding Genetics and the Fallacy of Biological Racism

Grade Level: High school

Next Generation Science Standards Performance Expectation: Ask questions to clarify relationships about the role of DNA and chromosomes in coding the instructions for characteristic traits passed from parents to offspring (HS-LS3–1).

Disciplinary Core Ideas: Variation of Traits (LS3.B)

a. In sexual reproduction, chromosomes can sometimes swap sections during the process of meiosis (cell division), thereby creating new genetic combinations and thus more genetic variation. Although DNA replication is tightly regulated and remarkably accurate, errors do occur and result in mutations, which are also a source of genetic variation. Environmental factors can also cause mutations in genes, and viable mutations are inherited. (HS-LS3–2).

b. Environmental factors also affect expression of traits, and hence affect the probability of occurrences of traits in a population. Thus, the variation and distribution of traits observed depends on both genetic and environmental factors (HS-LS3–2; HS-LS3–3).

Science and Engineering Practices

1. Analyzing and interpreting data
2. Engaging in argument from evidence

Crosscutting Concepts: Cause and effect
Empirical evidence is required to differentiate between cause and correlation and make claims about specific causes and effects (HS-LS3–1; HS-LS3–2).

Connections to Nature of Science: Science is a human endeavor
Science and engineering are influenced by society and society is influenced by science and engineering (HS-LS3–3).

Learning Objectives (for Two to Three Lessons)

1. **Explain the Basics of Genetics:** By the end of this lesson, students should be able to explain the role of DNA and chromosomes in coding for traits and how these are passed from parents to offspring.
2. **Recognize the Impact of the Environment on Traits:** Students will identify how environmental factors can affect the expression of traits and thus affect the probability of occurrences of traits in a population.
3. **Debunk Misconceptions Related to Race and Genetics Like Biological Racism:** Students will understand that people from the same racial group are not genetically uniform and that people from different races are not categorically different. They will comprehend that the concept of "race" is a social construct and not a biological determinant.
4. **Reflect on the Influence of Science and Society on Each Other:** Students will discuss how science is influenced by society and how it, in turn, influences society, in the context of scientific racism and genetics.
5. **Apply Their Understanding to Real-World Scenarios:** Students will apply their understanding of genetics and variation to real-world scenarios, such as personal genetic testing and historical events like the Dutch Hunger Winter.

Phenomenon: To address misconceptions and biological racism, the chosen phenomenon will be the human genome project and the genetic diversity observed among different racial groups. We'll discuss how the completion of the Human Genome Project has shown us that all humans are 99.9 percent identical in their genetic makeup.

> Imagine a school-wide talent show has been announced. The categories include singing, painting, sports, and coding. Upon hearing this, one of your classmates, Jay, makes a comment: "Well, we all know the Asian students will win the coding competition. They are just naturally better at it."
>
> His comment sparks a debate in your class. Some students agree, pointing out the significant achievements by Asians in the field of technology. Others disagree, arguing that talent has nothing to do with race.
>
> Later that day, you go home and tell your older sibling, a genetics major in college, about the incident. They tell you about the Human Genome Project and how it showed that all humans share 99.9 percent of their DNA, suggesting that there is more genetic diversity within racial groups than between them.
>
> Guiding Question: Based on what you've heard and read today, how much of who we are, our talents, and our capabilities do you think are determined by our race? And how might our understanding of genetics support or refute Jay's claim?

ENGAGE (20 minutes)

Begin the class by reading the phenomenon and reflecting on the situation. You can use the guiding question for that purpose. Then have a brief discussion about the recent surge of personal genetic testing services, like 23andMe, AncestryDNA, or FamilyTreeDNA, and how these tests provide insights about our ancestry.

Display a provocative question on the board: "Do you think your race determines who you are?" Encourage a short discussion, ensuring all views are heard and respected.

Student Behavior

Students listen attentively to the phenomenon being read and engage in a discussion about genetic testing services and the relationship between race and identity. They share their initial thoughts, listen to their peers' opinions, and begin to think critically about the topic. They are encouraged to be respectful and open to different viewpoints.

Teacher Behavior
In this stage, the teacher sets the tone for the lesson by creating a safe space for open discussion. The teacher begins by reading the phenomenon and guiding questions to the class, and then facilitates a brief discussion about personal genetic testing services. The teacher must actively listen to the students' perspectives, ensure that every voice is heard, and make sure that the discussion stays respectful and on track. The teacher also writes a provocative question on the board to engage students in critical thinking.

EXPLORE (60 minutes)
Divide the class into small groups and give each group a set of index cards with different human genetic traits written on them. You can use the examples below. Assign each group a different geographic region or population (for example, East Asia, Sub-Saharan Africa, Northern Europe, South America, etc.).

Begin with a presentation covering the basics of DNA and chromosomes, genes, and how they code for traits. Briefly explain Mendelian and non-Mendelian inheritance patterns using information sheets or a presentation. Explain how some traits such as eye color can be influenced by multiple genes, while others, like blood type, follow a simpler inheritance pattern. Show a video or use a simulation to visually illustrate these concepts.

Instruct each group to make predictions about what variations of traits are very frequent in their population or region, what are less frequent, and which affect around half of the population. They should base their initial predictions on their current knowledge and perceptions.

Now ask the groups to use the internet to research the actual prevalence of the traits in their assigned population. They should verify or correct their initial predictions based on real data. Encourage them to find sources that provide information about the genetic diversity within the population.

Each group should present their findings to the class. They should discuss how the actual genetic diversity compared to their initial perceptions and what surprised them. As a class, mark the global distribution of some of the traits discussed on a world map. This can be done on a drawing of the world map on the whiteboard or on a physical map. Students can create charts in a Post-it with the prevalence of traits they found online and put the Post-it on their assigned region. This can also be done on a shared digital map.

Conclude the activity with a class discussion about how genetic traits can vary widely within and between populations, and how societal perceptions do not always align with genetic reality.

Table 4.1.

Eye Color	Blood Type	Attached or Detached Earlobes	Ability to Roll Tongue
Description: The color of the iris, which can range from brown, blue, green, gray, to various shades in between. **Genetic Factors:** Multiple genes contribute to eye color, including OCA2 and HERC2.	**Description:** The classification of blood based on the presence or absence of antigens. The main blood types are A, B, AB, and O. **Genetic Factors:** Determined by the ABO gene; inheritance can be explained using Mendelian genetics.	**Description:** Earlobes can be either hanging free (detached) or attached directly to the side of the head. **Genetic Factors:** Traditionally thought to be a simple Mendelian trait, but recent evidence suggests multiple genes may be involved.	**Description:** Some people can roll their tongue into a tube shape, while others cannot. **Genetic Factors:** Often cited as an example of a simple genetic trait, but family studies suggest it is influenced by both genetic and environmental factors.
Lactose Tolerance	**Cilantro Taste Perception**	**Freckles**	**Hair Type (Curly or Straight)**
Description: The ability to digest lactose, the sugar found in milk, beyond childhood. **Genetic Factors:** Mostly influenced by the LCT gene; lactose tolerance is thought to have evolved in response to dairy farming.	**Description:** Some people find cilantro (coriander leaves) to taste soapy, while others do not. **Genetic Factors:** Genetic variants in the OR6A2 gene influence the perception of aldehydes, which are present in cilantro.	**Description:** Small, concentrated spots of melanin on the skin. **Genetic Factors:** Presence of freckles is influenced by multiple genes, including MC1R.	**Description:** The shape and texture of hair strands. **Genetic Factors:** Multiple genes contribute to hair type, including TCHH.

Student Behavior

Students work collaboratively in small groups, making predictions about genetic traits in different populations and then researching to verify or correct their predictions. They critically analyze data, discuss within their groups, and prepare short presentations. They actively participate in the class discussion and reflect on the genetic diversity and their initial perceptions.

Teacher Behavior

The teacher divides the class into small groups and hands out index cards with human genetic traits. The teacher gives a presentation about the basics of genetics, inheritance patterns, and provides guidelines for group activities.

The teacher moves around the classroom to support groups, answer questions, and ensure students are on task. The teacher helps to facilitate presentations of group findings and leads a class discussion on genetic diversity.

EXPLAIN (45 minutes)

Then introduce the topic of the Human Genome Project and its findings about human genetic diversity, emphasizing that all humans share 99.9 percent of their DNA and that there is more genetic diversity within racial groups than between them.

Next have students read the American Society of Human Genetics (ASHG) Statement Regarding Concepts of "Good Genes" and Human Genetics. Then facilitate a class discussion around these facts, encouraging students to reflect on how this information contrasts with societal perceptions of race and racial differences. As the discussion goes on, make sure to address the fallacy of scientific racism and the role of genetics in determining abilities.

Here are some guiding questions that could be used for this discussion:

- According to ASHG, how much genetic diversity exists between populations traditionally defined as "racial" or "ethnic" groups compared to within these groups?
- Why does ASHG emphasize the importance of considering environmental factors and social context when looking at health disparities between different racial and ethnic groups?
- Why do you think it's important for scientists to consider genetic diversity within and among populations rather than categorizing people by race?
- The ASHG statement highlights the idea that no single genetic variant is found in all members of one racial group and in no members of another group. How does this fact challenge common misconceptions about race and genetics?

Student Behavior

Students pay attention to the introduction of the Human Genome Project and actively participate in the discussion. They read the materials, think critically, and engage with the guiding questions. They reflect on societal perceptions of race and question their prior assumptions.

Teacher Behavior

The teacher introduces the Human Genome Project and shares key findings about human genetic diversity. The teacher facilitates a class discussion based on reading materials and guiding questions, ensuring that students understand the implications and challenge any preconceived notions. The teacher corrects misinformation and emphasizes the distinction between genetic facts and social constructs.

ELABORATE (30 minutes)
Have students work in the same groups or create new groups for this phase.

Provide an introduction to the Dutch Hunger Winter as a historical event that took place in the Netherlands during the winter of 1944–1945, during which there was a severe shortage of food.

Explain that this historical event is not only important from a historical perspective but is also a significant case study in understanding how environmental factors, such as malnutrition, can have lasting effects on gene expression and health.

Assign each group to research specific aspects of the Dutch Hunger Winter and its effects on gene expression, considering how this can affect the probability of occurrences of traits in a population. They could focus on the prenatal and postnatal effects, long-term health effects, or the scientific/physiological mechanisms behind these effects.

Encourage groups to use varied sources, including scientific articles, historical accounts, and interviews (if available). As an additional option, you can use some of the following questions to guide student investigations:

- What was the Dutch Hunger Winter? When did it occur and what were the circumstances that led to this famine?
- How did the famine affect pregnant women and their unborn children during the Dutch Hunger Winter?
- What are some of the long-term health effects observed in children who were in utero during the Dutch Hunger Winter?
- How does malnutrition impact gene expression? Are these changes temporary or can they have lasting effects?
- Can the effects of environmental factors on gene expression be passed down to subsequent generations? What evidence is there to support this?
- How does the Dutch Hunger Winter study inform our understanding of the relationship between environmental factors and genetic expression in a broader context?
- How do findings from the Dutch Hunger Winter challenge or support ideas about genetic determinism?

Student Behavior
Students work in groups to research the Dutch Hunger Winter and its effects on gene expression and health. They delve into historical accounts and scientific articles and engage in critical thinking to understand the relationship

between environmental factors and genetics. They participate in discussions and reflect on the implications of their findings.

Teacher Behavior
The teacher provides an introduction to the Dutch Hunger Winter, explaining its historical and scientific significance. The teacher assigns research topics to groups, provides guidelines, and ensures that students are using credible sources. The teacher may also facilitate sharing of the findings and lead a discussion on the environmental impact on genetics.

EVALUATE (15 minutes)
In the form of a quiz or an interactive game, assess students' understanding of the concepts discussed. Include questions that challenge the misconceptions addressed in the lesson.

Have a final discussion about the societal implications of misunderstanding genetic variation. Highlight the negative impacts of biological racism and the importance of science in debunking such harmful beliefs. You can use some of the following questions to guide this discussion:

- How can misconceptions about genetics be used to justify discrimination or prejudice? Can you think of any modern examples?
- Why is it important for individuals and societies to have an accurate understanding of human genetic variation?
- What role do media (movies, TV shows, news, etc.) play in perpetuating or combating misconceptions about genetics and race? Can you think of any specific examples?
- How might the belief that certain racial groups are genetically superior or inferior in certain aspects affect the opportunities and treatment of individuals within those groups?
- How can education and science be used as tools to combat biological racism and promote a more inclusive society?
- In what ways might the belief in fixed, unchangeable genetic traits impact a person's mindset and opportunities for growth and development?
- As a society, what steps can be taken to ensure that scientific information is not misused to promote discrimination or prejudice?
- What are some ethical considerations that should be taken into account when studying human genetics, especially in relation to different racial and ethnic groups?
- What can you, as students, do to promote genetic literacy and combat biological racism in your community?

End with a reflection activity where students write a paragraph on what they have learned, any changes in their previous beliefs, and the role they see for themselves in promoting genetic literacy in their communities.

Student Behavior
Students participate in the quiz or game, applying their new understandings to answer questions. They contribute to the final discussion, providing insights, and reflecting on the importance of genetic literacy in society. In the reflection activity, students write a paragraph on their learning, changes in beliefs, and roles in promoting genetic literacy in their communities.

Teacher Behavior
The teacher creates and administers a quiz or interactive game to assess students' understanding. The teacher leads a final discussion about the societal implications of misunderstanding genetic variation, providing real-world examples and stressing the importance of science in debunking biological racism. The teacher concludes the lesson with a reflection activity.

Reflection on This Lesson Plan
The lesson plan titled "Understanding Genetics and the Fallacy of Biological Racism" is intended to integrate science with social justice. By drawing connections between genetics and the social construct of race, the lesson offers students an opportunity to critically analyze both scientific concepts and social perceptions.

However, there are potential challenges in the implementation of this lesson. First, the topic of race is sensitive and requires tactful facilitation. Teachers should be mindful that students come from diverse backgrounds and may hold varying perspectives on race, some of which may be deeply rooted in personal experiences or family beliefs.

This sensitivity necessitates an environment where students feel safe and respected, so they can openly engage in discussions without fear of judgment or offense. Another challenge is the volume of information and complexity of concepts involved, which might be overwhelming for some students, particularly those who may not have a strong foundation in genetics.

Given these challenges, it is essential for educators to adopt certain strategies to maximize the effectiveness of the lesson. For instance, prior to the lesson, teachers should establish ground rules for discussions, emphasizing the importance of respect and open-mindedness. It may also be helpful for educators to undergo training in culturally responsive teaching strategies so that they are equipped to facilitate discussions on race constructively.

Additionally, teachers should consider scaffolding the content by breaking down complex ideas into simpler concepts and possibly spreading the lesson over several sessions. This would allow students to get familiar with the information gradually and make connections between genetics, race, and societal perceptions more effectively. Last, employing varied instructional methods, such as videos, group discussions, and hands-on activities, could cater to different learning styles and enhance engagement and understanding among students.

RESOURCES

Books

Kampourakis, K. (2023). *Ancestry reimagined: Dismantling the myth of genetic ethnicities.*

Aikenhead, G., and Michell, H. (2011). Bridging cultures: Indigenous and scientific ways of knowing nature.

Higgins, M. (2021). *Unsettling responsibility in science education: Indigenous science, deconstruction, and the multicultural science education debate* (p. 350). Springer Nature.

National Academies of Sciences, Engineering, and Medicine (2021). *Call to action for science education: Building opportunity for the future.*

Harden, K. P. (2021). *The genetic lottery: Why DNA matters for social equality.* Princeton University Press.

Atwater, M. M., Russell, M., and Butler, M. B. (Eds.). (2014). *Multicultural science education: Preparing teachers for equity and social justice.* Springer Netherlands.

Stephens, S. (2001). *Handbook for culturally responsive science curriculum.*

Articles

The NGSS-ification of too slow to notice: How to turn any unit into a phenomena-based, student-driven investigation. *Science Scope, 41*(6), 45–54.

Bobrowsky, M. (2018). Q: How can I make science fun and have students learn more by using phenomenon-based learning? *Science and Children, 56*(2), 70–73.

Lee, O. (2020). Making everyday phenomena phenomenal. *Science and Children, 58*(1), 56–61.

Watson, S. (2021). Culturally relevant pedagogy and the 5E lesson plan. *The Science Teacher, 89*(2), 56–61.

Olson, J. K., Levis, J. M., Vann, R., and Bruna, K. R. (2009). Enhancing science for ELLs: Science strategies for English language learners that benefit all students. *Science and Children, 46*(5), 46–48.

Miller, E., Lauffer, H. B., and Messina, P. (2014). NGSS for English language learners. *Science and Children, 51*(5), 55.

NSTA Position Statements

National Science Teachers Association (2000). Position Statement: Multicultural Science Education.
National Science Teachers Association (2019). Position Statement: Gender Equity in Science Education.
National Science Teachers Association (2009). Position Statement: Parent Involvement in Science Learning.
National Science Teachers Association (2010). Position Statement: Teaching Science in the Context of Societal and Personal Issues.

Websites

openscied.org
stemcareerscoalition.discoveryeducation.com
ngssphenomena.com
ca.pbslearningmedia.org
exploratorium.edu
learner.org

REFERENCES

Achieve, I. (2016). Using phenomena in NGSS-designed lessons and units. www.nextgenscience.org/sites/default/files/Using%20Phenomena%20in%20NGSS.pdf.
Aikenhead, G. S. (2001). Students' ease in crossing cultural borders into school science. *Science Education, 85*(2), 180–88.
Aikenhead, G. S., and Michell, H. (2011). *Bridging cultures: Indigenous and scientific ways of knowing nature.* Pearson.
Aronson, B., and Laughter, J. (2016). The theory and practice of culturally relevant education: A synthesis of research across content areas. *Review of Educational Research, 86*(1), 163–206.
Bang, M., and Medin, D. (2010). Cultural processes in science education: Supporting the navigation of multiple epistemologies. *Science Education, 94*(6), 1008–26.
Banks, J. A. (1993). Multicultural education: Historical development, dimensions, and practice. *Review of Research in Education, 19*, 3–49.
Barton, A. C. (2003). *Teaching science for social justice.* Teachers College Press.
Bencze, L., and Alsop, S. (2014). *Activist science and technology education.* Springer.
Bencze, L., and Carter, L. (2011). Globalizing students acting for the common good. *Journal of Research in Science Teaching, 48*(6), 648–69.
Brand, B. R., and Moore, S. J. (2011). Enhancing teachers' application of inquiry-based strategies using a constructivist sociocultural professional development model. *International Journal of Science Education, 33*(7), 889–913.
Brandt, A. M. (1978). Racism and research: The case of the Tuskegee Syphilis Study. *Hastings Center Report, 8*(6), 21–29.

Brandt, C. B. (2008). Discursive geographies in science: Space, identity, and scientific discourse among indigenous women in higher education. *Cultural Studies of Science Education, 3*(3), 703–30.

Brooks, J. G., and Brooks, M. G. (1999). *In search of understanding: The case for constructivist classrooms*. ASCD.

Cajete, G. A. (1999). *Igniting the sparkle: An Indigenous science education model*. Kivaki Press.

California Department of Education (2016). *Science framework for California public schools*. Sacramento, CA: CDE Press.

Clough, M. P. (2006). Learners' responses to the demands of conceptual change: Considerations for effective nature of science instruction. *Science & Education, 15*(5), 463–94.

Cummins, J. (2007). Rethinking monolingual instructional strategies in multilingual classrooms. *Canadian Journal of Applied Linguistics, 10*(2), 221–40.

Dewey, J. (1910). Science as subject-matter and as method. *Science, 31*(787), 121–27.

Donovan, B. M., Semmens, R., Keck, P., Brimhall, E., Busch, K. C., Weindling, M., Duncan, A., Stuhlsatz, M., Bracey, Z., Bloom, M., Kowalski, S., and Salazar, B. (2019). Toward a more humane genetics education: Learning about the social and quantitative complexities of human genetic variation research could reduce racial bias in adolescent and adult populations. *Science Education, 103*(3), 529–60.

Dover, A. G. (2013). Teaching for social justice: From conceptual frameworks to classroom practices. *Multicultural Perspectives, 15*(1), 3–11.

Driver, R., Asoko, H., Leach, J., Mortimer, E., and Scott, P. (1994). Constructing scientific knowledge in the classroom. *Educational Researcher, 23*(7), 5–12.

Gay, G. (2002). Preparing for culturally responsive teaching. *Journal of Teacher Education, 53*(2), 106–16.

Gay, G. (2010). *Culturally responsive teaching: Theory, research, and practice*. Teachers College Press.

Gay, G. (2013). Teaching to and through cultural diversity. *Curriculum Inquiry, 43*(1), 48–70.

Giroux, H. (2021). Critical pedagogy. In U. Bauer, U. H. Bittlingmayer, and A. Scherr (Eds.), *Handbuch Bildungs- und Erziehungssoziologie*. Springer.

Greenberg, J. (1990). *Problem-solving situations: A teacher's resource book*, Vol. 1. Grapevine.

Handelsman, J., Ebert-May, D., Beichner, R., Bruns, P., Chang, A., DeHaan, R., Gentile, J., Lauffer, S., Stewart, J., Tilghman, S., and Wood, W. (2005). Scientific teaching. *Science, 304*(5670), 521–22.

Hodson, D. (2011). *Looking to the future: Building a curriculum for social activism*. Sense Publishers.

Hoffman, K. M., Trawalter, S., Axt, J. R., and Oliver, M. N. (2016). Racial bias in pain assessment and treatment recommendations, and false beliefs about biological differences between blacks and whites. *Proceedings of the National Academy of Sciences, 113*(16), 4296–301.

Hoffmann, F. L., and Stake, J. E. (1998). Feminist pedagogy in theory and practice: An empirical investigation. *NWSA Journal, 10*(1), 79–97.

Johnson, D. W., and Johnson, R. T. (2009). An educational psychology success story: Social interdependence theory and cooperative learning. *Educational Researcher, 38*(5), 365–79.

Kampourakis, K. (2023). *Ancestry reimagined: Dismantling the myth of genetic ethnicities*. Oxford University Press.

Ladson-Billings, G., (1995). But that's just good teaching! The case for culturally relevant pedagogy. *Theory Into Practice* (3), 159.

Larivière, V., Ni, C., Gingras, Y., Cronin, B., and Sugimoto, C. R. (2013). Bibliometrics: Global gender disparities in science. *Nature News, 504*(7479), 211–13.

Lead States, N. (2013). *Next generation science standards: For states, by states*. National Academies Press.

Lee, O., and Fradd, S. H. (1998). Science for all, including students from non-English-language backgrounds. *Educational Researcher, 27*(4), 12–21.

Lee, O., Penfield, R., and Maerten-Rivera, J. (2009). Effects of fidelity of implementation on science achievement gains among English language learners. *Journal of Research in Science Teaching, 46*(7), 826–59.

Leonardo, Z. (2004). Critical social theory and transformative knowledge: The functions of criticism in quality education. *Educational Researcher, 33*(6), 11–18.

Lyons, T. (2006). Different countries, same science classes: Students' experiences of school science in their own words. *International Journal of Science Education, 28*(6), 591–613.

Maathai, W. (2004). *The Green Belt Movement: Sharing the approach and the experience*. Lantern Books.

Martin, E. (1991). The egg and the sperm: How science has constructed a romance based on stereotypical male-female roles. *Signs: Journal of Women in Culture and Society, 16*(3), 485–501.

Moje, E. B., Collazo, T., Carrillo, R., and Marx, R. W. (2001). "Maestro, what is 'quality'?" Language, literacy, and discourse in project-based science. *Journal of Research in Science Teaching, 38*(4), 469–98.

Nasir, N. S., Rosebery, A. S., Warren, B., and Lee, C. D. (2014). Learning as a cultural process: Achieving equity through diversity. In R. K. Sawyer (Ed.), *The Cambridge handbook of the learning sciences* (pp. 686–706). New York: Cambridge University Press.

National Research Council (2012). *A framework for K–12 science education: Practices, crosscutting concepts, and core ideas*. National Academies Press.

Neu, H. M., Lee, M., Pritts, J. D., Sherman, A. R., and Michel, S. L. (2020). Seeing the "unseeable," a student-led activity to identify metals in drinking water. *Journal of Chemical Education, 97*(10), 3690–96.

Richardson, V. (2003). Constructivist pedagogy. *Teachers College Record, 105*(9), 1623–40.

Rodriguez, A. J. (2015). What about a dimension of engagement, equity, and diversity practices? A critique of the Next Generation Science Standards. *Journal of Research in Science Teaching, 52*(7), 1031–51.

Sadler, T. D. (2011). Situating socio-scientific issues in classrooms as a means of achieving goals of science education. In T. Sadler (Eds.), *Socio-scientific issues in the classroom* (pp. 1–9). Springer.

Sayre, A. (1975). *Rosalind Franklin and DNA*. W. W. Norton & Company.

Scharff, D. P., Mathews, K. J., Jackson, P., Hoffsuemmer, J., Martin, E., and Edwards, D. (2010). More than Tuskegee: Understanding mistrust about research participation. *Journal of Health Care for the Poor and Underserved, 21*(3), 879–97.

Schinske, J., Perkins, H., Snyder, A., and Wyer, M. (2016). Scientist spotlight homework assignments shift students' stereotypes of scientists and enhance science identity in a diverse introductory science class. *CBE—Life Sciences Education, 15*(3), ar47.

Semken, S. (2005). Sense of place and place-based introductory geoscience teaching for American Indian and Alaska Native undergraduates. *Journal of Geoscience Education, 53*(2), 149–57.

Sinclair, H. (1990). Learning: The interactive re-creation of knowledge. In L. Steffe and T. Wood (Ed.), *Transforming early childhood mathematics education: An international perspective*. Hillsdale: Lawrence Erlbaum Press.

Sleeter, C. E. (2011). *The academic and social value of ethnic studies: A research review*. National Education Association Research Department.

Temple, R. (1998). *The genius of China: 3,000 years of science, discovery, and invention*. Inner Traditions.

Warren, B., Ballenger, C., Ogonowski, M., Rosebery, A. S., and Hudicourt-Barnes, J. (2001). Rethinking diversity in learning science: The logic of everyday sense-making. *Journal of Research in Science Teaching, 38*(5), 529–52.

Windschitl, M. (2002). Framing constructivism in practice as the negotiation of dilemmas: An analysis of the conceptual, pedagogical, cultural, and political challenges facing teachers. *Review of Educational Research, 72*(2), 131–75.

Witteman, H. O., Hendricks, M., Straus, S., and Tannenbaum, C. (2019). Are gender gaps due to evaluations of the applicant or the science? A natural experiment at a national funding agency. *The Lancet, 393*(10171), 531–40.

Zeidler, D. L. (2014). Socioscientific issues as a curriculum emphasis: Theory, research, and practice. In G. Lederman and S. Abell (Eds.), *Handbook of research on science education* (pp. 697–26). Routledge.

Chapter 5

Caring for Body *and* Soul in Physical Education

Derek R. Riddle

> To teach in a manner that respects and cares for the souls of our students is essential if we are to provide the necessary conditions where learning can most deeply and intimately begin.
>
> —hooks, 1994, p. 14

EXPECTED LEARNING OUTCOME

- Identify and integrate instructional strategies to promote culturally responsive teaching, social and emotional learning competencies, and a pedagogy of care specific to physical education.

The primary mission of physical education has centered on developing lifelong movers. In 2015, the Society of Health and Physical Educators (SHAPE) tasked physical educators to develop physical literacy in their students, which is "the ability, confidence, and desire to be physically active for life" (2019, p. 9). Thus, the primary mission of physical education is to empower and support K–12 students to become autonomous in maintaining and improving their physical health and being active throughout their lifetime. Unfortunately, this lofty aim has yet to be actualized.

The Center for Disease Control and Prevention (CDC, 2022a) recommends "children and adolescents ages 6 through 17 years should do 60 minutes (1 hour) or more of moderate-to-vigorous physical activity daily" (para. 2). Unfortunately, research has found that only "42 percent of children and only 8 percent of adolescents engage in moderate-to vigorous-intensity activity [within] 5 of the past 7 days [at the time of the administration of the survey] for at least 60 minutes each day" (CDC, 2022b, para. 3).

Low activity rates in children most often lead to inactivity and health complications later in life as adults. According to the CDC, obesity in adults, in March 2020, was roughly at 42 percent (CDC, 2022b, para. 1). Obesity can lead to heart disease, stroke, type 2 diabetes, and certain types of cancer, all of which are preventable and can lead to premature death (CDC, 2022b, para. 1). While there exist many initiatives and organizations working to curb the obesity epidemic, it may be pertinent to examine how physical education in schools can become a more effective lever in supporting active lifestyles among children and adolescents.

I am a teacher educator of physical education preservice teacher candidates, and one of the main barriers physical education teacher candidates report they encounter in student achievement is the lack of student motivation to participate in physical education courses. This chapter argues for adopting culturally responsive teaching practices and social and emotional learning competencies as methods, proven prior, to enhance student engagement and support student academic success in learning physical education curriculum.

Furthermore, this chapter advocates for adopting a pedagogy of care to support all physical education students, especially transgender students. Transgender youth have been at the forefront of discriminatory practices attested by the 650 pieces of anti-LGBTQ legislation proposed in 2023 (Miller, 2023). In physical education courses, perplexed physical educators can feel unsupported on how to best serve transgender students in the political hotbeds that unfortunately exist in today's schools and locker rooms.

Using the narratives of preservice and in-service teachers, this chapter will demonstrate how teachers attempt to incorporate culturally responsive teaching practices, social and emotional competencies, and a culture of care in physical education. The following section will be written as a single teacher narrative; however, the single perspective narrative represents many voices. This narrative will also highlight physical education teachers' failures and successes. The hope is to inspire more physical educators to reflect on how they might improve their pedagogy to center on care in a physical education space.

INSTRUCTIONAL STRATEGIES FOR CULTURALLY RESPONSIVE TEACHING IN PHYSICAL EDUCATION

Before I decided to adopt more culturally responsive teaching practices, I was traditionally taught to include activities in physical education such as running the mile, playing team sports, and dressing in specified uniforms to participate in class and/or receive credit for doing so. Over time, I learned these are not experiences that motivate students to participate in physical education. When student participation waned, I decided I needed to look at a different instructional approach. That is when I became familiar with the concept of culturally responsive teaching. Here are some lessons that helped me become more culturally responsive.

Lesson 1: Audit My Course and Seek Community Input for Curriculum Decisions

In order to begin the transition of creating a more culturally responsive physical education classroom, I began by considering the content and learning activities of my curriculum. As an example, in my state, California, physical education content standards requires high school students to learn the following three anchor standards:

1. Demonstrate knowledge of and competency in motor skills, movement patterns, and strategies needed to perform a variety of physical activities.
2. Achieve a level of physical fitness for health and performance while demonstrating knowledge of fitness concepts, principles, and strategies.
3. Demonstrate knowledge of psychological and sociological concepts, principles, and strategies that apply to the learning and performance of physical activity. (California Department of Education, 2005, p. 36)[1]

I began to think more about the first anchor standard. California-based physical education requires students to "demonstrate proficient movement skills in aquatic, rhythms/dance, and individual and dual activities" (California Department of Education, 2005, p. 36).

In my past practice, I would have interpreted *dual activities* to be synonymous with team sports. While this decision was not necessarily a poor curricular decision, the sports I typically chose for students to participate in were not always responsive to the types of sports my students had prior experiences with or were interested in. During my teacher preparation program, I was encouraged to take an audit about my current teaching philosophy and practices. When I audited my current courses, I realized I could be selecting team-based games that connected more to the community I served.

I began with surveying families and their students about culturally based games, dances, and other physical activities practiced within their cultures. I learned about various games from the families in my community. For example, I learned about a Mexican/Latin American–based game called *Basque Pelota*, which was similar to various court games like racquetball, tennis, and/or pickleball. I also learned that many of my students were familiar with equestrian-based (that is, rodeo) activities, which could also be used to meet the aforementioned standard. My course audit and community outreach increased student engagement and participation in my classroom and, ultimately, led to my students becoming lifelong movers in activities more relevant to their cultural identities.

Lesson 2: Develop High Expectations for All of My Students

It was easy for me to center my efforts on students who were motivated to participate, who dressed out each day, and who were athletically inclined. However, in reality, that meant only a small group of students were succeeding in my class, and it bothered me. Through various professional learning offerings through my school and in discussion with colleagues, I realized I needed to focus on having clear and high expectations for all students.

Unfortunately, in reflecting, I recognized I had work to do. My classroom environment felt more like an environment of compliance rather than competence. Dressing out and participation had become the primary measures for student success rather than on developing and demonstrating competence in the knowledge and skills of the curriculum. My students varied in their competence and confidence levels to participate in various physical activities, which impacted students' levels of motivation to participate.

Additionally, my more confident and competent students tended to participate more often and at higher levels, which caused a discrepancy in how I evaluated my students. Sadly, I defaulted to using participation and students dressing out as a measure of curricular success. Even then, the requirements for dressing out did not always match the norms for dress in certain cultures as well as caused financial burdens for students who came from lower socio-economic backgrounds.

It took some work to change my practice. One of the major shifts I made was to be more intentional in setting my learning goals. Once I was clear on my goal, I would then ask, "What barriers might students in my class have towards achieving this goal?" Typically, I could anticipate which of my students would encounter barriers to meeting the goal. Once I could identify the barriers, I would then reflect on whether those perceived/anticipated barriers were ones where students needed more support to be successful or if those barriers emerged because of my unrealistic expectations. I learned fostering high expectations is much different than setting unrealistic expectations. Once my goals were clear, I could create learning environments inclusive and accessible for all students to achieve.

CULTURALLY RESPONSIVE LESSON PLAN TEMPLATE

Title of Lesson:	*Using Offensive, Defensive, and Transition Strategies in Kabaddi*
Grade Level:	High school (9–10)

Content Standard(s):

1.4. Explain and demonstrate advanced offensive, defensive, and transition strategies in aquatic and individual and dual activities

Social Justice Standard: https://www.learningforjustice.org/frameworks/social-justice-standards

Students will examine diversity in social, cultural, political, and historical contexts rather than in ways that are superficial or oversimplified.

Objectives: *Students will be able to*

analyze and evaluate various offensive, defensive, and transition strategies to compete effectively in Kabaddi.

Anticipatory Set: *(How will student interest be sparked to engage in the lesson of the day?)*

Students will watch a recent clip of a Kabaddi world cup match. After students watch the clip, they will be asked to play the role of the coach of the team and devise a way each team could have defended or attacked better in that situation.
Clip: https://www.youtube.com/watch?v=Y-bq3adcnpA (2:35–2:50)

Relevancy: *(How will the content be made relevant to the students in the context you are teaching? What connections can be made to their experiences and cultures?)*

There is a growing population of Indian students in my class. The game Kabaddi is a sport that has grown in popularity insomuch as it now has its own international competition where teams from around the globe compete in a world cup. Most of my Indian students are familiar with the sport. Therefore, I can utilize their funds of knowledge to teach others in the classroom. Because the sport is like tag, all students will have some prior knowledge, so the sport is accessible to students who are non-Indian. The sport can be played on a spectrum from simple to complex, in terms of offensive, defensive, and transition strategies, which is the focus of today's lesson. I anticipate students will enjoy the collaboration, critical thinking, and competition as well as the opportunity to build cardiovascular endurance.

Academic Vocabulary: *(What academic vocabulary will be addressed in this lesson? How will it be taught and made comprehensible to ALL learners?)*

boundary lines, mid-line, play area, baulk line, bonus line, raider, antiraider
Students are familiar with the definition of these terms. As students are participating and designing offensive and defensive plays, they will be encouraged to use the vocabulary when discussing with their teams and answering check for understanding questions.

Lesson Overview: *(Please describe the steps for each part of the lesson. Also, in parentheses, put a time estimate for each segment of the lesson.)*

Students will begin by viewing the clip described in the anticipatory set. The teacher will ask students to consider how they would attack or defend in the situation they viewed. The teacher may follow up to encourage small and whole group discussion with questions such as:
  a. In what ways was the offensive/defensive approach effective/ineffective?
  b. What strategies might your team use on offense/defense? (5–7 minutes)

After the anticipatory set, students and teacher will walk out to the tennis courts to play Kabaddi. (3–5 minutes)

Students will do a brief warmup. (5 minutes)
  c. Three laps around a single tennis court
  d. Stretches specific to Kabaddi to prevent injury
     i. Calves
     ii. Hamstring
     iii. Thighs

Students will be divided into teams by randomization. (3–5 minutes)

Teams will play to 10. (Each game may last 7–10 minutes)

The instructor will ask students to play best out of three. (Total of 30 minutes)

At the end of the first match, students will work together to review their offensive, defensive, and transition strategies. They will work to revise their strategies and possibly formulate new ones as they compete in the subsequent matches. (3-minute huddle)

They can call the teacher over for support in their team huddle.

At the end of the set of three, if there is time, teams can play other teams in one single elimination match.

At the close of class, students will complete a reflection. They will respond to the following questions:
  e. What offensive strategies worked? Why?
  f. What defensive strategies worked? Why? (5 minutes)

They will turn their slips in and be dismissed to change. (5–7 minutes)

Materials Needed: *(Please list the materials that will be needed for this lesson.)*

Tennis courts without the nets
Whiteboards and markers

Universal Design for Learning: *(How will the principles of UDL be utilized throughout this lesson to give students voice and choice?)*

Because the game Kabaddi is a game that is culturally responsive to all learners (both Indian and non-Indian) due to its tag-like nature, this activity is universally designed to recruit interest to optimize the relevancy, value, and authenticity (7.2) of all students in the class. The nature of collaboration in the use of end-of-match huddles fosters collaboration and community (8.3). Moreover, the use of end-of-match huddles allows for mastery-oriented feedback (8.4) from their peers and instructor, when solicited. All of these principles align to enhance engagement with students.

Access: *(What strategies will be used throughout the lesson to allow students multiple entry points into understanding the concepts taught?)*

The video used for the anticipatory set is universally designed and allows access for all students regardless of prior knowledge and language. All students will be able to comprehend the input provided by the video. While student attire is important, student dress in the activity is not requisite for participation. Having collaborative groups with the option of using the instructor allows for multiple opportunities to learn offensive and defensive strategies in this game. Last, the lack of equipment needed in this game allows for all students to participate effectively.

Students with physical disabilities can also participate in the learning goal. As they will not be able to actively play, they can participate as coaches at the end-of-match huddles.

Higher-Order Thinking: *(In what ways will this lesson require students to utilize higher-order thinking? Please describe.)*

The lesson promotes students to think at the top two levels of Bloom's taxonomy:

Analyzing/evaluating game situations
Creating new strategies to compete

Assessments: *(How will each learning objective be assessed? What activities do you have planned to check for understanding approximately every 5 minutes of the lesson?)*

The instructor will monitor the huddles and look for students devising and reflecting on offensive and defensive strategies from the prior match to the next one. The end of lesson reflection will serve as a summative learning assessment of the intended objective.

Closure: *(What activity will you use to close this lesson and to assess students' understanding at the end of the period?)*

At the close of class, students will complete a reflection. They will respond to the following questions:
   a. What offensive strategies worked? Why?
   b. What defensive strategies worked? Why?

Instructional Strategies for Social and Emotional Learning Competencies in Physical Education

I must confess. I was an educator that brushed aside teaching social and emotional competencies to my students. I believed that these are skills to be taught at home rather than in the classroom—and besides, I need to get students exercising and did not feel I had time to incorporate social and emotional learning. Then I was introduced to social and emotional learning frameworks, and I learned that developing social and emotional competencies can increase students' achievement (Collaborative for Academic, Social, and Emotional Learning, 2023a). I also read this statement from my own professional learning and study:

> Too often, however, schools teach social and emotional skills outside the daily curriculum. Consider how much more relevant such skills would be if we embedded them in daily work, supporting students as they learn to cooperate effectively with a lab partner, set realistic writing goals, persevere through a tough math problem, or self-regulate well enough to allow others to speak in a class discussion. . . . Instead of viewing social and emotional learning as tangential—something to fit in around the edges of the curriculum—we should treat it as an integral part of our daily teaching for all students. (Anderson, 2015, para. 2–3)

This statement changed my perspective and caused me to realize that there are many important social and emotional competencies that students could learn in my class. It also made me realize that the times my students were not being successful were partially due to a lack of social and emotional skills required to meet my objective.

For me, social and emotional learning, much like culturally responsive teaching, should be a shared responsibility and partnership between parents and educators. There are social and emotional skills needed to be harmonious in a student's family life, and (while there is some congruence) there are specific discrete social and emotional skills to be learned to succeed in school. I was fortunate to be a member of my national organization, the Society of Health and Physical Educators (SHAPE). They created a crosswalk[2] to provide guidance for how to teach social and emotional competencies naturally in connection with the national physical education standards (Society of Health and Physical Educators, 2019). I provided an example from the SHAPE crosswalk as well as an example I created using the California content standards in table 5.1.

Now, I do not teach content and social and emotional competencies in silos. For example, when I teach the standard of motor skills and movement patterns through dance, it provides a perfect opportunity to simultaneously teach teamwork and collaborative problem solving, skills required for developing healthy relationships in personal and professional life.

Another article I received from SHAPE helped me outline how to more intentionally teach social and emotional learning competencies across the arc of my curriculum through the year. This teacher used the familiar physical education concept of progressions and created social and emotional learning progressions to be used throughout the year to become more intentional in developing these core competencies (Bragg, 2019).

For example, in the beginning of the year, he focuses on building community in his classroom. In order to build community, he pulls a variety of skills from all of the Collaborative for Academic, Social, and Emotional Learning (CASEL, 2023b) five core competencies such as "developing positive

Table 5.1. Integrating Social and Emotional Learning with Content Area Learning in Physical Education

	SHAPE America National Standards and Grade-Level Outcomes for K–12 Physical Education	CASEL Core Competencies and Related Skills
Anchor Standard/ Category	Standard 2: The physically literate individual applies knowledge of concepts, principles, strategies, and tactics related to movement and performance.	Responsible Decision Making: The ability to make constructive choices about personal behavior and social interactions based on ethical standards, safety concerns, and social norms. The realistic evaluation of consequences of various actions and a consideration of the well-being of oneself and others.
Substandard/Skill	S2.E3.5a: Applies movement concepts to strategy in game situations. California Content Standards	Analyzing Situations CASEL Core Competencies and Related Skills
Anchor Standard/ Category	Standard 1: Students demonstrate the motor skills and movement patterns needed to perform a variety of physical activities.	Relationship Skills: The ability to establish and maintain healthy and rewarding relationships with diverse individuals and groups. The ability to communicate clearly, listen well, cooperate with others, resist inappropriate social pressure, negotiate conflict constructively, and seek and offer help when needed.
Substandard/Skill	1.2: Create and perform a square dance.	Practicing Teamwork and Collaborative Problem Solving

Note: As cited in the Crosswalk for SHAPE America National Standards & Grade-Level Outcomes for K–12 Physical Education and CASEL Social and Emotional Learning Core Competencies (Society of Health and Physical Educators, 2019).

relationships" from *Relationship Skills* and "identifying social norms" from *Social Awareness*, to cite only a few of the possibilities (Bragg, 2019). As students in his class develop these competencies, he suggests that physical educators then move to another categorical progression and further develop students' social and emotional competencies to prepare students for deeper content learning. For instance, once a community is built, he then builds students communication skills, applying additional competencies and skills from the framework. Using this progression—much like using progression to teach students novice to advanced physical movements—allows physical educators to be intentional in developing social and emotional competencies cohesively with content learning.

I learned there are many opportunities for developing social and emotional competencies naturally within the physical education curriculum. These tools really helped me develop well-rounded students who learned to care as much for their social and emotional well-being as they did for their physical well-being. I was able to see many of my students mature over the year. In my experience, social and emotional learning was simple and natural to incorporate and I cannot imagine my practice in any other way now.

SOCIAL AND EMOTIONAL LEARNING LESSON PLAN TEMPLATE

Title of Lesson:	*Carnival of Physical Fitness*
Grade Level:	Seventh grade
Content Standard(s):	

5.2. Accept responsibility for individual improvement.

Note: This lesson is intended to work additionally to promote the acquisition of the social and emotional competency of "self-management, the abilities to manage one's emotions, thoughts, and behaviors effectively in different situations and to achieve goals and aspirations." Specifically, this lesson will promote the skills of exhibiting self-discipline and self-motivation, setting personal and collective goals, and using planning and organizational skills.

Social Justice Standard: https://www.learningforjustice.org/frameworks/social-justice-standards

Students will express pride, confidence, and healthy self-esteem without denying the value and dignity of other people.

Objectives: *Students will be able to*

demonstrate and explain improvement in activities related to physical fitness.

Anticipatory Set: *(How will student interest be sparked to engage in the lesson of the day?)*

When students walk into class, they will be given a "ticket" (that is, a map and a score card) for the Carnival of Physical Fitness. They will be given time to decide which fitness activities they want to participate in with the goal to show improvement in at least two of the five areas of physical fitness.

Relevancy: *(How will the content be made relevant to the students in the context you are teaching? What connections can be made to their experiences and cultures?)*

The lesson primarily promotes student choice which will optimize relevancy. Students will be able to select activities for which they have prior experience and ones they have high interest in.

Academic Vocabulary: *(What academic vocabulary will be addressed in this lesson? How will it be taught and made comprehensible to ALL learners?)*

body composition, flexibility, muscular strength, muscular endurance, cardiorespiratory endurance

Students will continue to be exposed to these terms as they have been in prior lessons. These terms will serve as the categories on their "ticket" that describes the stations for which they can attend to improve their physical fitness. This will be how they will receptively learn the terms. They will also be encouraged throughout discussions during the class session and their reflections at the end of class to use these terms in describing their performance. For example, they will be asked to articulate:

How did you improve or plan to improve your [body composition, flexibility, muscular strength, muscular endurance, and cardiorespiratory endurance] during this lesson and/or beyond it?

In this way students will produce these terms and further internalize them.

Lesson Overview: *(Please describe the steps for each part of the lesson. Also, in parentheses, put a time estimate for each segment of the lesson.)*

Students will enter class and engage in the anticipatory set. Students will need to complete at least one exercise in each of the five domains. They should select which exercises they will do from each of the five categories. They must also keep in mind that if a station is full, they will need to manage their time well. (3–5 minutes)

The teacher will explain that each station has an instruction card. Students will need to go quickly to their station, read the instruction card, and do the required exercise. Students will need to do the exercise twice. They will give their best attempt the first time and then do it again and seek improvement. The teacher will elicit and answer any questions. (3–5 minutes)

Allow students to begin their station work. The instructor will monitor stations and student work. (25–30 minutes)

At the close of the session, students will review their baselines and their second attempts. Students will reflect on their two scores and then set goals for personal improvement. The instructor will provide a date for the next fitness test practice where they will have another opportunity to show improvement. (5–7 minutes)

Materials Needed: *(Please list the materials that will be needed for this lesson.)*

Station instruction cards: There will be five stations for each physical fitness component. Stations will comprise activities and drills that students have participated in during class prior.
Maps of stations
Score cards

Universal Design for Learning: *(How will the principles of UDL be utilized throughout this lesson to give students voice and choice?)*

This lesson incorporates the following principles of UDL:
- Optimizing individual choice and autonomy (7.1): Students will be able to select the stations they are most interested in and would like to participate in to improve their physical fitness
- Clarify vocabulary and symbols (2.1): The instruction cards allow to reduce language barriers and become accessible for all students to effectively participate
- Activate or supply background knowledge (3.1): Because the activities are ones that have been done in class prior to this lesson, students will have the background knowledge to participate. Moreover, they have peers and the instructor who can help them during the process as well as use the card to supply background knowledge.

Access: *(What strategies will be used throughout the lesson to allow students multiple entry points into understanding the concepts taught?)*

The stations will be set up prior including equipment and instructional cards for students who need support in participating in the activities. Therefore, equipment needs will not serve as barriers. Students will be able to participate whether or not they have workout clothes. However, clothes will be provided if needed. The map and description of activities in the anticipatory set will be in multiple languages. Students will be able to use peer and instructor support throughout the lesson.

Higher-Order Thinking: *(In what ways will this lesson require students to utilize higher-order thinking? Please describe.)*

Students will be asked to analyze and evaluate their performance as they seek to improve their physical fitness.

Assessments: *(How will each learning objective be assessed? What activities do you have planned to check for understanding approximately every 5 minutes of the lesson?)*

The whole session station exercise activity is designed to foster students to accept responsibility for individual improvement. The completion of the closing reflection at the end will demonstrate how students accept responsibility for their improvement in their physical fitness.

Closure: *(What activity will you use to close this lesson and to assess students' understanding at the end of the period?)*

At the close of the session, students will review their baselines and their second attempts. Students will reflect on their two scores and then set goals for personal improvement. The instructor will provide a date for the next fitness test practice where they will have another opportunity to show improvement.

Applying a Pedagogy of Care in Physical Education

When I was asked about how I incorporate a pedagogy of care into my practice, I was a bit perplexed about the concept. It was a new term to me (and, perhaps, those reading the chapter). However, it may not be too unfamiliar in practice. Simply defined, a pedagogy of care is the strategies and mindsets teachers use to exhibit and build caring and positive relationships with all students (Palahicky et al., 2019). I believe all teachers desire to develop positive relationships with their students. Nevertheless, we are not always aware nor explicitly taught how to do so. I was taught and have learned from experiences over the years that developing a strong stance for a pedagogy of care may be the single greatest factor to support student success and development (Sparks, 2019).

There are many ways to practice a pedagogy of care, but I also have realized how important it is to be intentional, especially with students who identify as LGBTQ. Unfortunately, students who identify as LGBTQ may have encountered the antithesis of a pedagogy of care. It has been hard for me and my colleagues who are perplexed on how to create a more inclusive environment in physical education despite a culture of heteronormativity. Here are some lessons I learned about implementing a pedagogy of care with all students.

Lesson 1: Be Reflective

To start, I continually reflect on the following question, "If I was in this physical education class, would I feel cared for?" Oftentimes, this critical self-reflection provides me a new perspectives. Moreover, I take time to build relationships with students and elicit their honest feedback about their experiences in my physical education course. It provides me data to not only improve in providing care but also to be more culturally responsive and attuned to my student social and emotional needs.

Lesson 2: Be Mindful of Tonality

Some physical education classrooms can feel more like a military camp than a space to learn about how to become active and physically fit. This is a result of large class sizes. In the past, I would resort to management techniques such as yelling, blowing whistles, and highly structured routines, such as setting specified times to dress in workout uniforms or having students sit in rows. In this environment, it was difficult for my students to feel cared for when I was enforcing compliance. I realized I need to consider how to demonstrate care better.

I began having conversations before and after class to connect with and encourage students in appropriate ways. I started having students sit in a circle rather than rows. Additionally, I began using signals to get attention rather than a raised voice or a whistle. These strategies lead to a climate of care in physical education. Physical educators should be mindful of the tone they set in class and work to mitigate negative tones and replace them with more positive caring ones.

Lesson 3: Be Responsive

Like most academic subjects in secondary schools, students in physical education arrive late and/or without their needed materials. Students also may come to class with various levels of motivation to participate for a variety of reasons. How I responded to students in these situations made all the difference. I watched my colleagues and my mentor punish a student with unpleasant physical exercises (that is, pushups, running laps, etc.) for various behavioral issues such as tardiness, not wearing proper attire, and/or lack of participation. None of these demonstrate care to me. In fact, I noticed it significantly diminished it. Instead, I decided to make it a practice to learn more about students in these situations. I would inquire about the reasons for the tardiness, for not wearing proper attire, and/or for lack of participation. It always led to a more caring and compassionate response and relationship with my students.

There were lots of situations where being responsive was a better approach than being reactive or punitive. For example, I create my lesson activities to be responsive to the assets and needs of my students. Students who are not as developed in an activity are grouped in a way that supports their development and does not bring unnecessary attention to them, especially among more developed students in that activity. One class, I had a student with a physical deformity in his right hand. We were playing field hockey that day. I asked what position he would be comfortable playing. He was surprised because he assumed I would excuse him, but instead he expressed an eagerness to play goalkeeper. It ended up being a great experience for him.

I have colleagues who provide clothes and shoes for students. I also welcome students who are late or not fully dressed out rather than drawing negative attention to them. We just have a conversation at the appropriate time to address the concern and see how we can together find a solution. This is how I have practiced and observed others use a pedagogy of care.

Pedagogy of Care Practices for Students Who Identify as LGBTQ

Before delving into better practices that can demonstrate a pedagogy of care for students who identify as LGBTQ, it may be helpful to identify areas where students who identify as LGBTQ have felt unsafe (Kosciw et al., 2022). Roughly 15 percent of students who identified as LGBTQ stated they were prevented or discouraged from playing sports from either school staff or coaches (Kosciw et al., 2022). One-fourth of students who identified as LGBTQ had been prevented from using the locker room that aligned with their gender (Kosciw et al., 2022). Students who identify as LGBTQ are frequently encountering barriers to meeting the aims of and having access to physical education. What can be done to ensure a pedagogy of care is better practiced toward students who identify as LGBTQ in physical education?

While I am still learning much about how to foster a caring environment for students who identify as LGBTQ+, I found a few key strategies can be helpful to begin to help students who identify as LGBTQ feel cared for in the physical education classroom. I have a local chapter of the Gay, Lesbian & Straight Education Network (GLSEN), a national support and advocacy group for students who identify as LGBTQ and the teachers who educate them, at my school.

I have learned from their advisors and trainings they offered at my school that I could begin by adopting an LGBTQ+ inclusive curriculum, which included, but is not limited to, "positive representations of LGBTQ+ people, history, and events related to the class," "inclusive language," "gender-neutral clothing options," and a curriculum that avoids "gender-segregated activities" (The Gay, Lesbian & Straight Education Network, 2021, p. 3). In applying this professional learning, I now discuss athletes who identify as LGBTQ, address students in gender-inclusive language (for example, phrases like "welcome everyone" rather than "welcome young men and women"), and avoid activities where it is boys versus girls.

Additionally, GLSEN recommends physical educators get educated about the experiences of the students who identify as LGBTQ and also with their local policies related to their students who identify as LGBTQ (The Gay, Lesbian & Straight Education Network, 2021). We have been working to create a locker room culture where everyone is accepted. I have had conversations with all of my students about their experiences in my course. I found this is a helpful practice for me to improve but to also not single out students who identify as LGBTQ.

I also model how to introduce oneself using my preferred pronouns and inviting students who are comfortable doing so to share their pronouns (The Gay, Lesbian & Straight Education Network, 2021). I learned though that requiring all students to do so in class may lead to outing students that are not ready or comfortable to share that part of their identity.

Last, I provide curricular alternatives as well as flexible classroom policies for students who identify as LGBTQ. For instance, if they prefer an alternative space to change, I provide it (The Gay, Lesbian & Straight Education Network, 2021). If they prefer not to attend class due to harassment and bullying for a time, I provide alternative coursework and assignments (The Gay, Lesbian & Straight Education Network, 2021). Revisiting the previous principle of responsiveness, I show immediate responsiveness in the face of harassment and/or bullying of students who identify as LGBTQ. This has allowed me to create a space where all students feel safe, but more especially students who identify as LGBTQ (The Gay, Lesbian & Straight Education Network, 2021). While I am sure there are many other ways I can demonstrate a pedagogy of care for students who identify as LGBTQ, these practices have provided—so far—a solid foundation upon which I can build.

CONCLUSION

These teachers have provided an invaluable glimpse into how physical education spaces can be more culturally responsive, more socially and emotionally productive, and more intentionally caring. The educational landscape constantly changes. The field of education is becoming more aware of the need to respond to the diversity of students in current classrooms. It is an exciting period to be an educator amid such positive change. Physical educators have an opportunity before them: ride the waves of change like a great surfer would or become swallowed up in the tidal wave that may come down on them if they resist change.

Hopefully, this chapter inspires them to abolish any practices that are not culturally responsive, do not support social and emotional learning, and do not promote a pedagogy of care. These key pedagogical stepping stones will allow physical educators to climb to greater heights. Then, perhaps, the world will see a more physically active and healthier generation of people who were taught to become lifelong movers in cultural, social, and emotional sustaining ways.

READER TAKEAWAYS

- Physical educators should seek to work with families and students to create a curriculum more aligned to the culture, values, and practices of the community wherein they serve.

- Physical educators should understand that social and emotional learning is not an "extra" duty for them but rather that the physical education curriculum has many natural opportunities to teach social and emotional competencies.
- Physical educators should consider creating progressions for the social and emotional competencies they want to teach in an academic year.
- Physical educators should be mindful of how the tone and their responsiveness in their classrooms contribute to a climate of care and mitigate any practice that may reduce a student's perception of care in the physical education classroom.
- Physical educators should seek to adopt and become further educated on best practices for exhibiting a pedagogy of care toward students who identify as LGBTQ.

NOTES

1. These standards closely mirror the National Physical Education Standards (see https://www.shapeamerica.org/standards/pe/default.aspx), which can also be assumed are closely aligned to other physical education standards in other states in the United States. Therefore, it is hoped that the example generated using California content standards will have general applicalblility for readers in other states.

2. Reference to full crosswalk in the reference section of this chapter.

REFERENCES

Anderson, M. (2015). Social-emotional learning and academics: Better together. *Educational Leadership*, *73*(2). https://www.ascd.org/el/articles/social-emotional-learning-and-academics-better-together.

Bragg, K. (2019). *How to integrate social and emotional learning in PE to improve classroom climate.* SHAPE America Blog. https://blog.shapeamerica.org/2019/11/how-to-integrate-social-and-emotional-learning-in-pe/.

California Department of Education (2005). *Physical education model content standards for California Public Schools, Kindergarten through grade twelve.* https://www.cde.ca.gov/be/st/ss/documents/pestandards.pdf.

Centers for Disease Control and Prevention (2022a, July 26). *Physical activity guidelines for school-aged children and adolescents.* https://www.cdc.gov/healthyschools/physicalactivity/guidelines.htm#:~:text=Children%20and%20adolescents%20ages%206%20through%2017%20years%20should%20do,to%2Dvigorous%20physical%20activity%20daily.

Centers for Disease Control and Prevention (2022b, July 26). *Physical activity facts.* https://www.cdc.gov/healthyschools/physicalactivity/facts.htm.

Centers for Disease Control and Prevention (2022c, May 17). *Adult obesity facts.* https://www.cdc.gov/obesity/data/adult.html.

Collaborative for Academic, Social, and Emotional Learning (2023a). *What does the research Say?* https://casel.org/fundamentals-of-sel/what-does-the-research-say/.

Collaborative for Academic, Social, and Emotional Learning (2023b). *What is the CASEL framework?* https://casel.org/fundamentals-of-sel/what-is-the-casel-framework/.

Farrey, T., and Isard, R. (2015). Physical literacy in the United States: A model, strategic plan, and call to action. https://www.shapeamerica.org//Common/Uploaded%20files/uploads/pdfs/PhysicalLiteracy_AspenInstitute-FINAL.pdf.

hooks, b. (1994). *Teaching to transgress.* Routledge.

Kosciw, J. G., Clark, C. M., and Menard, L. (2022). *The 2021 national school climate survey: The experiences of LGBTQ+ youth in our nation's schools.* GLSEN. https://www.glsen.org/sites/default/files/2022-10/NSCS-2021-Full-Report.pdf.

Miller, S. (2023, March 31). "War" on LGBTQ existence: 8 ways the record onslaught of 650 bills targets the community. *USA Today.* https://www.usatoday.com/story/news/nation/2023/03/31/650-anti-lgbtq-bills-introduced-us/11552357002/.

Palahicky, S., DesBiens, D., Jeffery, K., and Webster, K. S. (2021). Pedagogical values in online and blended learning environments in higher education. In *Research anthology on developing effective online learning courses* (pp. 1316–38). IGI Global.

Society of Health and Physical Educators (2019). *Crosswalk for SHAPE America national standards & grade-level outcomes for K–12 physical education and CASEL social and emotional learning core competencies.* https://www.lahperd.org/assets/SHAPEResources/PhysEd-SEL-Crosswalk-final.pdf.

Sparks, S. D. (2019, March 12). Why teacher-student relationships matter. *Education Week.* https://www.edweek.org/teaching-learning/why-teacher-student-relationships-matter/2019/03.

The Gay, Lesbian & Straight Education Network (2021). *Game plan for physical education teachers: Creating safe and inclusive classrooms for LGBTQ+ students.* https://www.glsen.org/sites/default/files/ctg/GLSEN_CTG2021_PETeachers_Middle-High_Guide.pdf.

Chapter 6

Culturally Responsive Teaching in Music and Theater Classrooms

Daniel Bryan and Lindsay Bryan

The arts are not a frill. The arts are a response to our individuality and our nature and help to shape our identity. What is there that can transcend deep difference and stubborn divisions? The arts. They have wonderful universality. Art has the potential to unify. It can speak in many languages without a translator. The arts do not discriminate. The arts lift us up.

—Barbara Jordan

EXPECTED LEARNING OUTCOMES

- Readers will be able to empower students to use their voices.
- Readers will establish empathy in the classroom using a variety of practices.
- Readers will be able to create a classroom environment that is conducive to student engagement and success.

TEACHER NARRATIVE

There is a misconception that culturally responsive teaching refers only to acknowledging our differences in race. Culture in the classroom is abundant: it can refer to race, religion, socioeconomic status, gender identity, sexual preference, hobbies, athleticism, music preferences. and more. The list can go on in perpetuity. The performing arts, especially music and theater, as a discipline give silenced voices a microphone.

As we have gone through our careers, different acronyms are introduced every few years to reform, reshape, and reinvigorate education. Ultimately, we found that in the performing arts, we were already implementing these "new" techniques or designations that were supposedly on the cutting edge of pedagogy. Luckily, the arts, as an academic discipline, are inherently student centered and relationship focused.

When we were going through our credential programs, we did not have the terminology like "culturally responsive teaching" (CRT) or "social emotional learning" (SEL) because they did not exist, but the spirit behind these terms has always been at the epicenter of our programs. Through learning about CRT and SEL, arts practices have been validated among the core curricula.

When we returned to campus after the pandemic, Lindsay made relationships paramount in her theater classroom. Instead of reviewing the syllabus on the first day of class, students immediately began talking, sharing, and collaborating. There was a shift in protocol to create the ensemble first, and then talk about the norms needed to make the classroom a safe space for all artists to thrive in as opposed to dictatorial rules being reviewed.

With relationship building being the foundation of the class for the first few weeks, the other pieces fell into place. Once Lindsay knew her students, she was able to make the curriculum more relevant to their unique lens. For instance, when doing a Shakespeare unit, one of the students translated a sonnet into Vietnamese, their native language, and performed it for the class. In another example, students contributed ideas for a one-act play that represented them called "That's Our Folks!" and included folktales and poems from Iran, Afghanistan, China, El Salvador, and Mexico. Furthermore, students reimagined Maya Angelou poems and performed some selections in ASL. The result was an authentic celebration of the diversity of the students in the program at that time—a true example of CRT before the term became an educational buzzword.

Postpandemic, the job for Dan was singular in definition but massive in task: rebuild a nearly five-hundred-member band program for the entire district from scratch. During the pandemic, all aspects of the fledgling fifth- through eighth-grade program had been shut down; there was no timetable for a return to in-person learning, or if playing instruments indoors or outdoors was even going to be feasible.

At the root of it, the task was simple: use the same road map and routines that were used prepandemic and rebuild the program. Those procedures and strategies were already in place, but it came with an unexpected bonus: an opportunity to be more efficient, focus on the needs of individual campuses, and develop curriculum that better fit the community that was being served (read: toss out the generic music books that were not connecting with the student population).

The complex part: Who was the new "post-COVID" population? Were they going to come back with the same academic skills they had prior to our "break"? Would they learn at the same rate and be interested in learning? Would playing music have an appeal to a group who had been largely isolated for a year and half?

Two years back into in-person learning, Dan would learn that the answer was "yes," but the upper grades of the program (seventh and eighth grades) were going to need something different from the music they performed. Additionally, they were going to have to take the bigger steps of exploring band literature and trying to translate it into something meaningful for both themselves and their audiences. They needed to establish a connection between themselves and the music they were playing—it had to have personal meaning to them.

The performing arts took a huge hit with the pandemic as our performances were indefinitely postponed due to being superspreader events. Rebuilding our programs has made both of us focus on the relationship piece first and the curriculum second. As a result of changing our approaches, we are now able to go deeper through our curriculum because we are able to make it student centered and relevant.

MUSIC LESSON PLAN

Title of Lesson:	*What Is It? What Is It Made Of? What Does It Do?*
Grade Level:	6–12

Content Standard(s):

4.2 Enduring Understanding. Analyzing creators' context and how they manipulate elements of music provides insight into their intent and informs performance.
Essential Question: How does understanding the structure and context of musical works inform performance (or analysis)?
4.3 Enduring Understanding. Performers make interpretive decisions based on their understanding of context and expressive intent.
Essential Question: How do performers interpret musical works?

Social Justice Standards: https://www.learningforjustice.org/frameworks/social-justice-standards

Students will develop language and knowledge to accurately and respectfully describe how people (including themselves) are both similar to and different from each other and others in their identity groups.
Students will respectfully express curiosity about the history and lived experiences of others and will exchange ideas and beliefs in an open-minded way.
Students will respond to diversity by building empathy, respect, understanding, and connection.

Objectives: *Students will be able to*

identify what makes music work—what it is made of and why and how we connect to it.

Anticipatory Set: *(How will student interest be sparked to engage in the lesson of the day?)*

The lesson begins with the statement, "Genre means kind or type. Can you name a genre of music that people might listen to?"

Students will be played two to three listening examples (not included in the listening exercise). These should be examples that a vast majority of the class could recognize. Examples of this would be

1. music from a popular film (*Star Wars Main Titles* is always a good one),
2. music from a video game,
3. music from a popular kids TV show,
4. music from a frequently played commercial (recent Burger King Ads, as an example), or
5. music from videos played by a social media influencer.

Students will need a pen/pencil and paper to complete this assignment, or a simple Google form can be created for responses. They will be asked to

1. acknowledge if they have heard the selection before, and if so, what the name of it is;
2. identify as many instruments and/or voices as they can hear; and
3. identify a genre (classical, rock, etc.).

Each selection should be played for approximately 30 seconds. Students will be randomly selected to share what they have heard.

Relevancy: *(How will the content be made relevant to the students in the context you are teaching? What connections can be made to their experiences and cultures?)*

Relevancy: What do students know about the music they listen to and what instruments they play?

Connections: Students (and people in general) begin to connect to music in early childhood and often tie memories of family, upbringing, and culture to music. How can these connections be used to have deeper conversations about what they listen to or what they play?

Academic Vocabulary: *(What academic vocabulary will be addressed in this lesson? How will it be taught and made comprehensible to ALL learners?)*

Genre: kind or type. In music, examples would include: pop, rock, jazz, classical, etc.

Additional vocabulary that students discover can be written down in their notebooks/personal devices and discussed as a class with personal examples.

Lesson Overview: *(Please describe the steps for each part of the lesson. Also, in parentheses, put a time estimate for each segment of the lesson.)*

Anticipatory Set: Listening warmup (see previous for details). (5–7 minutes)

Activity 1: What Is It?
Part I: Students are played a 30-second clip of music and are asked to identify and write down what genre of music it is. This is brief: only a one- to two-word answer is needed. Play each clip, then give students a brief amount of time to reflect and respond. Depending on the number of selections you use, this can take 5 to 10 minutes.

Part II: Going selection by selection, students will be asked in a popcorn style (with random students called on) to identify the genre after each listening excerpt. This should go quickly, using "nonvolunteers" to give answers. Teachers should record each nonduplicate answer on a white board or screen for students to see. (5–10 minutes)

Activity 2: What Is It Made Of?
Part I: Students are played *the same* 30-second clip of music in the same order as the previous activity. In this second round, students are asked to identify the types of sounds they hear (voice, keyboard, trumpet, etc.). They should write or record as many as they can identify. Play each clip, then give students a brief amount of time to reflect and respond (this will take slightly longer than the previous exercise). Depending on the number of selections you use, this can take 7 to 12 minutes.

Part II: Going selection by selection, students will be asked to identify *just one* of the instruments they think they've heard. This should go quickly, using "nonvolunteers" to give answers. Teachers should record each original (nonduplicated) answer they get on a white board or screen for students to see. This list is in addition to the genre list that has already been created. (5–10 minutes)

Activity 3: What Does It Do/How Does It Feel?
This is, in my opinion, the heart of the assignment.

Part I: Students are played the same 30-second clip one last time and are asked two questions:
1. *How does it make you feel? What you're looking for here are short answers based on their emotional responses. What feelings do you get when you listen to the selection?*
2. *What does it remind you of? Does it bring up a fun memory? A sad memory? Does it remind you of something else? Another piece of music or something they saw on TV or the internet? Can they briefly describe it?*

Part II: *This is volunteers only.* Going selection by selection, students can volunteer their answers to one or both questions. Generally, I start with the first question, as it is not too personal, and reactions tend to be somewhat universal. (10–12 minutes)

Materials Needed: *(Please list the materials that will be needed for this lesson.)*

1. Recording of approximately ten to twelve pieces of music of varying styles (as described previously). This is best done with a playlist on a portable device.
2. Speaker of some kind with good quality playback (many portable Bluetooth speakers can do this).
3. Student needs (these assignments can be addressed in one of two ways: digital or "analog"):
   a. pencil/pen and paper, or
   b. tablet device.

Universal Design for Learning: *(How will the principles of UDL be utilized throughout this lesson to give students voice and choice?)*

The lesson, by design, is pretty accessible. Students can record responses in a variety of ways, based upon access to technology, individual learning styles, or 504/IEP plans.

Access: *(What strategies will be used throughout the lesson to allow students multiple entry points into understanding the concepts taught?)*

Several pedagogical strategies are used including listening, written responses and reflections, and class discussion. In order to have meaningful discourse, all students need to participate in the dialogue.

Higher-Order Thinking: *(In what ways will this lesson require students to utilize higher-order thinking? Please describe.)*

This assignment asks students to call upon personal/prior experience to describe kinds of music, instrumentation, and how it makes them feel. They will analyze and record their observations using a variety of prompts.

Assessments: *(How will each learning objective be assessed? What activities do you have planned to check for understanding approximately every 5 minutes of the lesson?)*

This is a very conversational/interactive activity that is very fast paced. Excerpts are played, and student input should be solicited after a very brief period of reflection for the students to consider the question. On average, you may solicit four to five responses per question (they are short answers).

Closure: *(What activity will you use to close this lesson and to assess students' understanding at the end of the period?)*

Ask students, "Why did we spend this amount of time on this activity? Why did we do this instead of having a lecture or playing an instrument?" Students will discuss the intention behind the assignment and will hopefully pull some, if not all, of the following points:
1. How much they already know about the music they listen to, and ways to listen to it differently. The lists that *they have created on the board are a reflection of this. They are using their vocabulary to describe the music they are listening to based on their own experiences.*
2. How music affects mood, and how what they know about music comes largely from their parents and their cultures.
3. How they can use this newly found knowledge to listen to and discover different kinds of music. If they play an instrument, how might this change how they play? Students have an opportunity to reinterpret music that they rehearse and perform in a way that better connects with themselves and their audience.

Reflection on Teaching the Music Lesson Plan

I have always found this lesson as a great way to begin a school year. The activity establishes what I hope is an open and welcoming classroom, where students feel comfortable expressing themselves and their opinions. This is important because our musical choices are an expression of us: our histories, our families, and our culture. To be able to do a deep dive on the music we are either playing or studying requires that people listen with open minds and empathy. More importantly, there is a need to connect to why and how we listen to the music we choose, and how to be open to hearing new things.

One of the great things I have found over the years of doing this assignment is seeing strangers in these classes connect instantly through a shared observation of a piece of music. In a thirty-second sampling of a tune, two students from completely different walks of life can share the same observation and make an instant connection.

Often, these observations are arrived at through a variety of experiences that culminate in the same moment to hear that "thing" in the same way. This realization starts the process of dismissing preconceived notions that exist about people that we have based upon appearance, an unfamiliar name, or some other standard that we might use to judge people. When we can speak about something universal like music using a shared language with total strangers, it makes it possible to have deeper conversations without fear of ridicule or anger. To get there, we start with something simple: thirty seconds of good music.

As an ensemble director, I have found that this assignment serves as a gateway to interpretation. From a playing standpoint, it is unlikely that you will be playing a single note of anything that you listen to that day. The point is to create dialogue and get students used to the practice of talking about what they hear. Music is not just the notes on the page; instead, it is what we *do* with the notes on the page.

Ironically, I have found that interpretation of a nonverbal language actually begins *with language*. Starting with music that students can talk about—the things they normally listen to—builds both vocabulary and analytic skills to get to the point of talking about the sounds that are coming from their instruments. Eventually, it can become a catalyst to talking about band and orchestra literature that helps students understand the sounds that they are hearing (and creating) in such a way as to cause them to "shape" the direction of a musical phrase.

Consider this: when we speak to other people in our native language, we know what words to emphasize to help drive a point home. The best instrumental music you listen to does the same thing: a saxophone soloist who brings "soul" to a sad melody, or an orchestra that makes Tchaikovsky's

Trepak dance. A composer can write the words "sad" and "dance" on a page as a directive to a performer, but it is through years of processing our language that we can *begin* to translate said language into the sounds that you hear great instrumentalists produce.

That "translation" begins with the music we know and having conversations about what we hear and what things sound like. If it sounds sad, what can we do to make our instruments sound sad? If it makes us dance, how do we make our instruments dance? If we think the piece of music we just listened to is fun, can we explore what makes it sound fun and see if we can apply it ourselves?

I have found that this assignment is ultimately an exercise in letting your defenses down. Sure, there is academic vocabulary and learning to listen to music beyond the lyrics, but it also encourages students to put into their own words what they are hearing and to not be afraid to identify the things that they hear to the best of their ability.

There are often missteps, guesses, and a lot of "I have no idea," but there is a lot of laughter, open dialogue, and thoughtful consideration of what others have to say and how they view the music they are taking in. Most importantly, there are a lot of connections made and commonalities found. It is a great way to commence a year of analysis, performance, or both.

THEATER LESSON PLAN

Title of Lesson:	*Empathetic Ensemble Exploration*
Grade Level:	6–12

Content Standard(s):

CONNECTING—Anchor Standard 10: Synthesize and relate knowledge and personal experiences to make art.
Enduring Understanding: Theater artists allow awareness of interrelationships between self and others to influence and inform their work.
Essential Question: What happens when theater artists foster understanding between self and others through critical awareness, social responsibility, and the exploration of empathy?

Social Justice Standards: https://www.learningforjustice.org/frameworks/social-justice-standards

Students will express pride, confidence, and healthy self-esteem without denying the value and dignity of other people.
Students will express comfort with people who are both similar to and different from them and engage respectfully with all people.

Objectives: *Students will be able to*

discuss the differences between empathy and sympathy, and understand that an ensemble is created when all voices are contributing and respected.

Anticipatory Set: *(How will student interest be sparked to engage in the lesson of the day?)*

Opening Discussion: Ask students what sympathy is and to give an example of a time when they were shown or showed sympathy. Ask if anyone knows what empathy is and to give an example (if possible!). Ask how they are similar and different. You can give them the definitions now if you do not want to show a video.

Definitions:
Sympathy: feeling pity and sorrow for someone's situation.
Empathy: the ability to understand and share the feelings of another person.

Video Option: If time and technological means are allotted, you can show a short video showing the differences between empathy and sympathy (I like "Dr. Brené Brown on Empathy vs Sympathy" available on YouTube [https://youtu.be/KZBTYViDPlQ] but there are tons of short videos that would work).
As you introduce the definitions or video, let students know that in a theater classroom, empathy is the foundation of everything we will do. Therefore, it is imperative that we all have a good understanding of what it is. The video will define and clarify sympathy and empathy. As you watch the video, note key ideas or examples you find help define these terms so you can share in our discussion.

Postdefinition/Video Discussion: Discuss the similarities and differences between sympathy and empathy by calling on student volunteers. After the discussion, have students write down the definitions in their theater notebooks and provide an example of each term (either a personal example or one another class member has shared).

Relevancy: *(How will the content be made relevant to the students in the context you are teaching? What connections can be made to their experiences and cultures?)*

Students will share examples of their own lives when sympathy and empathy were shown to them and how it made them feel. As we get through the activities, they will start to learn that all members of the ensemble are vital and that we only succeed when everyone participates and uses their voice.

Academic Vocabulary: *(What academic vocabulary will be addressed in this lesson? How will it be taught and made comprehensible to ALL learners?)*

Sympathy: feeling pity and sorrow for someone's situation.
Empathy: the ability to understand and share the feelings of another person.
Slating: introducing yourself prior to an audition.
Vocabulary will be written down for students to write down in their notebooks, discussed as a class with personal examples, and an optional video discussing the differences through a cartoon will be shown and discussed if time and technological means allow for this.

Lesson Overview: *(Please describe the steps for each part of the lesson. Also, in parentheses, put a time estimate for each segment of the lesson.)*

Reflection on Teaching the Theater Lesson Plan

It is surprising how many students already know what empathy is when we start discussing it in class . . . then I realize that they think it is the same as sympathy, so we have a great deal of relearning to do! This lesson is the first of several days of team building, communication development, problem solving, and continuing to build our empathetic ensemble in the classroom.

In this lesson, I started with giving the students think time to discuss, write, and reflect on the terms "empathy" and "sympathy." After watching the video and having a class discussion, I felt like the students were ready to start the "work" of the day by getting up to prepare mentally and physically for the tasks. Taking a few minutes to breathe reduces anxiety and gives the whole class a moment to get centered in the space. Stretching is an important element of my theater practice because they need to prepare their bodies to be active—we are not a sedentary class! I encourage them to note where they have tightness in their bodies and to recognize and validate how they are feeling when they are in the space.

Doing a daily check in where they say their names is important on many levels: I want to know what they want to be called (along with pronouns they use) because this space needs to be safe for them and they need to feel comfortable. Giving them the opportunity to share their identity is paramount. My students said what they were looking forward to that day and we had a range of answers from "seeing my friends at lunch" to "cuddling with my cat" to "watching *Dance Moms*." These little glimpses into their interests help me get to know the students while encouraging them to get to know one another.

The first activity was quick and easy because it did not take them a long time to figure out how to see who was taller. We had extra time, so I had them do the same Nonverbal Line Up according to birthday (month and day, not year) and that got trickier for them. We were 100 percent successful with the tallest to shortest line up but we had two students in the wrong spots when we lined up according to their birthday. When the students said their birthdays, it was fun to notice a Halloween birthday and two students with the same birthdays.

Human Knots is one of my favorite games because you really have to work together. In my class, I only had one student who chose not to hold hands with other people and they elected to help their group untangle their knot successfully. One group was really struggling and I ended up having them drop hands, take a big group breath, and restart. They easily got out of the knot on the second attempt.

Group Count was frustrating and wonderful. I love to see how they deal with the pressure of having to restart over and over. Sometimes, we did not even make it to two before we had to restart because there are some big alpha personalities that always want to lead. Once I brought this to their attention and talked about how the only way we can reach our goal is for each person to speak once and only once, they started to understand that they were helping by giving other students the opportunity to participate.

There was a moment about five minutes into the exercise when they got to ten and then two people said eleven and we had to restart. There was audible disappointment in the circle and I had to remind them that we need to respond with empathy. How would they feel if they made a mistake and their classmates got upset with them? I told them they would be failing a lot in this activity, and they were successful in the amount of times they had to restart. Failing is okay! It is how you handle it and get right back on up to do it again that is important. We got through our objective and kept going. We made it to forty-four before we had to restart.

When we achieved our goal, the group was ecstatic—I think counting to twenty-nine was a highlight of their day. Getting all the way to forty-four was greeted with enthusiasm, shouting, and high fives. There was no blame at the people who said forty-five at the same time—just pure excitement that they surpassed the goal. During our debrief of the whole lesson, the students made it clear that they were frustrated with me at moments because I took away their ability to speak in the Nonverbal Line Up (especially during the line up according to birthday), and they did not understand the point of Group Count at first.

We unpacked the objective and talked about the relationship of Group Count to empathic ensemble building and they started to come around. Group Count is all about resilience and working together—two things that are paramount in any ensemble. I use all of the activities in the lesson throughout the year, but I see the biggest growth in Group Count. As the ensemble gels and becomes cohesive, they will be able to count higher without the side coaching.

As I read their responses to why having empathy in a theater classroom is important, I saw a continuous thread of how empathy makes students feel comfortable and not judged. While it may have seemed like we were just playing games to an outsider, these activities help create a positive classroom atmosphere where we can take risks, fail, be vulnerable, and (ultimately) grow.

READER TAKEAWAYS

- The performing arts are unique in that our discipline is built on relationships.
- Successful ensembles are created with open dialogue that can exist when there is an environment of mutual respect.

- Encouraging empathetic classrooms promotes a more cohesive ensemble and class engagement.
- CRT and SEL practices are inherent in performing arts classrooms and ensembles as the nature of the discipline requires that students work together in a collaborative fashion to create the end product.

Chapter 7

Culturally Responsive Teaching with the Visual Arts

Lauren Burrow

> We do not have to choose between a rigorous lesson and a culturally responsive one. Our current political moment, and indeed our nation's history, demands both.
>
> —Clint Smith (2020)

EXPECTED LEARNING OUTCOMES

- Readers will gain perspective via one teacher educator's experience with the intersections of culturally relevant and responsive teaching and visual arts teaching for student learning rooted in the social justice–related topics of identity and advocacy.
- Readers will understand the definitions of culturally relevant and responsive teaching and how the two, collectively, are relevant to and realized through visual arts lessons.
- Readers will gain insights into practical suggestions for two visual arts lessons that consider culturally relevant and responsive teaching.

TEACHER NARRATIVE

Throughout my almost twenty years of PK–16 teaching, I have taught numerous individuals who hold a variety of identities—visible and not—including racialized, ethnic, cultural, linguistic, religious, ability, gender, sexual orientation, etc. And while I have always sought to teach with the "good intention" of welcoming all those students into classroom spaces that invite them to show up as their own, unique, true identities, I admit that I have not always been radically intentional about student inclusivity in my classrooms—and that is not okay, especially when teaching "other people's children" (Delpit, 2006).

In my current professional academic position, I teach future K–6 teachers in educator preparation courses at the college level, so my level of responsibility to be a better teacher to them feels infinitely more significant to me because I need them each to be a better teacher than I was to their future students. I am learning/*un*learning that guiding my college students through visual arts lessons rooted in the values and goals of culturally relevant and responsive teaching helps them in the present, as college *students*, and in the future as K–6 *teachers*.

By presenting CRT visual arts lessons for them to complete they both learn (1) who they are as a teacher, so they can better understand who they need to be when teaching—because they cannot teach who they do not understand—and (2) what CRT pedagogy can successfully achieve for all learners—because they cannot teach what they do not understand.

Throughout this chapter I will share my own personal journey toward learning/*un*learning about CRT—its principles and pedagogy—and provide examples of how I have successfully crafted visual arts lessons that showcase CRT in action. It is my hope, dear reader, that this chapter helps you be more intentional in your practice of culturally relevant and responsive teaching (at least through the visual arts) when teaching other people's children.

My Personal Background

I frequently tell my preservice elementary education teachers: knowing who you are and where you come from is important, because all of that *will* find its way into your classroom. Who you are and where you come from often influences what you know (and don't know!) and can impact who/what you stand for. Knowing who you are and where you come from can help you recognize the areas where you might instantly connect with your students while also prompting you to prepare for the areas where you need to learn/*un*learn so that you can be in a space where you are ready to authentically connect with and learn from your students and their families. Because while you cannot teach what you do not know, you certainly cannot teach *who* you do not know. So I'll start this chapter by introducing myself:

I am a white, cisgender Woman.
I am from color blindness and treating everyone the same.
I am from "hating the sin but loving the sinner."

I am from conservative politics that you don't talk about,
don't question, don't argue about.
I am from neutrality, balanced perspectives, equality,
and both sides have valid points.
I am from affirmative action is reverse racism and bootstrap mentality.
I am from we can agree to disagree (even when it comes to one's identity).
I am from whiteness and all its privileges.
I am from gendered roles and patriarchal pastures that fenced out feminism.
I am from the waters of white supremacy that I didn't even know
were drowning me, too.

I grew up in a large, metropolitan city full of diverse individuals in my schools, at my workplaces, and throughout my life. I also grew up with "niceness" and "color blindness" as my guiding principles for interacting with that city of diverse people: meaning, treat everyone politely and treat everyone the same. As a teacher educator, it was these practices that I had to *un*learn so that I could replace them with "kindness" and "color braveness" in order to be the conscientious, educated, effective teacher that my preservice elementary education teachers urgently deserve—one that recognizes, celebrates, and responds to their unique, multilayered, intersecting identities throughout the intentionality of my educator preparation curriculum—so that they, in turn, can become the teachers their future students deserve! In short, students (of all levels) need a curriculum full of culturally relevant and responsive teaching.

CRT *AND* CRT

In this chapter, my discussions of my own teaching practices (and those I am encouraging readers to commit to) come from my understanding of culturally relevant and culturally responsive teaching as based on the works of the esteemed Gloria Ladson-Billings and Geneva Gay. I see culturally relevant teaching and culturally responsive teaching as pedagogies that can work together to improve student learning through the acknowledgment and intentional inclusion of cultural assets—both from individuals and ideas that are in and out of the classroom.

While culturally *relevant* teaching is a way to "empower students intellectually, socially, emotionally, and politically by using cultural referents to impart knowledge, skills, and attitudes" (Ladson-Billings, 1994, pp. 17–18), culturally *responsive* teaching uses "the cultural knowledge, prior experiences, frames of reference, and performance styles of ethnically diverse students to make learning encounters more relevant to and effective for them"

(Gay, 2010, p. 36). So, essentially, culturally *relevant* teaching brings into the classroom the cultural assets of *others* to model diverse perspectives, successes, points of views, and experiences for student learning, while culturally *responsive* teaching capitalizes on the cultural assets of the students already in your classroom to model and share their unique, valuable perspectives, successes, points of view, and experiences with their peers.

For myself, my journey toward becoming a culturally responsive teacher is usually most easily achieved through culturally relevant teaching. Exposing students to a multitude of ideas, experiences, cultures, people, etc. is something I can preplan for and accomplish to some level of consistency.

Culturally responsive teaching, on the other hand, requires more time, more space, and more comfortability with uncertain and unplanned curriculum in my college classroom because my teaching has to be guided by and responsive to the students I am teaching. But visual arts lessons have helped me increasingly embrace and enact culturally relevant and responsive teaching (both as a college pedagogy for their own current learning *and* as an example of K–6 practice to be used with their own future learners) wherein my students and their created artworks become the class textbook each semester.

A CULTURALLY *RELEVANT UN*LEARNING MOMENT WHILE K–3 TEACHING

You probably noticed a shift between the themes of the first six lines of my introductory poem and its last three lines. That "life shift" was first prompted back in 2010 when planning a social studies unit for lower elementary grade students with my coteacher at a classical education school. Teaching a classical curriculum requires teachers to paint a broad, interconnected stroke across all subjects throughout a spiraled exposure to the history of our world, but it often approaches the entirety of our world's history from a Eurocentric perspective.

As a Black Woman originally born in the African country of Nigeria, my coteacher helped me push my planned lessons on medieval art to include artists and artworks beyond the traditional European examples, including Western Asia and Northern Africa. Specifically, she educated me about art from her home country of Nigeria so that we could prioritize teaching about art from the Yoruba people of Ife (pronounced ee-feh), a city-state in West Africa (now modern-day Nigeria). The artists of Ife flourished during the medieval period of the twelfth to the fifteenth centuries with "a refined and highly naturalistic sculptural tradition in stone, terracotta, brass, and copper and created a style unlike anything in Africa at the time" (The British Museum, 2023).

I did not know it at the time, but that was my first realization that *not* presenting culturally relevant lessons is a disservice to all students. As a result of this cotaught unit of study, I *un*learned my default to curriculum that looked like me and my experiences and learned what students can miss out on when multiple different cultures, knowledge, skills, and attitudes are not presented throughout your curriculum.

Additionally, I *un*learned my default to textbook knowledge and learned how curriculum becomes elevated and more authentic with input from the multiple different cultures, knowledge, and skills represented by the individuals in the classroom. This key *un*learning moment while coteaching in a K–3 classroom opened my mind and heart to many, many more *un*learning moments from a variety of formal and informal educators (including educators sharing their messages on social media, colleagues sharing their professional expertise, and local community members welcoming me to share in the learnings of their everyday experiences).

All my *un*learning became the foundation from which I crafted culturally relevant teaching as the primary pedagogy during my early years of teacher preparation at the college level—doing so by focusing my lessons on imparting knowledge acquisition, vocabulary, activities geared toward improving understanding of ideology, and critical conversations that urged preservice teacher to commit to the culturally relevant pedagogy that they were being taught with. But it took many more years of *un*learning to better understand how to also include culturally responsive teaching in my college classrooms—and it came in the form of my lifelong love of the arts.

CRT AND THE VISUAL ARTS

According to Changing Education Through the Arts (CETA), a John F. Kennedy Center for the Performing Arts program, "arts integration is an approach to teaching in which students construct and demonstrate understanding through an art form. Students engage in a creative process which connects an art form and another subject area and meets evolving objectives in both" (Silverstein and Layne, 2010, p. 1).

Fine arts integration (including visual art, music, performance art, etc.) promotes constructivist and constructionist approaches to learning as students draw on prior knowledge and experiences; engage in hands-on learning, have opportunities to learn from each other to improve understanding of self, others, and content; and build a positive classroom environment in which students are "encouraged and supported to take risks, explore possibilities, and where social, cooperative learning community is created and nurtured" (Silverstein and Layne, 2010, pp. 2–3).

In arts-integrated curriculum, the arts become the approach to teaching and the vehicle for learning. Students meet dual learning objectives when they engage in the creative process to explore connections between an art form and another subject area to gain greater understanding in both (Silverstein and Layne, 2010).

Incorporating and integrating the fine arts into the classroom encourages deeper levels of thinking, exploration, discovery, creativity, choice, and engagement. The arts engage diverse learners and offer students of all ability levels a way to communicate expressively about meaningful themes. "By their nature, the arts engage students in learning through observing, listening, and moving and offer learners various ways to acquire information and act on it to build understanding. They also offer a natural way to differentiate instruction as the arts offer multiple modes of representation, expression, and engagement" (Wolf, 2008, pp. 5–6).

How Visual Arts Lessons Accomplish CRT

According to Gay (2010) there are eight dimensions of culturally responsive teaching: validation, inclusion, multidimensional, empowering, transformative, emancipatory, humanistic, and ethical. These dimensions capitalize on students' interests; promote high standards of learning and bravery in risk taking for all students; situate the curriculum within overlapping racial, sociopolitical contexts in which teachers respect all students' ethnic and racialized identities and students can build cultural pride and awareness as a path toward intellectual liberation; and, ultimately, interrupt and dismantle the idea of "unbiased" education (Gay, 2010).

Creation and exploration of visual art can accomplish many culturally responsive teaching goals. Visual arts can be a highly effective medium for teaching social justice. The arts have historically communicated ideas about oppression and provided a way to reenvision the world free from injustice. Art can serve as a catalyst for wider discussions about social justice and nurture student growth, talent, and self-expression. (*Artistic expression showcase*, n.d.)

CULTURALLY *RESPONSIVE* LEARNING MOMENTS THAT TRANSFORMED MY COLLEGE TEACHING

Since 2020, the COVID-19 pandemic has altered personal, professional, and academic lives around the world. For myself, as a MotherScholar (Burrow et al., 2020), the early months of COVID-19—when I was simultaneously responsible for the health care of my own children (plus extended family) and the academic learning of other people's children—were confusing, difficult, and frustrating. And then in May 2020, the murder of George Floyd by Minnesota police officers added layers of grief, pain, outrage, and urgency to my personal responsibility for raising up White children who need to actively ally with Black and Brown children and my professional responsibility for training up mostly White teachers who would be teaching Black and Brown students. In a professional and personal world of constant uncertainty and unprecedented tragedy, I (like many others) found comfort, clarity, and connection through the visual arts.

On a national level, protest movements inspired by the tragic and racist murder of George Floyd "sparked a massive proliferation of spontaneous art to appear. . . . Tags and murals were suddenly everywhere in Minneapolis and Saint Paul. It was an amazing artistic expression of rage, pain, mourning and trauma and someone needed to document it." Examples of this and other social justice and equity public art can be found in the online George Floyd and Anti-Racist Street Art database (https://georgefloydstreetart.omeka.net/) and the Covid-19 Street Art database (https://covid19streetart.omeka.net/), which are maintained by the University of St. Thomas College of Arts and Sciences and Arts Midwest.

As a personal experience, searching out public artwork that conveyed messages of social justice became a routine that I shared with my children during the early quarantine periods of COVID-19. These familial adventures prompted critical conversations about current events and encouraged us to explore visual arts practices to express our own voices, concerns, and calls for action about political issues that matter, especially for those who hold global majority identities but are subjected to marginalized experiences.

As I have mentioned, in my teacher preparation courses, culturally responsive teaching often showed up as knowledge exposure to vocabulary, ideology, and critical conversations about the urgency with which I needed students to commit to being culturally responsive teachers. But teaching *about* CRT is only so effective and so relevant. It took the events and experiences of 2020 to help teach me that with the visual arts "we do not have to choose between a rigorous lesson and a culturally responsive one. Our current political moment, and indeed our nation's history, demands both" (Smith, 2020, n.p.).

So throughout the early stages of COVID-19, sharing artists' public art prompted necessary conversations within my online courses about the Truth that teaching is a political act; meanwhile, the act of art making created natural spaces for my students to connect with one another across the screen as they tried to make sense of an uncertain world in a virtual learning environment.

As the world has largely reemerged into shared physical work and learning spaces, I continue to commit to maintaining the powerful practice of art making for meaning making by devoting much of my class time to having my preservice teachers try out lessons that simultaneously lean into a CRT environment for their own learning while also modeling how to incorporate CRT into their own future classrooms. Allowing them the space and time to try out the lessons themselves makes it more meaningful to them as they see, firsthand, the benefits of CRT for understanding self and others.

TWO CULTURALLY RELEVANT AND RESPONSIVE VISUAL ART LESSONS

During this ongoing time of reemergence from the COVID-19 global pandemic and amid increasing attacks on personal civil liberties at federal and state levels, I have found visual arts lessons can act as authentic and critical elements of culturally relevant and responsive teaching. The two lessons shared in this chapter emphasize care as a way of achieving social justice standards.

The Southern Poverty Law Center's Learning for Justice's framework for antibias education includes a set of Social Justice Standards that "form the bedrock of how we think about instilling anti-bias, anti-racist principles into any classroom, subject, curricula or learning environment" (*Social Justice Standards*, n.d.). The Social Justice Standards are composed of four domains and these two visual art lessons focus on the first—"identity"—and last—"action."

The first lesson is meant to facilitate the following objectives within the identity anchor standard: students' development of positive social identities, recognition of others' identities, and expression of pride and confidence in their identity while still valuing the dignity of others' identities. The second lesson guides students toward the achievement of the following objectives within the action anchor standard: students' expression of empathy when people are negatively targeted based on their identities and recognition of their responsibility to take action against injustices. Together, the two visual art lessons are structured to promote both self-care through self-reflection and art expression and care for others through collective reflection and art creation.

CRT Visual Art Lesson 1: Self-Portraits

The first lesson shared in this chapter gives students the opportunity to create multiple visual art self-portraits to demonstrate text-to-self connections with a variety of children's books that focus on identity-affirming themes, such as the significance of one's name; racialized, ethnic, and cultural identity; the fashions we wear to signal to others our religious beliefs and personal/communal values; the complexity of mental health; and how the geography of where we come from impacts our experiences.

Additionally, I make efforts to ensure that the selected mentor texts highlight authors with gender, racialized, cultural, etc. identities beyond the dominant identity groups as a way to (1) showcase the voices, values, and experiences of minoritized individuals as valuable and knowledgeable sources of student learning in the classroom and (2) to connect students to individuals that look like them or present an identity that they can learn to appreciate more (see lesson 1 for recommended books and themes).

This lesson focuses intensely on the Social Justice Standard of identity while also promoting self-care in line with the Minneapolis Institute of Art's Center for Empathy and the Visual Arts' belief in "the power of art . . . to spark curiosity and creativity, connect people across cultural differences, and engage our individual and shared values" (*Empathy*, n.d., p. 1). The art making process of creating identity portraits in this lesson prompts students to critically consider their identities, values, interests, and beliefs and allows them space to show gentleness, care, and pride in who they are. And then, the concluding art showcase in which they share their self-portraits with peers helps all students gain a better understanding of the diversity of humans through a social justice lens that values all identities—the ones that mirror our own and the ones that we still need to learn from/about.

Title of Lesson:	*Connecting to Identity-Affirming Children's Books through Self-Portrait Creations*
Grade Level:	3–5

Content Standard(s):

Common Core State Standards

CCSS.ELA-LITERACY.RL.3.6. Distinguish their own point of view from that of the narrator or those of the characters.

CCSS.ELA-LITERACY.RL.4.9. Compare and contrast the treatment of similar themes and topics (for example, opposition of good and evil) and patterns of events (for example, the quest) in stories, myths, and traditional literature from different cultures.

CCSS.ELA-LITERACY.RL.5.7. Analyze how visual and multimedia elements contribute to the meaning, tone, or beauty of a text (for example, graphic novel, multimedia presentation of fiction, folktale, myth, poem).

CCSS.ELA-LITERACY.SL.3.1.D. Explain their own ideas and understanding in light of the discussion.

CCSS.ELA-LITERACY.SL.5.5. Include multimedia components (for example, graphics, sound) and visual displays in presentations when appropriate to enhance the development of main ideas or themes.

National Core Art Standards

Artistic Process: *Connecting*, Anchor Standard 10. Synthesize and relate knowledge and personal experiences to make art.

Artistic Process: *Connecting*, Anchor Standard 11. Relate artistic ideas and works with societal, cultural, and historical context to deepen understanding.

Social Justice Standard: https://www.learningforjustice.org/frameworks/social-justice-standards

Identity domain.
1. Students will develop positive social identities based on their membership in multiple groups in society.
2. Students will recognize that people's multiple identities interact and create unique and complex individuals.
3. Students will express pride, confidence, and healthy self-esteem without denying the value and dignity of other people.

Objectives: *Students will be able to*

identify personal connections to identity theme(s) discussed in a read mentor text(s),
compare and contrast their own identity(ies) to peers' identity(ies) when sharing their identity self-portraits, and
create a self-portrait that connects to the identity theme(s) discussed in a read mentor text(s).

Anticipatory Set: *(How will student interest be sparked to engage in the lesson of the day?)*

The teacher can play a "this or that" game with questions related to students' identities. For example: raise your hand if you have nicknames; stand on one foot if you do not have a nickname. Touch your head if you speak one language; touch your ears if you speak two languages; touch your shoulders if you speak three or more languages.

Relevancy: *(How will the content be made relevant to the students in the context you are teaching? What connections can be made to their experiences and cultures?)*

Students will be given the opportunity to create a self-portrait that shares their personal connections to the book themes of their choosing. Crafting the self-portrait will allow students to highlight and celebrate their personal experiences, cultures, etc. Sharing the self-portrait will allow all students to recognize commonalities and differences between peers' identities and their own.

Academic Vocabulary: *(What academic vocabulary will be addressed in this lesson? How will it be taught and made comprehensible to ALL learners?)*

theme, identity

The literary term "theme" has been taught previously and is being reinforced and reviewed through the discussion of read mentor texts intentionally chosen to highlight themes related to students' identities.

The social concept "identity" may need to be discussed with students. *Learning for Justice's* interactive lesson about identity can be accessed here: https://www.learningforjustice.org/magazine/spring-2019/digging-deep-into-the-social-justice-standards-identity. The concept of identity will be reinforced and reviewed through the discussion of read mentor texts intentionally chosen to highlight themes related to students' identities. The teacher can model personal examples using the *Learning for Justice's* interactive lesson (linked previously) to discuss the visible and invisible and personal versus social characteristics that make up their own identity.

The teacher can also discuss specific elements of identity relevant to the themes of the read mentor texts (for example, racialized identity, linguistic identity, ability, etc.).

Lesson Overview: *(Please describe the steps for each part of the lesson. Also, in parentheses, put a time estimate for each segment of the lesson.)*

Warmup: Teacher reviews previously read mentor texts (see "Materials Needed" for suggested thematic books) using a "picture walk" to highlight key ideas related to the book's identity theme. The teacher can project book covers/illustrations on the class board to visually remind students of the read texts.
Note: Multiple books can be read about *one* identity theme or multiple identity themes can be discussed using one book per theme. It is recommended that the amount of books/amount of themes discussed be determined based on the teacher's understanding of students' abilities and interests.
This lesson can also become a multiday lesson with one theme tackled per day.
(5–10 minutes, depending on number of mentor texts)

Guided Practice: Teacher and students identify the central theme in each of the read texts (see "Warmup"). The teacher can record the central theme for each book next to the book cover projected on the class board.
After identifying the central theme of each read text, teacher and students brainstorm examples of personal connections to each of the read mentor texts' identity themes. Teacher records examples for all students to view (this can act as inspiration, commonality, and/or recognition of differences). The teacher should explain/reiterate how a "nonconnection" is still a connection. For example, a student may not enjoy yams at their dinner table like Anna Hibicus (from the text *Anna Hibiscus' Song*) does, but they can still connect to the theme of culturally influenced food by identifying what they frequently eat/enjoy eating at school, home, etc. The teacher should guide students to acknowledge differences without judgment when connecting to the themes. For example, some male students may not wear their hair long, but other male students may enjoy how their long hair represents strength in their Indigenous tribe.
Example discussion prompts based on themes associated with the Suggested Mentor Texts (in "Materials Needed"):

- **THEME: NAMES**
    - *your name*
    - *a nickname*
    - *your friends' names*
    - *your pets' names*
    - *names in your residence*
    - *teacher names*
    - *street names you pass on way to school*
- **THEME: WHAT YOU SEE IN THE MIRROR (could include racialized and ethnic identity, body size, etc.)**
    - *how you like to wear your hair*
    - *your eye color*
    - *why you love the skin you're in*
    - *who in your family you look like or don't look like*
    - *when you look in the mirror you love what you see*
- **THEME: FASHION (to show off our culture: beliefs, values, etc.)—RELIGIOUS WEAR / SPORTS UNIFORMS / SOCIAL CLUB LOGOS / FAVE OUTFITS / DRESS TO IMPRESS**
    - *your favorite outfit to wear for good luck*
    - *do you wear glasses?*

- *do you wear a uniform for a sport?*
- *your favorite outfit to wear to a celebration*
- *an outfit you don't like wearing*
- *your favorite piece of clothing*
- *something special someone gave you to wear*
- *something you wear because of your religion*
- **THEME: FEELINGS**
  - *where you go when you are mad*
  - *name someone who can always make you laugh*
  - *name a song that makes you happy*
  - *what do you do when you are sad*
- **THEME: WHERE I'M FROM / TRAVEL / LIFE MAPS (for example, daily schedules; significant places; maps of your heart, stomach, brain; etc.)**
  - *a map of your neighborhood*
  - *all the places you've lived*
  - *where you want to travel to*
  - *your daily routine*
  - *your meditation steps*
  - *flags of the countries that are dear to you*
  - *who/what fills up your heart*
  - *foods that comfort you, recipes filled with memories*

Once the class has brainstormed personal connections to the texts' themes, the class participates in a discussion about the various art styles that could be used to present different elements of their identity. The teacher can model abbreviated examples of each suggested visual art style using their own personal connections to each theme. For example, the teacher could cut out letters from various magazine headlines to collage their various names that are used in various contexts (for example, *Mx. Smith* in class with students and *Ace* at home with friends).
(15 minutes)

Independent Practice: Students create a self-portrait that shares symbols/ideas that reflect the identity theme(s) discussed in the read mentor text(s).
Students can create multiple self-portraits—one for each identity theme they wish to connect with—or students can create a single, collective self-portrait that incorporates multiple elements of their various identities.
(20–25 minutes)

Closure: In peer pairs, students can share one to two identity elements exhibited in their artworks.
In a whole class discussion, one to two students can share what they learned about their partner peer from their identity self-portrait and then discuss the commonalities/differences they have with their peer partner.
The teacher can project their own finished example to model discussion of identity theme connections presented in their artwork. Students can discuss the rubric evaluation of the teacher's example and then take time to self-reflect about the quality and accuracy of their own work against the rubric.
Students will submit their self-portrait to the teacher and verbally identify an identity they are proud of in their artwork.
(10 minutes)

Materials Needed: *(Please list the materials that will be needed for this lesson.)*

Recommended Visual Art-Making Materials:
- Paper (variety of colors and types)
- Writing / coloring tools (for example, markers, pens, paints, highlighters, chalk, etc.)
- Collage materials (for example, photographs, magazines, textured papers, etc.)
- Attaching tools (for example, glue, tape, etc.)
- Transforming materials (for example, clay, foil, etc.)
- Editing tools (for example, scissors, hole punchers, etc.)

Suggested Children's Books by Self-Portrait Theme:
THEME: NAMES (could include racialized and ethnic identity, body size, etc.)
- *My Name Is Not Isabella* by Jennifer Fosberry
- *My Name Is Yoon* by Helen Recorvits
- *Your Name Is a Song* by Jamilah Thompkins-Bigelow

THEME: WHAT YOU SEE IN THE MIRROR
- *Hair Love* by Matthew A. Cherry
- *Princess Puff* by Ariel Jones
- *Eyes that Kiss in the Corners* by Joanna Ho
- *Laxmi's Mooch* by Shelly Anand

THEME: FASHION (to show off our culture: beliefs, values, etc.)—RELIGIOUS WEAR / SPORTS UNIFORMS / SOCIAL CLUB LOGOS / FAVE OUTFITS / DRESS TO IMPRESS
- *Mommy's Khimar* by Jamilah Thompkins-Bigelow
- *Not All Princesses Dress in Pink* by Jane Yolen and Heidi Elisabet Yolen Stemple
- *Julián Is a Mermaid* by Jessica Love

THEME: FEELINGS
- *When Sophie Gets Angry—Really, Really Angry* by Molly Bang
- *Exactly You! The Shape of your Feelings* by Sarah Krajewski
- *Anna Hibiscus' Song* by Atinuke and Lauren Tobia

THEME: WHERE I'M FROM / TRAVEL / LIFE MAPS (for example, daily schedules; significant places; maps of your heart, stomach, brain; etc.)
- *My Map Book* by Sara Fanelli
- *Milo Imagines the World* by Matt de la Pena
- *My Two Border Towns* by David Bowles

Universal Design for Learning: *(How will the principles of UDL be utilized throughout this lesson to give students voice and choice?)*

Students will have a choice on what to share about themselves in connection to the discussed book themes. They also can choose how they want to express their connections to the book themes.

Access: *(What strategies will be used throughout the lesson to allow students multiple entry points into understanding the concepts taught?)*

- Teacher provides multiple mentor texts about one theme or several mentor texts about multiple themes to prompt student thinking.
- Teacher reads the mentor text aloud (previous lesson) and then reviews plots/themes with students.
- Student discussion and teacher confirmation of mentor text themes are identified prior to artwork creation.

- Student and teacher discussion of potential visual art styles for use in the self-portrait work occurs prior to artwork creation.
- Mentor texts can be made available for students to review during their independent work.
- Students needing assistance with their personal connections to text(s) and/or choice of artwork styles for self-portrait can receive direct teacher guidance and/or refer to teacher-created examples.

Higher-Order Thinking: *(In what ways will this lesson require students to utilize higher-order thinking? Please describe.)*

- Students will need to apply their knowledge of themes and understanding of identity to identify them in mentor text(s).
- Students will evaluate and decide on the most effective visual art style for conveying their personal connections to mentor text(s) identity themes.
- Students will create a self-portrait that uses symbols and other artistic elements to convey abstract ideas.

Assessments: *(How will each learning objective be assessed? What activities do you have planned to check for understanding approximately every 5 minutes of the lesson?)*

During guided practice, the teacher will model examples of potential visual art styles that can be used to express connection to each of the mentor texts' themes. The teacher will invite students to evaluate the teacher's examples to determine how well each visual art style conveys personal connections to the texts' themes.

During independent work, the teacher will walk the room to monitor if any students need additional support and respond, accordingly. For example, the teacher might offer review of or tips for particular visual art styles and/or offer thought prompts to help students' searching for personal connections to the texts.

The completed self-portraits will count as a summative assessment. Checking for understanding can be evaluated on a rubric that identifies a student's progress along a scale of emerging, progressing, accomplishing, or exceeding in the following categorie
- Content: *How well does the student's work convey ideas/symbols relevant to themes discussed in the book readings?*
- Appearance: *How well does the work reflect effort or care in presentation?*
- Connection to Central Texts: *How well does the work connect to the themes discussed in the central texts?*

Closure: *(What activity will you use to close this lesson and to assess students' understanding at the end of the period?)*

Students will submit their self-portrait to the teacher and verbally identify an identity they are proud of in their artwork.
(5 minutes)

CRT Visual Art Lesson #: Art for Advocacy

The second lesson in this chapter uses an art elicitation process to help guide students toward the creation of a visual art piece that harnesses visual literacy to educate others about and call them to action for a social (in)justice issue that the student artmaker cares most about (see lesson 2 for details). I originally learned about the art looking practice that I use in this lesson to prompt student self-reflection during a summer 2021 professional development taught by educators and artists associated with the Smithsonian National Gallery of Art in Washington, DC.

Since then, I have adapted that learned practice into an "art elicitation" process to help my colleagues and own children engage in art looking to help with critical self-reflection about the complex and significant professional and personal impacts of COVID-19 on who we are, what/who we value, and what/who we care most about (Burrow and Burrow, 2023, p. 192; Burrow et al., 2023).

This lesson focuses intensely on the Social Justice Standard of action as a practice and invites care for others that exemplifies Learning for Justice's assertion that visual arts can be a "powerful, hands-on way to . . . both educate and perpetuate change" (*Be the change* . . . , n.d.). Ultimately, the art elicitation activity creates space for the "students [to] have central and active roles as meaning makers . . . to develop the capacity to reflect on what they are learning and to use it as they interpret and create works of art" (Stevenson and Deasy, 2005, p. 37) while their final advocacy artworks take up the space that students should when demonstrating "empathy and compassion [which] are crucial as we care for others" (*Empathy*, n.d.).

Title of Lesson:	**Art Analysis and Art Creation for Advocacy**
Grade Level:	**6–8**
Content Standard(s):	

Common Core State Standards
CCSS.ELA-LITERACY.SL.6.2. Interpret information presented in diverse media and formats (for example, visually, quantitatively, orally) and explain how it contributes to a topic, text, or issue under study.
CCSS.ELA-LITERACY.SL.6.5. Include multimedia components (for example, graphics, images, music, sound) and visual displays in presentations to clarify information.
CCSS.ELA-LITERACY.W.6.1. Write arguments to support claims with clear reasons and relevant evidence.
CCSS.ELA-LITERACY.SL.7.2. Analyze the main ideas and supporting details presented in diverse media and formats (for example, visually, quantitatively, orally) and explain how the ideas clarify a topic, text, or issue under study.
CCSS.ELA-LITERACY.SL.7.5. Include multimedia components and visual displays in presentations to clarify claims and findings and emphasize salient points.
CCSS.ELA-LITERACY.W.7.1. Write arguments to support claims with clear reasons and relevant evidence.
CCSS.ELA-LITERACY.SL.8.5. Integrate multimedia and visual displays into presentations to clarify information, strengthen claims and evidence, and add interest.
CCSS.ELA-LITERACY.W.8.1. Write arguments to support claims with clear reasons and relevant evidence.

National Core Art Standards
Artistic Process: *Responding,* **Anchor Standard 7.** Perceive and analyze artistic work.
Artistic Process: *Responding,* **Anchor Standard 8.** Interpret intent and meaning in artistic work.
Artistic Process: *Connecting,* **Anchor Standard 10.** Synthesize and relate knowledge and personal experiences to make art.
Artistic Process: *Connecting,* **Anchor Standard 11.** Relate artistic ideas and works with societal, cultural, and historical context to deepen understanding.

Social Justice Standard: https://www.learningforjustice.org/frameworks/social-justice-standards

Justice domain.
1. Students will recognize unfairness on the individual level (for example, biased speech) and injustice at the institutional or systemic level (for example, discrimination).
2. Students will analyze the harmful impact of bias and injustice on the world, historically and today.
3. Students will identify figures, groups, events, and a variety of strategies and philosophies relevant to the history of social justice around the world.

Action domain.
1. Students will recognize their own responsibility to stand up to exclusion, prejudice, and injustice.
2. Students will speak up with courage and respect when they or someone else has been hurt or wronged by bias.

Objectives: *Students will be able to*

identify personal connections to current social (in)justice issues through an art looking activity;
research past and current community support related to responding to, reforming their identified social (in)justice issue;
identify their own role in assisting in the response to, reformation of their identified social (in)justice issue; and
create an artistic call to action (that is, public artwork) related to their identified social (in)justice issue.

Anticipatory Set: *(How will student interest be sparked to engage in the lesson of the day?)*

The teacher can share images from the online George Floyd and Anti-Racist Street Art database and the Covid-19 Street Art database, which contains photos of public art focused on social justice and equity. The sites are maintained by the University of St. Thomas College of Arts and Sciences and Arts Midwest. Whole class "lightning discussion" can be prompted by asking students to quick write all the messages they think the artworks are trying to convey.

Relevancy: *(How will the content be made relevant to the students in the context you are teaching? What connections can be made to their experiences and cultures?)*

Students will be prompted to complete an art looking activity meant to help them self-identify a social (in)justice issue that matters most to them. Students' final projects will be the creation of an artwork that shares a call to action for the social (in)justice issue they felt personally connected to/that felt most relevant to them. Crafting and sharing the Advocacy Artwork will help students realize their role in and effectiveness in civic action, as a youth.

Academic Vocabulary: *(What academic vocabulary will be addressed in this lesson? How will it be taught and made comprehensible to ALL learners?)*

- **Advocacy**
- **Informal advocacy**

Liz Agbor-Tabi, vice president of global policy at *Global Citizen*, works as an advocate by collaborating with world leaders to encourage them to put policies in place that ensure everybody's needs are met and rights are protected, with an emphasis on marginalized groups and people in poverty.

She defines "advocacy" as "an act of service, it is using your voice to influence decision-makers and demanding change that works for the benefit of humanity."

The teacher can discuss personal (or student) examples of advocacy that they have engaged in / seen students engage in. The teacher can also prompt student discussion of advocacy they have seen public figures engage in and/or examples of advocacy they, themselves, have engaged in.

The Center for Excellence in Disabilities at West Virginia University defines "informal advocacy" as "when people like parents, friends, family members or agencies speak out and advocate for vulnerable people this is termed informal advocacy."

Lesson Overview: *(Please describe the steps for each part of the lesson. Also, in parentheses, put a time estimate for each segment of the lesson.)*

Warmup: The Teacher projects on a class board the *Thirty-Six Views of Mount Fuji* (Japanese: 富嶽三十六), a series of landscape prints by the Japanese ukiyo-e artist Katsushika Hokusai (1760–1849).

The teacher invites students to quickly scan the artworks series and asks for student discussion of what they notice in one, some, and/or all the artworks. The teacher then highlights (if not already discussed by students) that Mount Fuji is depicted in all thirty-six artworks—from different locations and in various seasons and weather conditions.

(5 minutes)

Guided Practice: The teacher presents six specific pieces from the Hokusai art series for closer viewing and as a means of prompting student self-reflection about what social (in)justice issues matter most to them.

The teacher first presents Hokusai's *The Great Wave off Kanagawa*. The teacher prompts students to look at the artwork for 30–60 seconds in silence and then invites students to turn and talk with a peer partner about what they see (colors, content, art style, etc.). Students are then asked to interpret and find meaning in the work of art by making connections to social (in)justice issues with the following writing prompt: **Like this "Great Wave," what social (in)justice issues overwhelm you and or people (groups of people) you know?**

Next, the teacher presents Hokusai's *Yoshida at Tōkaidō*. The teacher prompts students to look at the artwork for 30–60 seconds in silence and then invites students to turn and talk with a peer partner about what they see (colors, content, art style, etc.). Students are then asked to interpret and find meaning in the work of art by making connections to social (in)justice issues with the following writing prompt: **Like those gathered in this Town Hall, who do you think are most impacted by the social (in)justice issues that you previously identified.**

Next, the teacher presents Hokusai's *Kajikazawa in Kai Province*. The teacher prompts students with the silent looking-paired discussion practice from before. Students then participate in the next reflective writing prompt: **Like these fishermen, identify the one social (in)justice issue that you are willing to struggle/fight for and discuss why. (This will be your Mt. Fuji.)**

Next, the teacher presents Hokusai's *Enoshima in Sagami Province*. The teacher prompts students with the silent looking-paired discussion practice from before. Students again participate in a reflective writing prompt: **Like the collective work in the artwork, which individuals, organizations, and businesses in your community are already supporting actions for positive change for your identified social (in)justice issue (your Mt. Fuji)?**

Next, the teacher presents Hokusai's *Sazai Hall—Temple of Five Hundred Rakan*. The teacher prompts students with the silent looking-paired discussion practice from before. Students answer the following reflective writing prompt: **Like the onlookers in the artwork, who are the people you think need to pay more attention to/do more to change this social (in)justice?**

Finally, the teacher presents Hokusai's *Under Mannen Bridge at Fukagawa*. The teacher prompts students with the silent looking-paired discussion practice from before. Students again respond to a reflective writing prompt: **Thinking of the bridge as a metaphor, what actions would need to be taken to move from the current state of your social (in)justice issue toward positive change for your identified social (in)justice issue?**

(20–30 minutes)

Independent Practice: Students return to their responses from the art looking activity and take time to update, clarify, expand, and/or correct any of their initial responses. This could include time devoted to external research, peer discussion, independent investigation, and/or teacher-guided knowledge awareness (especially surrounding existing community assets).

Students synthesize their reflections that led to an identified social (in)justice issue that matters to them and any additional research completed to create an artwork that educates others about "their Mt. Fuji" (social [in]justice issue) and includes a simple call to action.

(30–45 minutes; additional time may be necessary to complete external research)

Closure: In peer pairs, students can share their Advocacy Artworks.

In a whole class discussion, a few students can share about how the art elicitation process helped them to identify a social (in)justice issue and/or discuss why the social (in)justice issue they chose matters most to them.

Students will submit their Advocacy Artwork to the teacher and verbally commit to sharing their artwork with someone in their life in order to educate them about their chosen social (in)justice issue.

(15–20 minutes)

Materials Needed: *(Please list the materials that will be needed for this lesson.)*

Copy of the *Thirty-Six Views of Mount Fuji* (Japanese: 富嶽三十六), a series of landscape prints by the Japanese ukiyo-e artist Katsushika Hokusai (1760–1849). Copies of each of the artworks can be found here: https://en.wikipedia.org/wiki/Thirty-six_Views_of_Mount_Fuji.

Recommended Visual Art-Making Materials:
- Paper (variety of colors and types)
- Writing/coloring tools (for example, markers, pens, paints, highlighters, chalk, etc.)
- Collage materials (for example, photographs, magazines, textured papers, etc.)
- Attaching tools (for example, glue, tape, etc.)
- Transforming materials (for example, clay, foil, etc.)
- Editing tools (for example, scissors, hole punchers, etc.)

Universal Design for Learning: *(How will the principles of UDL be utilized throughout this lesson to give students voice and choice?)*

Students will have a choice on which topic they want to advocate for. They also can choose how they want to express their advocacy through artwork.

Access: *(What strategies will be used throughout the lesson to allow students multiple entry points into understanding the concepts taught?)*

- Teacher provides multiple examples of public artworks that focus on social justice issues to connect students to the practice of art as advocacy.
- Teacher provides multiple clarifying prompts to assist students in narrowing down which social (in)justice issue matters most to them.
- Teacher provides students with additional time to complete external research and/or peer discussions to further investigate their social (in)justice issue beyond the "drafting stage" completed during the art elicitation.
- Examples of public artworks that focus on social justice issues can be available to students for review during their independent work.
- Students needing assistance with their personal connections to social (in)justice issues and/or choice of artwork styles for their Advocacy Artwork can receive direct teacher guidance and/or peer support.

Higher-Order Thinking: *(In what ways will this lesson require students to utilize higher-order thinking? Please describe.)*

- Students will need to demonstrate empathy and understanding to reflect on social (in)justice issues.
- Students will evaluate and decide on the most effective visual art style for conveying their education about and call to action for their identified social (in)justice issue.
- Students will create an Advocacy Artwork that both educates and calls the viewer to action on a specific social (in)justice issue.

Assessments: *(How will each learning objective be assessed? What activities do you have planned to check for understanding approximately every 5 minutes of the lesson?)*

During independent work, the teacher will walk the room to monitor if any students need additional support and respond accordingly. For example, the teacher might offer review of or tips for particular visual art styles and/or offer thought prompts to help students' searching for more up-to-date, verified information about social (in)justice issues.

The completed Advocacy Artwork will count as a summative assessment. Checking for understanding can be evaluated on a rubric that identifies a student's progress along a scale of emerging, progressing, accomplishing, or exceeding in the following categories:

- Content: *How well does the student's work convey ideas/actions relevant to their identified social (in)justice issue?*
- Appearance: *How well does the work reflect effort or care in presentation?*
- Connection to Central Issue: *How well does the work connect to the identified social (in)justice issue?*

Closure: *(What activity will you use to close this lesson and to assess students' understanding at the end of the period?)*

Students will submit their Advocacy Artwork to the teacher and verbally commit to sharing their artwork with someone in their life in order to educate them about their chosen social (in)justice issue.
(5 minutes)

CULTURALLY RELEVANT AND RESPONSIVE *UN*LEARNING AND LEARNING FROM TEACHING CRT VISUAL ART LESSONS

I shared earlier that my own journey toward understanding and inclusion of culturally relevant and responsive teaching is the result of years and years of personal and professional *un*learning. And while these shared lessons demonstrate that CRT can be enacted through visual arts assignments that promote hands-on learning, critical self-reflection, and civic change makers, I admit that I am still learning and *un*learning how to better position myself to more faithfully and authentically to achieve the values and goals of a classroom committed to CRT.

Personal Reflections on Teaching the Self-Portrait Lesson

After teaching this lesson as the introductory assignment for the past two years in my fine arts teacher preparation course, I have found preservice teacher engagement with this lesson to be an excellent model for We Need Diverse Books' claim that teachers' commitments to diverse classroom libraries that prominently and intentionally feature characters that proudly embody a wide range of racialized, cultural, ethnic, gender, sexual orientation, linguistic, and disabilities identities (n.d.) is an urgently critical commitment to make so that all students feel welcomed, seen, and included in classrooms. Time and time again, this lesson successfully prioritizes space for my students to take pride in their own overlapping, intersecting identities while also growing in their understanding and appreciation of their peers (and future students') identities, too.

I will also note that teaching this lesson has helped my own growth in understanding the spaces that must be created when committing to culturally relevant and responsive teaching. I have always intended the lesson to serve as an introduction to the importance of acknowledging and celebrating one's own identity, so that in turn students can empathize with, seek to understand, and respect peers' identities. It is my hope that this assignment can serve as a start to our semester-long creation of a safer, braver space in which to discuss, as humans, the social (in)justices that impact all of us in different ways.

Figure 7.1. A preservice elementary education student in Dr. Burrow's Fine Arts for Elementary Education course creates a self-portrait that showcases how they personally connected to the identity-affirming themes throughout the shared children's books My Map Book by Sara Fanelli, Mommy's Khimar by Jamilah Thompkins-Bigelow, and When Sophie Gets Angry—Really, Really Angry by Molly Bang.

During my most recent semester of teaching my fine arts course, a Black student helped me pause and consider which identities I was actually making brave spaces for, which identities I was creating truly comfortable spaces for in my classroom with this self-portrait project. During the guided practice

This self-portrait was inspired by the book, Hair Love. I have extremely curly hair and it is often the first thing people notice about me. I wanted to show that my hair is a big part of who I am, and that I am prod of it. I did not add any facial features to my self-portrait, because I really wanted my hair to stand out.

Figure 7.2. A preservice elementary education student in Dr. Burrow's Fine Arts for Elementary Education course creates a self-portrait that showcases how they personally connected to the identity-affirming theme throughout the shared children's book Hair Love by Matthew A. Cherry.

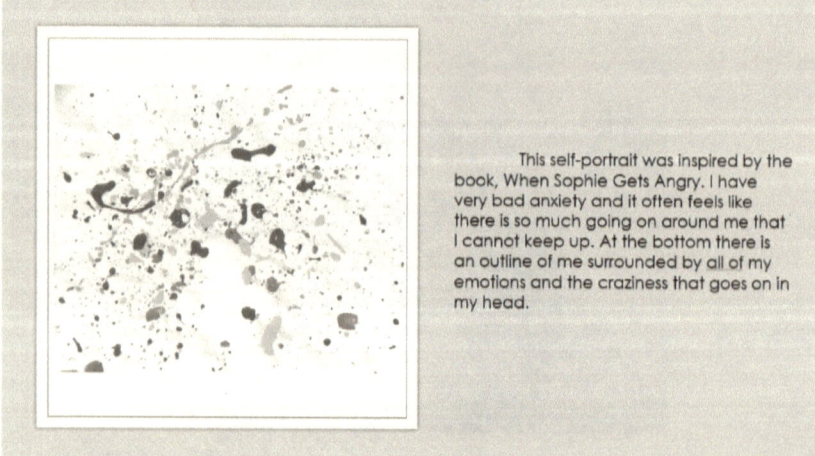

This self-portrait was inspired by the book, When Sophie Gets Angry. I have very bad anxiety and it often feels like there is so much going on around me that I cannot keep up. At the bottom there is an outline of me surrounded by all of my emotions and the craziness that goes on in my head.

Figure 7.3. A preservice elementary education student in Dr. Burrow's Fine Arts for Elementary Education course creates a self-portrait that showcases how they personally connected to the identity-affirming theme throughout the shared children's book When Sophie Gets Angry—Really, Really Angry by Molly Bang.

time in class, the student asked me if it was okay if they included the racially derogatory names that they had been called throughout their life on their self-portrait in a graffiti art style—they were worried that seeing those names in writing might offend or make their White peers uncomfortable.

While I reassured them that I was okay with their self-portrait being an authentic representation of their identity, I also took time to discuss how their final art piece could convey a more empowered statement in which they took back the lies and harm of those names and proudly overlapped them with the names and nicknames that they cherished about themselves. This exchange helped me see that as a White teacher, my lessons will always default to make space for the identities that look like mine, which also happens to look like the majority of my elementary education college students, which also mirrors the 80 percent of White women who currently teach in K–6 classrooms across our nation (National Center for Education Statistics, 2021); therefore, it is essential that I try harder to intentionally prioritize space for the voices, values, and knowledge of my Black and Brown preservice teacher (a racialized identity desperately needed in our public schools for the benefit of all students [Bond et al., 2015]) when completing visual art projects like this one.

Personal Reflections of Teaching the Art for Advocacy Lesson

As previously mentioned, I had used art elicitation with both my youngest son and fellow professional colleagues as a personal and scholarly method for emotional self-reflections about our experiences during the early stage of COVID-19, but in my teacher preparation course I chose to turn the process into an assignment for external reflection and knowledge sharing about current social (in)justices—because teachers must learn to care about the politics and take actions on the issues that impact them, their students, their schools, and their communities.

What I have learned from teaching this lesson is that teachers care, they truly want to care and make a difference; however, largely due to their White identities, many of my elementary education preservice teachers are woefully unaware of the multitude of social (in)justice issues that are targeting the education profession, teachers, and their future students. I am learning to reconnect my college students back to their initial course artwork project of self-portraits as a personally relevant starting point for investing in the investigation of social (in)justices linked to classrooms full of diverse identities. This lesson is becoming an authentic way for me to prompt my students who hold dominant cultural, racialized, linguistic, religious, etc. identities to learn more about their privileges while also demonstrating to my students with minoritized identities the collective power their communities already hold.

READER TAKEAWAYS

- Culturally relevant and responsive teaching benefits all students by guiding teachers toward the creation of meaningful, significant learning experiences rooted in cultural values and voices that students can more readily connect with and urgently need to learn from.
- The visual arts provide an engaging, authentic way to pursue CRT in classrooms.
- The engagement in self-expression that visual arts creation promotes can help students teach each other as they share different perspectives and voice their own cultural knowledge and experiences.
- Teaching with the visual arts accomplishes CRT goals of linking students' personal experiences to the curriculum by connecting to students' identities and tackling authentic problems that matter to the identities of their groups and others.'

REFERENCES

Activity: Self-care through art (n.d.). Minneapolis Institute of Art. https://new.artsmia.org/activity-self-care-through-art/.

Artistic expression showcase (n.d.). Learning for Justice. https://www.learningforjustice.org/classroom-resources/student-tasks/do-something/artistic-expression-showcase.

Be the change . . . (n.d.). Learning for Justice. https://www.learningforjustice.org/classroom-resources/student-tasks/do-something/be-the-change.

Bond, B., Quintero, E., Casey, L., and Di Carlo, M. (2015). *The state of teacher diversity executive summary*. Albert Shanker Institute. https://www.shankerinstitute.org/resource/state-teacher-diversity-executive-summary.

Burrow, L. E., and Burrow, E. S. (2023). Noticing: A story of a mother's and son's discussions about the pandemic. In L. R. Ennis (Ed.), *Are the kids alright?: The impact of the pandemic on children and their families* (pp. 183–200). Demeter Press.

Burrow, L. E., Cross, C. J., and Olson Beal, H. K. (2023). Art looking within MotherScholarhood: Art elicitation for self-reflections and sense-making. *Journal of the Motherhood Initiative: Learning from the Pandemic: Possibilities and Challenges for Mothers and Families, 14*(1).

Burrow, L. E., Cross, C. J., Olson Beal, H. K., and Smith, S. (2020). The skits, sketches, and stories of MotherScholars. *The Qualitative Report, 25*(12), 4245–73. https://nsuworks.nova.edu/tqr/vol25/iss12/4.

Delpit, L. (2006). *Other people's children: Cultural conflict in the classroom*. The New Press.

Empathy (n.d.). Minneapolis Institute of Art. https://new.artsmia.org/empathy/.

Gay, G. (2010). *Culturally responsive teaching: Theory, research, and practice*. New York: Teachers College Press.

Ladson-Billings, G. (1994). *The dreamkeepers*. Jossey-Bass Publishing Co.

National Center for Education Statistics (2021). Table 208.20. Public and private elementary and secondary teachers, enrollment, pupil/teacher ratios, and new teacher hires: Selected years, fall 1955 through fall 2030 [Data table]. In *Digest of education statistics*. US Department of Education, Institute of Education Sciences. https://nces.ed.gov/programs/digest/d21/tables/dt21_208.20.asp

Silverstein, L. B., and Layne, S. (2010). Defining arts integration. The John F. Kennedy Center for the Performing Arts.

Smith, C. (2020). How culturally responsive lessons teach critical thinking. *Learning for Justice, 64*. https://www.learningforjustice.org/magazine/spring-2020/how-culturally-responsive-lessons-teach-critical-thinking.

Social Justice Standards (n.d.). Learning for Justice. https://www.learningforjustice.org/frameworks/social-justice-standards.

Stevenson, L. M., and Deasy, R. (2005). Third space: When learning matters. Washington, DC: Arts Education Partnership.

The British Museum. (2023). *Kingdom of Ife: Sculptures from West Africa*. Khan Academy: Art of Africa. https://www.khanacademy.org/humanities/art-africa/west-africa/nigeria/a/kingdom-of-ife-sculptures-from-west-africa#:~:text=Ife%20%28pronounced%20ee-feh%29%20is%20today%20regarded%20as%20the,culture%2C%20combining%20technical%20accomplishment%20with%20strong%20aesthetic%20appeal.

The Kennedy Center's Changing Education Through the Arts (CETA) (2008). *Key features*. The Kennedy Center. https://www.kennedy-center.org/globalassets/education/networks-conferences--research/networks--strategic-leadership/changing-education-through-the-arts-schools/ceta-learn-more-key_features_modelschools_10-08.pdf.

We need diverse books. We Need Diverse Books. https://diversebooks.org/.

Wolf, D. P. (2008). Building and evaluating "freedom machines": When is arts education a setting for equitable learning? In D. Glass (Ed.), *The contours of inclusion frameworks and tools for Evaluating Arts in Education* (pp. 5–6). Essay distributed by ERIC Clearinghouse.

Chapter 8

Cultural Inclusivity and Gamification

Addressing Diversity in the Twenty-First-Century World Language Classroom

Jon McFarland

In every job that must be done, there is an element of fun. You find the fun and—SNAP!—the job's a game!

—Mary Poppins

EXPECTED LEARNING OUTCOMES

- Readers will gain insight into how gamification can increase cultural inclusivity in the classroom as a means to develop culturally responsive teaching practices.
- Readers will gain an awareness of various gamifying elements that are culturally responsive and that increase student engagement.

TEACHER NARRATIVE

Past Reflections of a Former French Teacher

I have spoken to many adults who have mentioned to me in passing conversation about learning another language in secondary school, "*Yeah, I took four years of* ____ *(insert world language of choice here) in high school, but I can barely speak a word of it.*" Those words would always crush me as a French teacher of over two decades, as if they were personally attacking me as an educator and my efforts to get students interested in the French language.

The reality of second language learning in past decades is that many of us remember learning a world language in a very traditionally humdrum manner. The "drill and kill" method of memorizing verb conjugations and rote exercises of constant vocabulary repetition plague many world language learners with all-not-so-good memories that resemble high school nightmares rather than the beloved visions of language learning with which most educators hope students leave their classes.

As a young child attending a French-English bilingual school in Hawaii of all places, I remember learning French interactively through songs, play, and games. However in high school, I, too, succumbed to the boring traditional methods of language learning my teachers implemented. *When was it decided that the game elements used in language learning that were so impactful in my youth no longer applied in secondary school?*

Aside from my elementary school years, much of the world language teaching I witnessed was focused on reading and writing competency with a lack of practical and realistic oral proficiency. Vocabulary memorization and grammar development was often done with little to no contextual meaning through lived experiences. I was taught this way in high school, and when I did my student teaching at a public high school near the university I was attending, I was expected to teach the same way. I knew that world language teaching needed a revamp, but as a brand new teacher, I did not have the know-with-all to do it . . . yet.

In 2003, I started working at a Title I public high school with a diverse student population where more than half of all students received free and reduced lunches. Over 85 percent of my students were English learners at some point in their educational journey, and almost 90 percent of them were Spanish heritage speakers.

We had a high failure and dropout rate at our school, and my students faced multiple challenges including socioeconomic disadvantages, racial disparities, and gang violence. Most kids who took my French classes already spoke Spanish at home and wanted to be multilingual. I was able to engage most students with my witty repartee and ability to make fun of myself all in the target language, but I wanted to engage *all* of my students. I knew that I needed to adjust my approaches to curriculum design and delivery, so I dove into the research.

With the growing diversity of student populations in US public high schools, educators are finding it imperative to address the many forms of heterogeneity. Whether it be academic or cultural heterogeneity (Cheng, 2000; Dupriez et al., 2008), research has shown that not all students learn the same way (Armstrong, 2009).

Simply put, one size does not fit all. In addition, many twenty-first-century learners are digital natives, those who do not know life without computerized technology (that is, laptops, cell phones, tablets, etc.) and have very different learning experiences than previous generations due to greater exposure to technological advancement (Bennett et al., 2007; Prensky, 2001; Van Eck, 2006). This led me to consider two driving terms that influenced my curricular design, pedagogical delivery, and development of a new learning framework.

CULTURAL INCLUSIVITY DEFINED

Inclusivity is not a new concept in education but has been highly popularized by disability studies and the integration of special needs students in the mainstream classroom (McKinney and Lowenhaupt, 2013). Although scholarly attention has been given to inclusivity as it relates to students of different subgroups such as those representing special education, minority groups, women, and sexual orientation (DeLuca, 2013), no solid definition of inclusivity equally addresses all subgroups (Artiles, 2011; Trifonas, 2003).

This led me to examine the intersection of culture and inclusion by adopting the term "cultural inclusivity" as it focuses on the diverse cultures of different ethnic, racial, gender, and sexual identity groups. Cultural inclusivity is operationalized here as a means of representing historically marginalized subgroups that are not represented by an individualized education plan (IEP) that addresses the special educational needs of previously diagnosed/tested students (California Department of Education, 2009).

I define "cultural inclusivity" as a sociological viewpoint that integrates, accepts, and celebrates the positive influences of different ethnic, racial, gender, and sexual identities on the development of the diverse educational experiences of twenty-first-century learners within a global community.

This redefines normalcy (DiPardo and Fehn, 2000) to include and accept the cultures of nondominant groups, and thereby views cultural difference as the new normal (Russell and Truong, 2001). Cultural inclusivity examines the twenty-first-century learner through the lens of a tiered worldview that values the individual student and what they can achieve within their local community and who is capable of having a positive, global impact on society. Incorporating cultural inclusivity as a pedagogical perspective has afforded my students varied opportunities and has provided means through which cultural and identity expression can take place in the educational experiences of twenty-first-century learners.

GAMIFICATION AS A TEACHING METHOD

"Gamification" is a relatively new term in education that first originated in the fields of business and marketing (Lee and Hammer, 2011; Linder and Zichermann, 2010). The definition of "gamification" has been greatly debated throughout the past ten years and continues to be operationalized differently in scholarly work (Deterding et al., 2011).

For definitional clarity, I adopt Kapp's (2012) explanation of gamification as it relates to education. He states that gamification is composed of "using game-based mechanics, aesthetics, and game-thinking to engage people, motivate action, promote learning, and solve problems" (p. 10). As far as I am concerned, there is not a teacher out there who does not want that happening for their students.

Methods of gamification in education vary from the use of avatars (Sheldon, 2004), leaderboards (Nah et al., 2014), accumulation of experience points via leveling (Chen et al., 2013; Nah et al., 2013), and badges (Abramovich, Schunn, and Higashi, 2013) as a means of incentivizing increased student engagement with subject matter content. Gamification can also help students increase their intellectual capital, which normally refers to the intellectual property owned and exploited by businesses (Petty and Guthrie, 2000), yet from an educational viewpoint, I refer to it as the acquisition of scholastic and pragmatic knowledge acquired through educational experience, which may in turn affect one's cultural capital and professional trajectory in society (Bourdieu, 1998).

All the while, gamification helps to develop critical thinking skills. Scriven and Paul (1987) define critical thinking as "the intellectually disciplined process of actively and skilfully conceptualizing, applying, analysing, synthesizing, and/or evaluating information gathered from, or generated by, observation, experience, reflection, reasoning, or communication, as a guide to belief and action" (Critical thinking as defined by the National Council for Excellence in Critical Thinking, 1987). Such skills are becoming increasingly valuable as student curriculum and assessment practices are adapting to align with Common Core State Standards (California Department of Education, 2014) and promoting inquiry-based learning (Films for the Sciences et al., 2005).

GAMIFICATION AND THE BENEFITS TO CULTURAL INCLUSIVITY

Gamified pedagogical practices can benefit students and teachers alike as gamification breaches the ethnic, sexual, and gender divide with creativity and game mentality. There exists an educational paradigm shift from a traditional perspective of a teacher-based curriculum to one that emphasizes play through the use of technology in a student-centered exploratory environment (de Freitas and Liarokapis, 2011).

Although most research on gamification emphasizes technology usage, gamified pedagogical practices using little to no technology have also shown to be beneficial in motivating student curricular engagement (McFarland, 2017, 2020). Gamified student group work can help promote the breakdown of cultural barriers and labels that normally divide students by different identity groups by deemphasizing cultural differences and unifying students with a common performance-based goal (Wiggins, 1998).

It was not until 2008 that I developed and introduced Fantasy French to my high school students, which was a gamified curricular framework, before gamification became popular in educational spaces. The theme of Fantasy French was based on my love of Dungeons & Dragons (D&D) that I played as a kid. The framework included a general leveling up system based on points players (aka students) accumulated throughout the game (that is, course).

In addition, each player had the choice of what type of character they played (regardless of sex and gender) throughout the semester that possessed associated powers that they could manipulate and use for their advantage throughout game play (that is, academic semester). The characters or avatars they could play included ranger, bard, healer, or sorcerer. Throughout the next eight years, I implemented my gamified framework and tweaked particular elements to equitably serve my students and their learning. Table 8.1.

Table 8.1. Welcome to Fantasy French

For the following class, you will take part in an intricately designed game. In many video games, you are required to complete certain tasks that advance you toward a goal. In the process of achieving that goal, you earn points for each step you complete. How easily you make it through the game and how many points you accumulate depend on how well you apply yourself, how much you practice, and the skills you ultimately develop.

General Levels of Fantasy French

Once you pass a level, you unlock your reward. You may redeem your rewards in any order you choose.

Game Score	Level	Reward	Your Score	Date Achieved	Date Reward Redeemed
0–50	1				
51–150	2	Extra life on an adventure (*1 life = 2pts)			
151–300	3	Free quest pass (≤12pts)			
301–400	4	Post-it note on an adventure			

(continued)

Table 8.1. (continued)

Game Score	Level	Reward	Your Score	Date Achieved	Date Reward Redeemed
401–550	5	5 minutes to use notes on an adventure			
551–700	6	Flashcard on an adventure			
701–850	7	Double points on one adventure problem			
851–1,100	8	Double quest pass			
1,101–1,600	9	10 bonus points on an adventure			
1,601–2,500	10	Adventure pass (≤25pts)			

Some helpful rules for players of the gamified class to understand:
1. Players (students) are *always* playing the game and have the opportunity to earn points that will help increase levels.
2. There are external (general and specific) rewards for increasing levels. Some rewards are specific for the character you play, while others are general for the class.
3. Player "powers" may be used on others within your established guild (group). When you have achieved certain levels within the game, you may use your player powers on yourself when indicated in the reward.
4. The rules of engagement in the game will remain consistent, yet if any changes arise, all players will be notified in advance.
5. You may also choose to grant a gift to another player with one of your rewards.
6. The ways to earn points in the game are limitless! Besides the assigned class material, some additional ways are
   - viewing videos, movies, news clips, etc. and writing a synopsis in French;
   - creating voice threads (voicethread.com) in French on your topic of interest;
   - reporting news articles in French and writing a synopsis;
   - writing additional essays, notes, or presentations from other classes in French;
   - starting up a discussion thread on our learning management system within your guild on a topic of interest;
   - posting self-made videos on a topic of interest in French; and
   - narrating an animated story in French, etc.

One year, in an attempt to increase student collaboration and community, I had students create their own "guilds" within the class. Each guild was composed of no more than four students who had individually chosen their own particular type of character they would play. In D&D, guilds are organized groups of artisans or characters who specialize in certain crafts, and typically they do not intermingle with characters of other crafts in the same guild; however, it was an opportunity to introduce different vocabulary that students would normally not receive in traditional world language settings.

Plus, I intentionally chose to use culturally sensitive terminology to ensure that all students felt equally represented in the educational setting. Players were encouraged to build alliances with others they may not have normally worked to collaboratively assist one another in group activities by manipulating their specialized character powers when it best suited them.

Table 8.2. Specific Player Levels of Fantasy French

As a player in the game (that is, class), you ultimately have many choices to make throughout the game that will make you points and raise your levels. The first choice you must make is the type of character you wish to be within the game. Each type of character has its strengths and different abilities that can be applied in the game:

the bard (le/la barde):
- an eloquent communicator and gifted musician
- powers include: provides extra percentage points to oral presentations; providing keys to assessment "traps"

the sorcerer (le sorcier/la sorcière):
- a learned character with extensive knowledge and high intelligence
- powers include: casting spells of foresight, invisibility, and other spells that affect others and oneself

the ranger (le gendarme à cheval):
- a character of high constitution, skill, and perseverance in tasks; good trackers
- powers include: increased endurance and extension of due dates for a group or oneself

the healer (le guérisseur/la guérisseuse):
- connection to the divine
- good group supporter
- powers include: granted with the ability to give lives to others in a group and oneself

Once you pass a level, you unlock your reward. You may redeem your rewards in any order you choose.

Game Score	Level	**Bard** (le/la barde):	**Ranger** (le gendarme à cheval):	**Sorcerer** (le sorcier/la sorcière):	**Healer** (le guérisseur/la guérisseuse):
0–50	1				
51–150	2	+5% on song/poem activity to other	1 day quest extension to other (up to 10pts)	+5% on web tool activity to other	2 lives to others (*1 life = 2pts)
151–300	3	+5% on group oral presentation	1 day group extension	+5% on writing activity to other	2 lives to others
301–400	4	1 trap key for self	1 day quest extension to self (≤12pts)	sight spell on adventure (1 min)	2 lives to self
401–550	5	+5% on song/poem activity	defeat 1 adventure question for self	1 teacher quest spell (≤12pts)	1 "divine" answer on adventure

(continued)

Table 8.2. (continued)

Game Score	Level	**Bard** (le/la barde):	**Ranger** (le gendarme à cheval):	**Sorcerer** (le sorcier/la sorcière):	**Healer** (le guérisseur/la guérisseuse):
551–700	6	singing hypnotic spell on 1 adventure question	defeat 1 quest for self (≤12pts)	persuasion spell on 1 adventure question	3 lives to others
701–850	7	1 trap key for self	+10% on 1 quest for self	+10% on web tool activity	3 lives to self
851–1,100	8	+10% on group oral presentation	defeat 1 quest for self and other (≤20pts)	1 invisible quest spell for self & other (≤20pts)	1 "divine" answer on adventure
1,101–1,600	9	singing hypnotic spell on 3 adventure questions	+10% on 1 adventure	sight spell on adventure (2 min)	9 lives to self
1,601–2,500	10	1 trap key to share with class (≤25pts)	defeat of 1 adventure for class (≤50pts)	1 invisible adventure for class (≤50pts)	grant 10 lives to whole class on adventure

I encouraged student agency and autonomy by having all players choose the type of fantastical characters they resonated with the most. Many students often played characters that demonstrated qualities they thought represented their own personalities and dispositions regardless of sex and gender. All students would then design what their avatar would look like, whether it be a drawing or digitally mastered, and display them around the classroom alongside their guild mates.

Keeping to the fantastical theme of D&D, many students played characters that defied traditional gender roles, represented mythical characters of their cultural heritage, or embraced androgynous neutrality. Game culture was established within the class as each group was expected to create a guild name and a symbolic representation of the group.

Students were also allowed to create nicknames for themselves as a form of self-identity within the game, which allowed for self-representation transcendent of marginalization. Multiple topics of the class content addressed issues of racial, gender, and sexuality stereotyping, which helped students of all identity groups to critically evaluate problems of equity and cultural inclusivity.

When gamified, differentiated instruction (Tomlinson, 1999, 2001) develops educational equity for all students regardless of cultural identity through a reculturation of the attitudes and beliefs about how things are done in the classroom or addressed through the curriculum (Anthony, 2011; Hemmings, 2012). With class content established as a game through which all students unify toward the common goal of overcoming quests and adventures (that is, class tasks and assessments), cultural identity difference is demarginalized with the adopted game culture. Guilds worked together on group projects and were rewarded for high scores on adventures with incentives that could have been used to benefit the guild as a whole.

This established game culture helps break down negative stereotypes sometimes associated with particular identity groups (Conchas, 2001). Gamified methods of instruction drastically reduces, if not eliminates, identity marginalization in the classroom by promoting a unified game culture where students are united together to meet and overcome the challenges of the game established via the curriculum and gamified social environment. The established game culture promotes performance-based unity regardless of race, ethnicity, gender, or sexual identity.

Gamifying my classes for the past nine years of teaching French at my former high school was not always successful. Some students, parents, and administration had difficulty buying into the gamified concept of the class, and they thought that we were just going to play games in class all day. I needed to explain the difference between game-based learning (what they thought was happening in the class) and gamification (what was really going on).

Game-based learning is when educators take closed-system games (for example, Monopoly, Scrabble, etc.) and use them in class to have students address particular learning goals. For example, teachers could have students play Monopoly to teach them about money management, property taxes, or inflation. Gamification, on the other hand, is when teachers weave the elements of games (for example, leaderboards, avatars, badges, incentives, etc.) throughout their curricula without jeopardizing course rigor.

Because gamification was a relatively new trend for teachers in my former school district at the time, it took some time before district administrators knew enough to provide any teacher training on gamification theory and changes to traditional pedagogical philosophy. In most cases, teacher interest remained greater than the implementation of such gamified methods. Conversely, many educators dismissed gamification as a legitimate pedagogical methodology and mistook its approach as traditional forms of play that may not add to the educational experience (Tulloch, 2014). I have learned many tips on how to successfully gamify throughout the years. Here are my top ten tips on gamifying your curriculum.

TEN TIPS FOR GAMIFYING THE CURRICULUM

1. Step out of the box.

Applying gamification methods to an academic curriculum is a major step toward an innovative way to teach content. Because gamified methodology is such a paradigm shift in the way many educators view teaching, it can be somewhat difficult to embrace and get comfortable with at first for all involved (for example, teachers, students, parents, administrators). By recognizing the educational paradigm shift in the ways that twenty-first-century learners seek, find, and produce information differently from previous generations, educators step out of the traditional box of how to teach their students.

Agency is an instrumental aspect in motivating players of games. Agency provides students a greater choice as to how they wish to engage in the gamified course. For example, teachers might give students the choice of homework activities to complete by requiring three out of five weekly exercises, and students can earn extra points for doing more than required. Educators might also offer earned homework passes or provide "extra lives" (that is, bonus points) for surpassing expectations on projects or presentations that students decide when to use. Additionally, teachers can devise a list of incentives that students could "purchase" with earned experience points from demonstrating positive behavior or completing coursework.

2. The what leads to the how.

It is important for teachers who are gamifying to reflect on where their students are academically, and where they want their *student-players* to be at the end of their game. By identifying *what* gamification is being used for, it will be easier for educators to determine *how* their gamified framework should be set up. For example, a language teacher having difficulties with classroom management might establish a gamified framework with incentives that focus heavily on classroom behavior modification. How a gamified framework is established depends on teachers' pedagogical needs and objectives.

3. Consider your student population.

It is important to know the curricular needs and motivations of the student populations for whom the gamified framework is created. One framework may not be effective for all student populations, which is why teachers should consider the types of incentives to offer student-players. While some teachers may need to provide more tangible rewards for greater immediacy (for example, choice of seat, extra bathroom pass, extra computer time, or edible treats) to better deal with disciplinary issues, others are apt to implement more intangible rewards (for example, homework passes or extra experience points) for student-players who are more academically motivated and concerned with how the gamified framework will affect their overall grades. Incorporating a bit of both tangible and intangible rewards will help address a diverse class population.

4. Create a theme.

Students know when teachers enjoy teaching the class, and they are more likely to be interested in a curriculum where teachers create a storyline or follow a particular theme. Thematizing the curriculum demonstrates the instructors' imaginative side and their willingness to create an interesting platform for the course content. Educators could consider themes such as different time periods in history (that is, artistic, philosophical, or literary movements, various feudal systems, or succession of kings and queens) to represent units in the course or cultural (super)hero themes such as Belgium's Tintin, France's *Asterix et Obélix*, or any number of the DC or Marvel Comic heroes in which student-players must face challenges (for example, projects, dialogues in the target language, oral presentations, literary analyses, or assessments of different sorts) and defeat the threat of villains who deter their success in the game. Moreover, themes may arise from popular culture and what students are interested in at the time (for example, various team sports, popular television programs, characters from *manga* [Japanese comics], or icons of *k-pop* [Korean pop music]).

5. Change your vocabulary.

Once a theme for the course is chosen, associated vocabulary is essential for student buy-in. Homework, quizzes, and tests are negatively correlated by many students. To help increase student buy-in, consider creating more positive associations with these activities. Additionally, when introduced in the target language, world language and English language development educators expose new vocabulary to student-players that may never surface otherwise. Homework can be a quest or an adventure. Quizzes might be missions, and tests could become challenges or operations. Projects might be considered ventures or exploits, and students are players.

Vocabulary changes for negatively associated activities help students to immerse themselves in the teacher's envisioned gamified theme for the course. However, it will take students some time to adjust to these new vocabulary associations, and student buy-in is impeded if they are not referred to often. Hence, when teachers decide to implement new vocabulary references for particular activities in their frameworks, it is important to commit to continually referencing the new terms. Newly adopted terminology that helps build upon the theme of a gamified framework is quickly forgotten, along with the benefits of the established framework when not reinforced by the system creator.

6. Make the game doable.

In the game world, there exist some very complex games with highly involved storylines, themes, and plot twists that offer a plethora of incentives for successful engagement. However, such models may not be ideal for creating a curricular gamified framework. It is imperative to consider the time and effort needed, not only to build the curricular framework but to upkeep it.

If the gamified system is too complex, it becomes a burden to play for both teacher and student-player alike. If the game is too complex, students will become confused and perhaps lose interest early on. Plus, teachers will need to upkeep the records of the game; therefore, the game should be manageable, and not be tedious and take too much time—the game is meant to enhance the curriculum, not burden teachers.

7. Incentivize early on.

Successful games promote opportunities to earn incentives early on as a hook to entice player buy-in. Without buy-in early on in games, a player will quickly lose interest and give up. A successful curricular gamified framework starts with a simple reward that compels the student-player to continue engaging within the gamified system. Rewards would then exponentially increase in worth and become more difficult to attain as the gamified curriculum progresses.

Leveling up is a gamified method that provides game players incentives for completing certain levels or achieving the indicated amount of experience points. Once that level is achieved, players may access the associated rewards for that level, which may be used when they choose. However, players must be strategic when utilizing their rewards because each reward is only accessible once. To increase class collegiality, teachers may allow student-players to gift one of their rewards to another classmate. With multiple choices embedded in the gamified framework, student-players need to be cognizant of *how* and *when* they will use their earned rewards to enhance their academic experience.

8. Be consistent.

Gamified frameworks are only motivating to student-players when played. If the game is not referenced or played regularly where students witness their own success within the game system, they will forget about it and lose touch with the initial motivation that the gamified system offered in the first place. Therefore, once teachers have developed their gamified framework with themes, associated vocabulary, and incentives, they should have written explanations of the gamified system, how student-players can earn rewards throughout the course, and a way for them to track their own scores along the way. This affords student-players more responsibility and accountability for their own gamified experience when engaging with the course curriculum.

9. Be flexible.

Keep in mind that most games are not stagnant and evolve with the players. Educators may find that they need to switch things up and change elements of their gamified frameworks to address the needs of the student-players. By being flexible to changes with the applied game elements, teachers are more likely to address the academic needs of their population and keep students interested and engaged with the gamified curriculum.

Adjusting point distributions, setting new rules of engagement, and adding or eliminating certain rewards based on what incentivizes their students are all ways of adapting to the student-player population. In addition, teachers may wish to limit their curricular games to academic quarters, trimesters, or semesters to allow for modifications at the end of grading periods, as well as to afford student-players the ability to evaluate their previous game play, provide helpful feedback to teachers, and start anew for another grading period.

10. Technology is just a tool.

While using technology can greatly enhance the experience of a gamified framework, it remains a tool through which curricular instruction is transmitted. Some educators may feel more comfortable manipulating various technologies or have better tech access with their student-players than others, depending on school resources and the student populations with which they work.

Linking the results from activities of preexisting gamified internet tools such as Quizlet Live or Quizizz to a gamified curriculum enhances the variety of game-like opportunities for academic success. If using educational technology to enhance the gamified experience in one's classes, it is critical that educators do their due diligence by receiving training and working with such technologies to assure they are utilizing them with cultural inclusivity in mind. It is better to be proficient at one or two robust tech tools that our students will utilize regularly than to dabble in using multiple tools ever so often. In doing so, teachers will better prepare future generations of twenty-first-century learners who will be united via performance rather than separated by identity difference.

Technology is not a requirement for implementing successful academic gamification. Teachers can set up leaderboards that use newly adopted gamified vocabulary to dress the walls of their classrooms. Leaderboards demonstrate physical representation of each student-player and their progression through the gamified course. Using avatars to represent student-players includes an additional element of personal creativity and imagination to the gamified curriculum, certainly when student-players are able to accessorize and manipulate their own avatars.

CONCLUSION

Cultural inclusivity is not usually thought of in association with gamification. However, good game and curriculum design does not negate the importance of cultural diversity for twenty-first-century learners. Cultural inclusivity is defined as it pertains to the varying demographic of twenty-first-century learners in American schools today.

Our students do not exist in silos; they are complex individuals with complex backgrounds. The more educators understand their students, the more teachers are able to address the diverse educational needs of marginalized twenty-first-century learners and implement best teaching practices to serve them.

Oftentimes educators think of addressing race and ethnicity as a means to be culturally responsive, but I learned from Zaretta Hammond (2015) that the elements of gamification I used in my classes to engage students through themes, collaboration, and gamelike interactions can increase students' attention and focus. Not to mention, student culture manifests through their academic, linguistic, and familial funds of knowledge that also emerge through the intersectionality of race, ethnicity, religion, gender, and sexuality.

CULTURALLY RESPONSIVE LESSON PLAN 1

Title of Lesson:	*Self, National, and Personal Identity*
Grade Level:	**Grades 10–12; French 2**

Content Standard(s):

This lesson pulls from the California Common Core State Standards for World Languages.

WL.CM1.I. Demonstrate understanding of the main idea and some details on some informal topics related to self and the immediate environment. Demonstrate understanding of sentences and strings of sentences in authentic texts that are spoken, written, or signed.

WL.CL2.I. Experience, recognize, and explore the relationships among typical age-appropriate target cultures' products, practices, and perspectives in culturally appropriate ways in transactional situations and some informal settings.

Social Justice Standard: https://www.learningforjustice.org/frameworks/social-justice-standards

ID.9–12.1: I have a positive view of myself, including an awareness of and comfort with my membership in multiple groups in society.

DI.9–12.7: I have the language and knowledge to accurately and respectfully describe how people (including myself) are both similar to and different from each other and others in their identity groups.

Objectives: *Students will be able to*

verbally express their understanding of the poem "L'homme qui te resemble" by René Philombe through small group discussion,

identify the use of the imperative tense (*l'impératif*) in authentic literary texts and verbally explain the underlying symbolism of its use in the poem "L'homme qui te ressemble," and

create a word cloud that expresses their personal identity to be used as a visual for an oral presentation.

Anticipatory Set: *(How will student interest be sparked to engage in the lesson of the day?)*

Leading up to this lesson, students will have been exposed to and worked with previous language content reviewed in the poem including colors, geography, and body parts.

To "hook" the students into this lesson, play a short video clip of the poem "L'homme qui te ressemble" being recited aloud from a fourth-grade bilingual class from Lycée Françahealthise de la Nouvelle Orléans on YouTube. Some suggestions on how to use the video for the anticipatory set:

1. Have students watch the video clip of the recited poem and ask students to make mental notes on the specific words (for example, nouns) they understood. (2 minutes)

2. Students work with class partners to verbalize and list on paper all the words they heard from the poem. (2 minutes)
   a. To gamify: Students are grouped in small groups of four and are numbered 1 through 4 for each group. Each group is provided a small student whiteboard and Expo pen. They are given 1 minute to brainstorm all together before the teacher calls a number between 1 and 4. The student assigned to the number called will now need to quickly list on the whiteboard all the words discussed from their group without any other group member touching the board. Other group members may only speak in the target language to the member writing on the board for words to count. When time is called, the group with the most words on their board spelled correctly and that are not duplicated by other groups wins an incentive (for example, extra points, piece of candy, advance on a leaderboard, etc.).
3. Together as a class, students share out the words they heard in the target language while the teacher writes them on the board classifying them into colors, geography, and body parts that demarcate the strophes in the poem and to help students recognize the different topics addressed in relation to the poet. (5 minutes)

Relevancy: *(How will the content be made relevant to the students in the context you are teaching? What connections can be made to their experiences and cultures?)*

The anticipatory set leads into reading the poem, conducting poetic analysis that remains in the target language, and the use of the poem's vocabulary to make connections to students' lived experiences and identities. The discussion that follows allows teachers to dive deeper into multiple topics including race, ethnicity, how we identify (that is, as individuals, as family members, as members of a community, etc.), marginalization, and equal treatment for all people, depending on the trajectory of the conversation and where the teacher and students wants to take it.

Academic Vocabulary: *(What academic vocabulary will be addressed in this lesson? How will it be taught and made comprehensible to ALL learners?)*

Students will be pulling from prior knowledge of vocabulary discussed before this lesson, which may lead to the introduction of new vocabulary and phrases in relation to identity. Examples include:
Je suis d'origine mexicaine / espagnole, etc. → (I am of Mexican origin.)
Je suis mexicain(e). → (I am Mexican.)
la nationalité → nationality
l'ethnicité → ethnicity
Other academic vocabulary resources include: Nationalités et Identités

Lesson Overview: *(Please describe the steps for each part of the lesson. Also, in parentheses, put a time estimate for each segment of the lesson.)*

1. Anticipatory set (5–10 minutes)
2. Read "L'homme qui te ressemble" and do poetic analysis with class (20–30 minutes)
   a. Break up the poem in strophes to help students understand how each one addresses different categories of identification.
   b. Provide guided note taking on the analysis of the poem by projecting the poem on the board; read it aloud with poetic emphasis.
   c. Provide guiding questions for students to unpack their understanding with partners near them.

Cultural Inclusivity and Gamification 167

3. Students create a Self-Identity Word Cloud by using a word cloud generator of their choice. Each word cloud must have at least ten different words (nouns or adjectives) students would use to describe their self-identify. Students must include their first and last name on the word cloud (*not as part of the ten required words). Students may use any digital word cloud generator of their choice (for example, beautiful.ai, Word Cloud Generator, or Word Art, etc.). (10–15 minutes)
4. Exit ticket: Provide three words that you will use as part of your word cloud and the categories associated with those words (for example, portoricain → ethnicité, frère → famille, américain → nationalité). (2–3 minutes)

Materials Needed: *(Please list the materials that will be needed for this lesson.)*

The teacher will need internet access for the YouTube video (anticipatory set) and digital display through overhead projection with audio, copies of the poem "L'homme qui te ressemble" by René Philombe, whiteboard markers, and student whiteboards.

Students will need paper, writing utensils, and highlighters for students to take notes and their Chromebooks (school-issued laptops).

*If students do not have access to computers for the Self-Identity Word Cloud, then this activity can be completed on poster paper using glue, scissors, and disposable magazines for images and lettering as an art project that represents the student in a personal way. Include colored string and wiring for students to create personalized mobiles. Student work can then be hung around the class environment to celebrate student identities.

Universal Design for Learning: *(How will the principles of UDL be utilized throughout this lesson to give students voice and choice?)*

To address UDL principles, this lesson affords students multiple means of representation with the introduction of the poem "L'homme qui te ressemble" with the video, the teacher reading the poem aloud, and students reading it themselves. This allows students to be exposed to the target language and the represented vocabulary multiple times to enhance listening and reading comprehension. Students are also provided multiple opportunities throughout the lesson to unpack their thought process with partner or small group discussions through teacher-directed and guided questioning.

Other ways teachers can employ UDL principles with this lesson:
1. Enlarge the font of the poem for better ease of reading.
2. If using PowerPoint or other visual display for presenting the material, utilize complimentary pictures on slides to help students make linguistic associations with visual representation; limit words on slides and animate any important vocabulary for students to follow along when note taking.
3. Promote translanguaging practices with students by allowing them to take notes in the language of their preference. While I tend to teach my French classes completely in the target language, sometimes allowing students to access their native languages in brief partner discussion to help process their understanding of the target language can help with their language development.

Access: *(What strategies will be used throughout the lesson to allow students multiple entry points into understanding the concepts taught?)*

This lesson is intentional at having students utilize the four modalities of learning including reading, writing, listening, and speaking in the target language at the developmental level of the students by utilizing the vocabulary and grammatical structures that are in their linguistic repertoire.

Higher-Order Thinking: *(In what ways will this lesson require students to utilize higher-order thinking? Please describe.)*

Students will be led and guided to implement higher-order thinking through poetic analysis, develop an increased vocabulary that associates with the categories of self-identification depicted in the poem, and use the poetic and discursive influence of the lesson to delve into reflective representation through personalized vocabulary for self-identification.

Assessments: *(How will each learning objective be assessed? What activities do you have planned to check for understanding approximately every 5 minutes of the lesson?)*

This lesson affords the teacher the opportunity to insert multiple checks for understanding (CFU) from the anticipatory set and all through the poetic analysis. Most of the CFUs come in the form of responding to probing questions from the teacher throughout the lesson. The exit ticket allows the teacher to see if students understand the classification of vocabulary with regards to the multiple ways we self-identify.

This lesson embeds multiple formative assessments, but the Self-Identity Word Cloud, which may or may not be completed during one class period, is meant to be the catalyst for the summative assessment, which involves a complex oral presentation on self-identification in which the word cloud is their visual artifact.

*This lesson plan can be adapted to a more advanced class as well. For assessment ideas that follow the same vein as this lesson with self-identification, see Qu'est-ce que c'est l'identité?

Closure: *(What activity will you use to close this lesson and to assess students' understanding at the end of the period?)*

For closure, I use the exit ticket in which students provide a minimum of three nouns or adjectives that they will use as part of their word cloud; however, they need to demonstrate their understanding of various categories associated with those words (for example, portoricain → ethnicité, frère → famille, américain → nationalité).

CULTURALLY RESPONSIVE LESSON PLAN 2

Title of Lesson:	*Existential Crisis*
Grade Level:	**11–12; (French 3–4/4AP)**

Content Standard(s):

All World Language Standards come from the California Common Core State Standards for World Languages.

WL.CM4. Initiate opportunities to use culturally authentic, real-world, and academic language in most informal and formal settings within target language communities in the United States and around the world.

WL.CL3.A. Describe and explain similarities and differences among products, practices, and perspectives of general public interest in the mainstream cultures of the United States, the students' own cultures, and the target cultures.
WL.CN1.A. Acquire, exchange, and present information in the target language on factual topics of public interest and general academic content across disciplines.

Social Justice Standard: https://www.learningforjustice.org/frameworks/social-justice-standards

JU.9–12.11. I relate to all people as individuals rather than representatives of groups and can identify stereotypes when I see or hear them.
DI.9–12.10. I understand that diversity includes the impact of unequal power relations on the development of group identities and cultures.

Objectives: *Students will be able to*

demonstrate their understanding of Sartrian existentialism as depicted in the play Huis Clos by analyzing a portion of scene 5 including Garcin's final monologue (scene 5, p. 93 of text) in small group and whole class discussion; and

express their opinion and interpretation of what hell is like through a written exit ticket (as part of a guided higher-order thinking activity) after reading and watching a brief video excerpt of Garcin's monologue performed in the 1954 film of Huis Clos.

Anticipatory Set: *(How will student interest be sparked to engage in the lesson of the day?)*

This lesson is meant to be a final lesson in a larger unit on French existentialism and Sartrian philosophical views. Students would have already been exposed to the life and history and Jean-Paul Sartre (*see Greatest Philosopher in History - Jean Paul Sartre) and finished reading and discussing the first four scenes of Sartre's play *Huis Clos*. There is a plethora of resources online for teachers who wish to keep all video material in the target language (for example, Résumé illustré - Huis Clos); however, due to the difficulty of the content itself, it may be beneficial to provide students with introductory resources either in English or in their first language (L1). If time does not permit reading the entire play, the use of an excerpt from scene 5 would suffice with prior introduction to existential thought and the impact this philosophical movement had on literature, art, and film in the mid-twentieth century.

1. For this lesson, the anticipatory set might be various images of hell taken from a general online image search that the teacher displays at the beginning of class for them to reflect on when responding to the question: What do you see? (Que voyez-vous?) In their notes, students individually test their prior knowledge of vocabulary studied and discussed in relation to the previous scenes of Huis Clos and religious/cultural thought. This gets them prepped for thinking deeper on their perceptions of what hell is (based on their cultural backgrounds) as opposed to what they see in the image. (2 minutes)
2. Students then work with class partners to verbalize and list on paper all the words they observed. (2 minutes)
   a. To gamify: Students are grouped in small groups of four and are numbered 1–4 for each group. Each group is provided a small student whiteboard and Expo pen. They are given 1 minute to brainstorm all together before the teacher calls a number between 1 and 4. The student assigned to the number called will now

need to quickly list on the whiteboard all the words discussed from their group without any other group member touching the board. Other group members may only speak in the target language to the member writing on the board for words to count. When time is called, the group with the most words on their board spelled correctly and that are not duplicated by other groups wins an incentive (for example, extra points, piece of candy, advance on a leaderboard, etc.).
3. Together as a class, students share out the words they generated in the target language while the teacher writes them on the board, following up with other clarifying or probing questions, makes corrections when necessary, and introduces new vocabulary that may arise. (5–10 minutes)

Relevancy: *(How will the content be made relevant to the students in the context you are teaching? What connections can be made to their experiences and cultures?)*

This lesson asks students to analyze the concept of hell as it is depicted in existential philosophy and pull from their own cultural backgrounds (that is, moral perceptions of good and evil, religious viewpoints, etc.) and various ideologies that contribute to a contemporary depiction of hell. The texts (that is, written play and film) are used as tools for students to better understand the Sartrian concept of hell and be able to defend or refute the depiction of hell in *Huis Clos*.

Academic Vocabulary: *(What academic vocabulary will be addressed in this lesson? How will it be taught and made comprehensible to ALL learners?)*

This lesson specifically focuses on key terms read and heard used in the film from scene 5 of the play. Garcin's final monologue expresses existential philosophical views that students must understand in order to verbally discuss Sartre's version of hell as depicted in the play and provide written interpretation of what hell is to them and why based on their own philosophical, religious, and/or cultural beliefs. Some key terms include: *lâche* → coward; *enfer* → hell; *la mort* → death; *la honte* → *shame*.

This lesson builds upon previous lessons that use *Huis Clos* as a literary text and film. There are many new vocabulary words that will arise through the reading and the film. I have created supplementary lists of vocabulary using Quizlet called Huis Clos (vocabulaire supplémentaire) et la violence that teachers may wish to use when discussing this text. Quizlet is a wonderful digital tool that affords students multiple means to review vocabulary associated with this lesson.

To gamify: Consider using the varied gamified options provided when using Quizlet. See the linked example of Quizlet: En Enfer that allows students to review vocabulary through gameful means and to experience safe failure by being able to redo the assessment if proficiency is not reached the first time around.

Lesson Overview: *(Please describe the steps for each part of the lesson. Also, in parentheses, put a time estimate for each segment of the lesson.)*

Due to the complexity of the content and need for adequate checks for understanding, this lesson may take up to two full days to complete.
1. Anticipatory set (10–12 minutes)
2. Pass out hard copies of the HOT Activity (en français) for students to develop and demonstrate higher-order thinking skills through scaffolded instruction, guided note taking, partner talk, and whole class discussion; explain the instructions of HOT activity before showing the video clip.

3. Introduce an excerpt of scene 5 of Huis Clos, film 1954 (1:27.00–1:31.54), which includes Garcin's final monologue (1:29.40–1:30.40) without closed captioning and have students complete the first section Observer of the HOT activity individually; discuss their initial list with a partner and add to the list; share with the class their observation. (10–12 minutes)
4. Review the same video scene again now with closed captioning and have students complete the second section Décrire of the HOT activity individually; discuss their initial descriptions with a partner and add to their own sheets; share with the class their descriptions. (10–12 minutes)
5. Have students then complete the third section Interpreter using the similar structure as previously that affords multiple checks for understanding. (10–12 minutes)
6. Introduce the written excerpt of Garcin's final monologue (that is, displayed on the whiteboard, shared digitally with students, and on hard copy). (15–20 minutes)
   a. Students read the excerpt individually; highlight or note any unknown terms in the text.
   b. Students discuss their understanding of terms in context (that is, deductive reasoning, prior knowledge of morphology, possible cognates, etc.).
   c. The teacher then may read aloud the final monologue or have a student do so and discuss or clarify any unknown terms in the text by offering synonyms or antonyms of each in the target language which only increases students' vocabulary and linguistic repertoire in the target language.
7. Students complete the section Synthétiser as part of their exit ticket in which they utilize pertinent terminology that was discussed and used in class. (5–10 minutes)
8. Introduce the culminating project and summative assessment Mise en Scène: En Enfer. (10 minutes)

Materials Needed: *(Please list the materials that will be needed for this lesson.)*

For this lesson, the teacher and students will use Jean-Paul Sartre's *Huis Clos* (the original text found free online) and the black and white video *Huis Clos* (1954). I found that downloading small chunks of the play worked well going through the play with students; see *Huis Clos* (1954 film) shared folder of downloaded video clips of whole play. Students will also need digital or hard copy access to the HOT Activity either in English or in French and use any preferred note taking tools including pens, pencils, highlighters, etc.

Universal Design for Learning: *(How will the principles of UDL be utilized throughout this lesson to give students voice and choice?)*

To address UDL principles, this lesson affords students multiple means of representation with the written text, with the video, the teacher reading the monologue aloud, and students reading it themselves. This allows students to be exposed to the target language and the represented vocabulary multiple times to enhance listening and reading comprehension. Students are also provided multiple opportunities throughout the lesson to unpack their thought process with partner or small group discussions through teacher-directed and guided questioning and the use of a graphic organizer.

Other ways teachers can employ UDL principles with this lesson:
1. Provide digital and hard copies of the textual excerpt from the play to allow for note taking in the students' preferred manner. Show students how to take notes through digital means with various Google extensions or online applications.
2. Display the theatrical excerpt on the whiteboard to use when reading aloud (teacher and/or student) and use various colors and highlighting tools to visually annotate the text and model how note taking should be completed for maximum comprehension.
3. If using PowerPoint or other visual display for presenting the material, utilize complementary pictures on slides to help students make linguistic associations with visual representations; limit words on slides and animate any important vocabulary for students to follow along when note taking.
4. Promote translanguaging practices with students by allowing them to take notes in the language of their preference. While I tend to teach my French classes completely in the target language, sometimes allowing students to access their native languages in a brief partner discussion to help process their understanding of the target language can help with their language development.
5. Utilize closed captioning (in English and/or French) with video clips presented for students with hearing impairments and for improved reading/listening comprehension. Consider slowing the playback speed to 0.75 for students to better understand the complexity of language at a slower rate for improved comprehensibility.

Access: *(What strategies will be used throughout the lesson to allow students multiple entry points into understanding the concepts taught?)*

This lesson is intentional at having students utilize the four modalities of learning including reading, writing, listening, and speaking in the target language at the developmental level of the students by utilizing the vocabulary and grammatical structures that are in their linguistic repertoire.

Higher-Order Thinking: *(In what ways will this lesson require students to utilize higher-order thinking? Please describe.)*

The goal of this lesson is to get students to reach levels of higher-order thinking (HOT) through scaffolded exercises done throughout the class. To help the teacher guide students through the development of HOT, I have provided a graphic organizer to be used in English and/or in French.

Assessments: *(How will each learning objective be assessed? What activities do you have planned to check for understanding approximately every 5 minutes of the lesson?)*

This lesson affords the teacher to insert multiple checks for understanding (CFU) from the anticipatory set and all through the literary/film analysis. Most of the CFUs come in the form of responding to probing questions from the teacher and students throughout the lesson. The exit ticket allows the teacher to see if students can properly use the vocabulary in context of the play, express their understanding of the philosophical tenets of existentialism, analyze the symbolism strewn throughout the scene, and provide their interpretation of hell by pulling from their own cultural backgrounds to support stated opinions.

The formal or summative assessment used to complete the unit of existentialism would be a small group dialogue (*see Mise en Scène: En Enfer) that asks students to create their own dramatic interpretation of hell and the existential angst of the three characters in the play.

Closure: *(What activity will you use to close this lesson and to assess students' understanding at the end of the period?)*

For closure, I use the section Synthétser of the HOT Activity (linked previously) as an exit ticket in which students are asked to synthesize the meaning of what it means to be in hell or how individuals experience hell in a minimum of five comprehensive sentences using the vocabulary and grammatical structures previously discussed and covered in class.

An alternative closure exit ticket question might be: *D'après vous, qu'est-ce qui est l'enfer? Est-ce la vérité de dire "L'enfer, c'est les Autres"? Expliquez-vous.* → According to you, what is hell? Is it true to say that "Hell, it is Others?" Explain.

READER TAKEAWAYS

- Cultural inclusivity extends beyond race and ethnicity to include religious beliefs, gender, and sexual identities.
- Educators should promote cultural inclusivity to address varying student inequalities that may exist in and out of the classroom.
- Implementing gamification in one's curricular framework is one method of promoting cultural inclusivity and being culturally responsive to all students.
- Educators can implement gamification with or without the use of technology.

REFERENCES

Abramovich, S., Schunn, C., and Higashi, R. M. (2013). Are badges useful in education?: It depends upon the type of badge and expertise of learner. *Educational Technology Research and Development, 61*(2), 217–32. doi: 10.1007/s11423-013-9289-2.

Anthony, S. L. (2011). Year two study of a community, school, and university partnership for urban schools: identifying resources which support the academic achievement for African American students. http://cdm15799.contentdm.oclc.org/cdm/ref/collection/p15799coll127/id/656449.

Armstrong, T. (2009). *Multiple intelligences in the classroom*. Alexandria: ASCD.

Artiles, A. J. (2011). Toward an interdisciplinary understanding of educational equity and difference the case of the racialization of ability. *Educational researcher, 40*(9), 431–45.

Bennett, S., Maton, K., and Kervin, L. (2007). The "digital natives" debate: A critical review of the evidence. *British Journal of Educational Technology, 39*(5), 775–86.

Bourdieu, P. (1998). *The state nobility: Elite schools in the field of power*. Stanford University Press.

Chen, Z., Po-Yao, C., Hsu, M., and Chin-Hung, T. (2013). Level up, my-pet: The effects of level-up mechanism of educational agents on student learning. *Journal of Educational Technology & Society, 16*(4), 111–n/a.

Cheng, Y. C. (2000). Cultural factors in educational effectiveness: A framework for comparative research. *School Leadership & Management, 20*(2), 207–25.

Conchas, G. (2001). Structuring failure and success: Understanding the variability in Latino school engagement. *Harvard Educational Review, 71*(3), 475–505.

Critical thinking as defined by the National Council for Excellence in Critical Thinking (1987). Retrieved November 27, 2014, from http://www.criticalthinking.org/pages/defining-critical-thinking/766.

de Freitas, S., and Liarokapis, F. (2011). Serious games: A new paradigm for education? In *Serious games and edutainment applications* (pp. 9–23): Springer.

DeLuca, C. (2013). Toward an interdisciplinary framework for educational inclusivity. *Canadian Journal of Education/Revue canadienne de l'éducation, 36*(1), 305–48.

Deterding, S., Dixon, D., Khaled, R., and Nacke, L. (2011). *From game design elements to gamefulness: Defining gamification.* Paper presented at the Proceedings of the Fifteenth International Academic MindTrek Conference: Envisioning Future Media Environments.

DiPardo, A., and Fehn, B. (2000). Depoliticizing multicultural education: The return to normalcy in a predominantly white high school. *Theory & Research in Social Education, 28*(2), 170–92.

Dupriez, V., Dumay, X., and Vause, A. (2008). How do school systems manage pupils' heterogeneity? *Comparative Education Review, 52*(2), 245–73.

California Department of Education (2009). Inclusion works! Creating child care programs that promote belonging for children with special needs. http://www.cde.ca.gov/sp/cd/re/documents/inclusionworks.pdf.

California Department of Education (2014). What are the common core standards? Retrieved April 1, 2014, from http://www.cde.ca.gov/re/cc/tl/whatareccss.asp.

Films for the Sciences, Films Media, and Claudia Levin, P. (2005). Educating to end inequity. New York: Films Media Group.

Hammond, Z. (2015, April 1). 3 tips to make any lesson culturally responsive. *Cult of Pedagogy*. https://www.cultofpedagogy.com/culturally-responsive-teaching-strategies/.

Hemmings, A. (2012). Four Rs for urban high school reform: Re-envisioning, reculturation, restructuring, and remoralization. *Improving Schools, 15*(3), 198–210.

Kapp, K. M. (2012). *The gamification of learning and instruction: Game-based methods and strategies for training and education*. San Francisco, CA: Pfeiffer.

Lee, J. J., and Hammer, J. (2011). Gamification in education: What, how, why bother? *Academic Exchange Quarterly, 15*(2), 146.

Linder, J., and Zichermann, G. (2010). *Game-based marketing: Inspire customer loyalty through rewards, challenges, and contests*: John Wiley & Sons.

McFarland, J. (2017). *Teacher perspectives on the implementation of gamification in a high school curriculum* (Order No. 10254484). Available from ProQuest Dissertations & Theses A&I; ProQuest Dissertations & Theses Global; ProQuest Dissertations & Theses Global A&I: The Humanities and Social Sciences Collection (1868502325). https://ezproxy.callutheran.edu/login?url=http://search.proquest.com.ezproxy.callutheran.edu/docview/1868502325?accountid=9839.

McFarland, J. (2020). Leveling up for the teacher-practitioner: Design & implementation of a gamified application. *Schools: Studies in Education, 17*(1), 115–35. https://doi.org/10.1086/708359.

McKinney, S. A., and Lowenhaupt, R. J. (2013). New directions for socially just educational leadership: Lessons from disability studies. In *Handbook of research on educational leadership for equity and diversity* (pp. 309–326). Routledge.

Nah, F. F.-H., Telaprolu, V. R., Rallapalli, S., and Venkata, P. R. (2013). Gamification of education using computer games. In *Human interface and the management of information. Information and interaction for learning, culture, collaboration and business* (pp. 99–107). Springer.

Nah, F. F.-H., Zeng, Q., Telaprolu, V. R., Ayyappa, A. P., and Eschenbrenner, B. (2014). Gamification of education: A review of literature. In *HCI in business* (pp. 401–9). Springer.

Petty, R., and Guthrie, J. (2000). Intellectual capital literature review: Measurement, reporting and management. *Journal of Intellectual Capital, 1*(2), 155–76.

Prensky, M. (2001). Digital natives, digital immigrants part 1. *On the Horizon, 9*(5), 1–6.

Russell, S. T., and Truong, N. L. (2001). Adolescent sexual orientation, race and ethnicity, and school environments: A national study of sexual minority youth of color. In *Troubling intersections of race and sexuality: Queer students of color and anti-oppressive education* (pp. 113–30). Rowman & Littlefield.

Sheldon, L. (2004). *Character development and storytelling for games*. Boston, MA: Course Technology Crisp.

Tomlinson, C. A. (1999). Mapping a route toward differentiated instruction. *Educational leadership, 57*, 12–17.

Tomlinson, C. A. (2001). *How to differentiate instruction in mixed-ability classrooms*: ASCD.

Trifonas, P. (2003). Pedagogies of difference: Locating otherness. In P. Trifonas (Ed.), *Pedagogies of difference: Rethinking education for social change* (pp. 1–9). New York: RoutledgeFalmer.

Tulloch, R. (2014). Reconceptualising gamification: Play and pedagogy. *Digital Culture & Education, 6*(4), 317–33.

Van Eck, R. (2006). Digital game-based learning: It's not just the digital natives who are restless. *Educause Review, 41*(2), 16.

Wiggins, G. P. (1998). *Educative assessment: Designing assessments to inform and improve student performance*. Volume 1. San Francisco, CA: Jossey-Bass.

Chapter 9

Culturally Responsive Teaching in a Virtual Classroom

Heather Dean

We should all know that diversity makes for a rich tapestry, and we must understand that all the threads of the tapestry are equal in value no matter what their color is.

—Maya Angelou

EXPECTED LEARNING OUTCOMES

- Readers will gain perspective via one teacher's experience with virtual teaching during COVID-19.
- Readers will understand the definition of culturally responsive teaching.
- Readers will gain insights into practical suggestions for the design of a virtual classroom that considers culturally responsive teaching.
- Readers will gain insights into practical suggestions for culturally responsive teaching in a virtual classroom.

TEACHER NARRATIVE

From Lucy Borba, Third-Year Teacher

A quote I recently found spoke to me. It goes like this: "The art of life lies in a constant readjustment to our surroundings'" (Kakuzō Okakura, *The Book of Tea*). This quote has embodied my teaching career, especially since COVID and distance learning. I began my teaching career in the middle of a school year. That in itself is challenging. Then the World Health Organization declared the coronavirus a global pandemic and weeks later Governor Newsom shut down schools.

I was just beginning to get into the groove of having a routine, getting into the final unit of our English class, and getting to know the students. No one knew what to expect; we were all on the same page trying to figure out how to teach through a screen. Plus, we teachers were told not to worry about the students who were happy with their grade. We only had to concern ourselves with those students who were failing.

Every day we checked for assignments being turned in and graded them. Every day we posted assignments online for those students who were failing. Every day we were reaching out to students who were failing. All of this happening at the same time of uncertainties of what will take place for the next school year.

Fast forward a few months, hundreds of emails, more tabs open on your computer researching how to teach virtually than you know what to do with, and finally having the certainty that you are teaching from your empty classroom. Our district did everything possible to make sure no child was left behind due to lack of internet access, but we still had students who were not able to attend class.

Our district also did everything possible to make sure no child was left behind due to not having a device, but we still had high school students who had to give up their device to their younger siblings so they could attend school. Additionally, the high school student was left to supervise their younger siblings; they were the adult in the house. If anything, distance learning placed a spotlight on the inequities that our students face on a daily basis when it comes to technology and attending school.

Every day of teaching was a reflection of what went well, what did not go well, what could have gone better, and what needs to change. The obvious change was getting our students back into their desks and in our classrooms, but that was not going to happen until much later. As we know, nothing can get done in a hurry; therefore, I knew I needed to make small changes and take baby steps.

In reflecting on my routine and reaching out to my colleagues on campus and in the Induction Program (yes, I was going through that as well), one small change I made was to create a playlist of songs. The songs were from all genres and played while students "entered" the classroom. In the chat box, I would have students say "great song" or "Wow! You listen to this kind of music?!" Students would begin to request songs and I would add them to the playlist (as long as they were appropriate for school).

Finally, I also discovered that students just want to know that we want them to be there, that we care about them and that they are loved. In order to do that I wanted to make sure students saw that. My slides would be displayed showing messages of inclusion such as "Everyone is welcome" and "I'm so glad you are here today!" and "Multilingualism is my superpower."

I saw some change with my ELD students, but the most change happened with my college prep students. With these small changes, I was able to make connections with students through a computer screen. Some would turn on their cameras and talk to me before class. Others would start to turn on their cameras to talk to one another. Still others would begin to feel comfortable with writing in the chat with either a classmate or with me. Finally, others felt comfortable enough to write in the chat that they were having a hard time with everything. I would take the time the student needed to be there for them and if I got to my lesson, I got to it. If I did not get to the lesson, I did not get to the lesson. The mental health of my students was my priority at that time.

As I reflect back on the journey of distance learning I realize it made me a better teacher. It made me hypersensitive to what the students say in my classroom about what is going on in their lives, especially when it comes to their mental health. Distance learning has given me the permission to reflect back onto how lessons went in my class. What went well for me to duplicate it? What needs to be changed? What needs to be scratched completely? It also gave me the permission to ask myself "how are *you* feeling today?"

I end with this saying that has been told to me throughout my time in the classroom, virtually and in person: you cannot pour into your students if *your* cup is not overflowing. Your mental health is just as important as your students.' Allow yourself the freedom to just do you and be happy in the profession in which you love and are passionate about.

CULTURALLY RESPONSIVE TEACHING DEFINED, AND REDEFINED

Gloria Ladson-Billings (1995) articulated and defined culturally relevant pedagogy as being composed of three components:

1. Student Learning: The students' intellectual growth and moral development but also their ability to problem solve and reason.
2. Cultural Competence: Skills that support students to affirm and appreciate their culture of origin while developing fluency in at least one other culture.
3. Critical Consciousness: The ability to identify, analyze, and solve real-world problems, especially those that result in societal inequalities.

Geneva Gay (2010), a professor of education at the University of Washington, defines culturally responsive teaching (CRT) as "using cultural knowledge, prior experiences, frames of reference, and performance styles of ethnically diverse students to make learning encounters more relevant and effective for them. It teaches to and through the strengths of these students."

Essentially, both of these definitions provide directional support for educators in empowering their students. While effective educators intuitively understand that relationships are at the heart of creating a pathway to learning, CRT helps to define the necessity of this for underserved populations of students and begins to support teachers in understanding how to penetrate existing barriers in order to propel all students forward.

In 2019, the COVID pandemic highlighted the need for CRT in a dramatic way. As schools across the nation were forced into virtual learning environments, the gaps in need became increasingly obvious. The digital divide became a barrier for the success of many students; however, a disproportionate number of these students were Black teens.

According to the American Consortium for Equity in Education, "a quarter of Black teens say they can't always finish their homework . . . whereas just 4 percent of White teens and 6 percent of Latinx teens say they have the same problem" (2020). This inequity likely has contributed to further gaps in education among minority students as K–12 education has returned to pre-COVID practices.

Within this context, CRT needs to continue to be defined for all educators but also redefined in light of the impact of COVID. Educators need to be given a toolbox to support them in understanding best practices, methods for implementation, and time for reflection on their evolving CRT pedagogy.

BEST PRACTICES FOR THE DESIGN OF A CULTURALLY RELEVANT VIRTUAL CLASSROOM

Even prior to COVID-19, distance learning was the fastest growing mode of learning (Vaughan et al., 2013). However, all modes of distance (synchronous, asynchronous, and hybrid) learning exploded with the COVID pandemic.

The Community of Inquiry (CoI) Framework (figure 9.1) can support educators in their design of online learning experiences. Within this framework, the learning experience is defined by three presences: cognitive, social, and teaching (Garrison et al., 2000).

The cognitive presence is defined as the meaning making through discourse, reflection, and critical thinking. Social presence is the creating of a safe learning environment characterized by the building of a community where all participants feel safe and comfortable to share and ask questions.

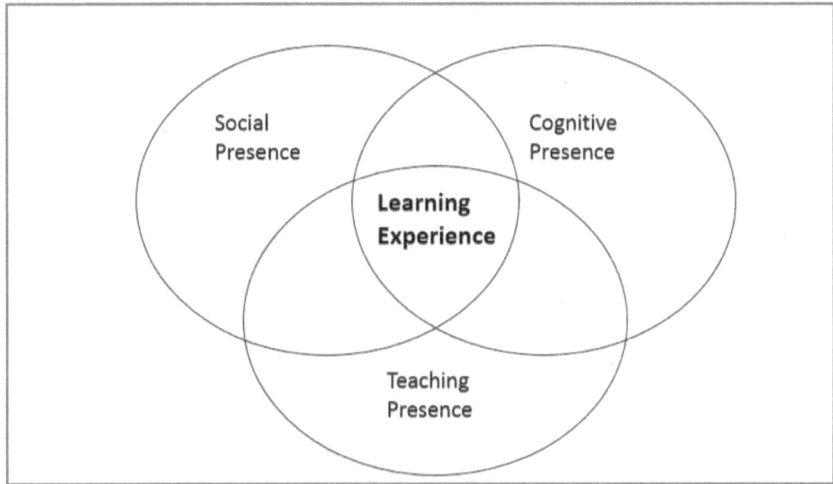

Figure 9.1. Community of Inquiry Framework.

Finally, the teaching presence consists of several components. First is the design and organization of the learning experience. Next is the design of the learning experience to provide opportunities for discourse and engagement among the students and between the student and teacher. Finally is the direct instruction from the teacher to share their expertise.

The interaction of these three components creates the learning experience for the student and all three aspects must be considered in order to develop an effective online learning experience.

Culturally Relevant Pedagogy in an Online Modality

Within the CRT framework, virtual instructors must strive to meet the various components of CRT (student learning, cultural competence, and critical consciousness) within diverse modalities. This can prove to be more challenging within the limitations of an online environment; however, with intentional efforts, these limitations can be overcome.

Pedagogy must be included that supports an understanding of various learning styles as well as various communication styles. Some specific strategies to consider include video introductions, weekly overviews/agendas, video grade feedback, and synchronous live meetings (Montelongo, 2019).

Design of Online Learning Courses

Prior to students enrolling in the course, an online educator must invest substantial time into designing and organizing the online course in a manner that is conducive to student learning and success. Garrison et al. state, "Designing a blended learning experience should start with organizing the content and activities. In addition, clear objectives for content and performance expectations will ensure a productive educational experience . . . it is crucial that the course outline, assignments, and grading rubric be posted well before the course begins" (2000, 35).

Finally, the online educator needs to lean on student feedback for continued reflection on their practices and organization of the learning management system (LMS), syllabus, and tentative schedule in order to promote continual improvement (Garrison, 2000, 43).

Teacher Impact

Success of online modalities of learning greatly depends on several factors within the control of the online teacher. It is essential that the instructor remains organized in their learning management system, materials, and teaching. Students easily become frustrated when materials have conflicting information and/or the educator is underprepared for the specific challenges of an online course.

Furthermore, it is essential that the professor be accessible via email, Zoom office hours, or other avenues of connecting in order for students to feel engaged, cared for, and supported in their learning. Relationships are essential to the success of the virtual classroom (Fink, 2016). Without access to the instructor, students will likely falter and feel disconnected from their learning.

The Use of Technology Tools

Educators teaching online need to invest time in understanding the technology tools available to enhance their instruction and increase student engagement (Montelongo, 2019). While the LMS provides a foundation and shell for the course, this should not be the lone form of technology use in an online course. More information about technology will be presented toward the end of the chapter.

BEST PRACTICES FOR CULTURALLY RESPONSIVE TEACHING IN A VIRTUAL CLASSROOM

High-Impact Practices

Virtual learning is often viewed from a deficit perspective; however, continued research and pedagogical exploration are proving that virtual learning is not only a matter of convenience but also an option for rigorous learning opportunities (Montelongo, 2019). Virtual instruction can successfully implement culturally relevant teaching practices as well. An initial place to start is to consider ways to build a community of learners, both between students and between student and teacher.

Building a Community of Learners

Transitioning from practices of community building that many educators are accustomed to within face-to-face environments to the virtual environment may prove challenging; however, the virtual environment does allow for community building that is impactful and effective with the use of a bit of ingenuity and trial and error. Keep reading for some ideas!

Icebreakers

Everyone cringes when they hear that icebreakers are on the agenda, and yet they support relationships and increase class-wide community. In one of my recent classes, I introduced the icebreaker two truths and a lie, a popular get-to-know-you activity where each student creates three personal statements in which one is a lie. Then other students have to determine the lie.

First, I modeled this. My three statements are shown in figure 9.2.

Then I gave students five minutes to write their three statements and then placed them in breakout rooms of approximately four students to share out. At the end of class, each student had to email me an answer to the prompt showing in figure 9.3.

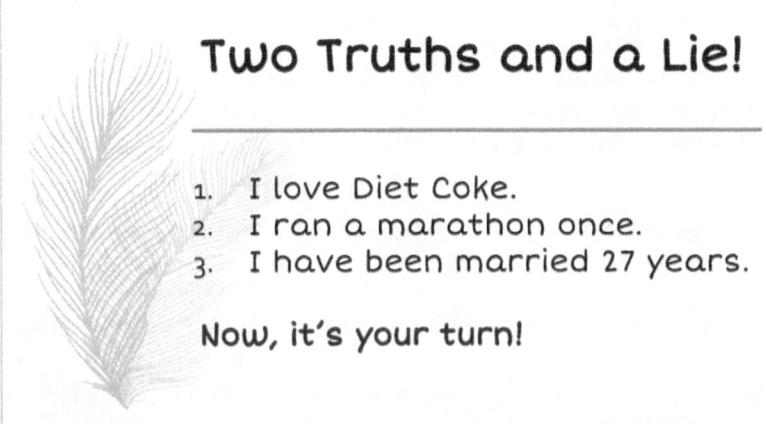

Figure 9.2. Two Truths and a Lie.

Exit Ticket

Share <u>one</u> of the following:
- Something you wanted to say today that you didn't say
- Question you have
- Something you enjoyed about class today
- Something about class that could have been better for you

Figure 9.3. Exit Ticket

Reading through my students' responses to the exit ticket, I was surprised to receive positive feedback regarding the icebreaker activity. The following is a sample of a few of my students' thoughts:

> I also really liked the little ice breaker you had us do. I have always thought it's important to start with ice breakers, so we get to know other people in our class and find similar interests between one another. I'm really excited to see what this course will be like this semester!

> Normally I hate icebreaker activities like most people do. Today though, I had fun and had a good time during our icebreaker activity in our break-out rooms. I liked the group that I got put into and we had a fun conversation while playing the two truths and one lie game.

> I really enjoyed the class today in general, and one of the parts that I enjoyed from the class was when we got separated into discussion groups to talk about the two truths and a lie. I had a fun time with it and got to know some of my peers. ☺

> I also enjoyed how you gave us the opportunity to do the ice breaker with other students because it gives us the courage to make new connections that way!

While it is rare for people to be excited by the prospect of icebreaker activities, the feedback from my students confirms that these types of community-building activities are necessary to improve the culture and comfortability within the class.

Group Introductions

Assignments to facilitate group introductions early in the semester facilitate community building as well. In one of the classes I teach, students are assigned to groups and given a due date to introduce themselves to the class in three slides. This allows each student to introduce themselves and their interests and share important photos from their life. This allows me as a teacher to know my students in a more personal way and supports me in planning class sessions with my students' unique personalities and interests in mind.

Entry Ticket Check-In

Brief entry ticket check-ins can be a great way to assess the well-being of your students as well as to assess student understanding on new topics. Entry tickets can be done in a variety of ways by asking simple questions that students can answer in the chat or in breakout rooms. These check-ins can be tied into social-emotional well-being, individual interests, or the curriculum.

During the pandemic, many educators developed creative ways to check in with students. For example, in figure 9.4, students would rate how they are feeling on a scale of cat. These types of activities can lower the affective

Figure 9.4. How Are You Feeling Today Chart.

filters of our students by allowing them to share their current state of being as well as to understand the wide array of emotions and feelings that the community of learners are bringing to the current class session.

In the next example with SpongeBob, I had my student teachers tie their answers to how they were doing in their field work. In the chat and in a class discussion, students shared why they rated themselves the way they did. This conversation allowed my class of student teachers to hear perspectives of others in their same situation, helping them understand they are not alone.

This quick exercise helped me as an instructor understand the areas my students were finding success in as well as other areas that they were struggling in. Listening to the perspectives and experiences of my students helps to inform my future instruction based on their needs.

The Use of Breakout Rooms

In the traditional classroom, students form relationships naturally with informal conversations throughout the class as well as by being in close proximity to one another. These relationships still need to be nurtured in the virtual classroom but will take a bit more intention to do so.

The use of breakout rooms allows for students to begin to know one another in a smaller setting. Instructors should be strategic in providing regular opportunities for students to interact in breakout rooms. For the time to be effective, instructors should give clear instructions as to what students should accomplish during this time and what they should be prepared to do upon return to the whole session class.

Figure 9.5. Field Work Chat: How's It Going?

Early in the semester, I incorporate time in these breakout sessions for students to introduce themselves. I also think it is important to mix and match the groups. In my class of student teachers, I have four ways I routinely create my groups.

- By professional learning groups (English teacher candidates, math teacher candidates, etc.)
- By interdisciplinary teams (groups composed of an English teacher, math teacher, science teacher, and a history teacher)
- Random groups (selected by me; sometimes I will put them in groups by the district they are student teaching in or where they live)
- Random groups (selected by the computer)

This allows students to interact with and learn from the collective class community.

I have also found that students benefit from class time devoted to students meeting in predetermined groups prior to the whole class meeting to work on collective tasks and support one another throughout the course. My student teachers have a high-stakes performance task they must pass to be credentialed. Routinely, I schedule thirty to forty-five minutes for students to meet in groups to peer edit and discuss this task. They record their session and send it to me to receive credit for this portion of the class.

When I review these recordings, students are diligent in accomplishing the task they have been given; however, they also have natural conversations, commiserate with one another, and support one another in relationship to other course objectives. Feedback from students proves that this time is valuable to them, supports their growth, and is manageable because the time they meet is embedded within our course time.

Routines and Procedures

Routines and procedures are essential to the success of an online class. According to Pamela Cantor, our brains are "prediction machines that like order" (2020). Students of all ages benefit from understanding the patterns and expectations of the class. During the first class, the instructor can support the students by discussing the organization of the LMS, sharing the best methods and times for contacting the instructor for support and help, and by sharing the basic structures and routines of the class including how class time will be spent, how work will be turned in, and how student collaboration will be facilitated.

The following are some additional structures and routines that may benefit the online class:

Use of Time Before and After Zoom/Online Platform

The time before the online class begins is prime time to greet students and support the students in feeling comfortable with an instructor that they won't likely ever see in person. This time prior to class and again at the end of class is also a time for students to ask questions that they may not feel comfortable asking in a group or are more private in nature.

Use of Camera

In a virtual environment, teaching to blank black boxes is the lowest form of teaching. I strongly believe online teaching can never be optimal without the routine use of cameras to foster relationships, to hold students accountable for learning, and to give the instructor visual cues as to how the students are responding to the presented material.

For example, the use of cameras allows the instructor to gauge the class's understanding of the concept being taught. Nodding heads, smiles, and tilted heads all support an instructor in assessing the understanding of a class and help the teacher make in-the-moment instructional decisions.

The camera also acts to build routines for certain instructional strategies. In my class, when I have students complete a quick write or other individual activities that require time to process, I have my students turn off their cameras. They are instructed to turn on their cameras again once they have completed the assignment. This simple routine acts as a great tool for the instructor to allow adequate time for students to complete various tasks while also giving students time to process without the added pressure of having the camera on.

Guest Speakers

Maintaining engagement and interest in the online class takes extra effort. The routine of inviting in guest speakers from time to time can allow students to learn from others. Guest speakers will present and engage students in ways that differ from the routine instruction and help maintain interest in the content of the course.

Expert Question and Answer Time

In most classes, students are more engaged when their own questions guide instruction. Time is well spent to devote instructional time to allowing for question and answer sessions with an expert panel. When I taught eighth-grade English, we studied the Holocaust and read both *The Diary of Anne Frank* and *Night*. As a culminating activity, a panel of Holocaust survivors came in and shared with students. While this was in a traditional classroom, these types of activities still hold value in the online modality.

In my current role as a teacher educator, my student teachers benefit from planned time to ask questions to a panel of practitioners about the day-to-day questions they have as they learn to manage a class, design a lesson plan, and balance all of their responsibilities.

Breaks, Brain Breaks, and Activity Changes

Learning is optimized when we allow a time for general breaks to stretch and go to the restroom as well as brain breaks to reenergize our learning. Depending on our age, we can only actively process information for twelve to twenty minutes. In a typical middle school period, the brain processes for twelve to fifteen minutes before it cycles down for ten minutes (Hammon, 2015). This is an important consideration in the traditional classroom, but it is vital in the virtual classroom as well.

There are many benefits to planned breaks and changes in activities. Switching up what we do in class eases exhaustion levels, lowers frustration levels, and helps to refresh the mind for new learning (Immordino-Yang et al., 2012).

Simple breaks that allow for movement, whether to allow for a bathroom break or an incorporated activity, increase blood flow to the brain, which helps with attention and focus.

Research shows that students learn more quickly after they have exercised. In one study, students learned vocabulary words 20 percent faster after exercising (Schmidt-Kassow et al., 2013).

Additionally, the brain is attracted to novelty. The brain stays alert when there is a certain amount of change within the structure of the class. Sometimes, the modifications can be very simple. Perhaps you tend to use Google Slides and decide to incorporate Pear Deck for a lesson, or rather than using the chat feature in Google, you use mentimeter to gather responses.

Here are some links to activities that allow for brain breaks:

- https://quickdraw.withgoogle.com/
  This application prompts users to sketch, on their phone or other device, simple images. While the user is sketching, the application will guess what has been drawn. This provides a quick and easy break for students and can also be used to introduce the topic of sketch noting.
- https://www.youtube.com/watch?v=W2e5Sm5xisw
  There are many videos like this on YouTube. This is a Name That Tune activity and can be used in a variety of ways in a virtual classroom. Use it as a quick entry activity, brain break, or transitional activity.

- https://www.youtube.com/watch?v=cZdO2e8K29o
  This video walks students through a three-minute instructional video to create an origami butterfly.
- https://www.youtube.com/watch?v=c1Ndym-IsQg

This video is a short meditation that may be useful to embed within an online class as well.

Incorporating breaks into the online class will support students' attention level and engagement and is an important component to the successful lesson planning of online educators.

Have Fun Structuring Your Online Class

Online teaching allows for flexibility in course delivery. In the last few years, as I have taught exclusively online, I have learned that Zoom fatigue is, in fact, very real. To alleviate this with my students, I have tried various ways of structuring my online class to maintain engagement and interactivity.

One strategy that has been successful for me is to structure my teaching schedule to have two synchronous courses followed by an asynchronous course. While I understand that this may not be possible for all situations, as educators, we should be comfortable in trying out new pathways to teaching.

My students have enjoyed that we meet as a community two times in a row and interact together and see one another; however, they appreciate that every third session is asynchronous. This allows them some flexibility as to when they complete the work and gives them a break from being online.

To keep students organized during our asynchronous sessions, I provide Google Slides similar to what they are accustomed to seeing during our synchronous sessions; however, they are also given a link to a Google Form. This Google Form is utilized to gather their answers to questions I have embedded throughout the asynchronous Google Slides.

Pedagogical Practices and Choices

The pedagogical practices and choices designed by the online educator are essential to promoting a CRT environment. Some methods are easy to implement. Instructors can incorporate readings from various perspectives and cultures as well as using the Zoom background to showcase various images and art from a multitude of cultures. (AVID Open Access, 2022). However, other ideas may take more planning. Please read on for additional ideas.

Voice and Choice

Voice and choice are important in all types of learning but must not be ignored in the online class. Voice and choice allow students the freedom to explore topics of interest to them while staying within the guidelines provided by the instructor. Voice and choice also allow students to demonstrate their learning in a variety of ways from traditional assessments to project-based learning opportunities. Allowing students agency in this way supports CRT.

Build Vocabulary

Inequities in academic settings often stem from students' differing access and understanding of academic vocabulary. According to the Common Core State Standards, "It is widely accepted among researchers that the difference in students' vocabulary levels is a key factor in disparities in academic achievement . . . but that vocabulary instruction has been neither frequent nor systematic in most schools" (2014).

The culturally responsive teacher, whether in a face-to-face or virtual setting, will invest time in supporting students in the development of academic vocabulary. Wordle and Tagul are wonderful tools that can support both instructor and student in targeting academic vocabulary. These sites create word clouds from documents. The more often a word is used, the larger it appears within the word cloud. Teachers can use this to create a visual of important vocabulary words that should be pretaught to students before delving into a complex text. Furthermore, students may find these sites supportive of their writing in identifying word choices that they may overuse in their academic writing. Please continue reading for a sample of vocabulary acquisition strategies that can be helpful in many learning environments.

KIM Strategy   This strategy utilizes the acronym KIM to support the learning of new vocabulary.

- K: **K**ey vocabulary
- I: **I**mportant information/user-friendly definition
- M: Visual that acts as a **m**emory device

Then students should write a context-rich sentence to show understanding of the vocabulary word.

In a traditional setting, flashcards work great for this exercise and become a study tool to support students in learning the new vocabulary words. However, this can also be utilized virtually by creating the KIM graphic organizer within a Google Document or Google Slides. Students can work on this independently or within small groups.

K Key Idea	I Information	M Memory Clue
democracy	a system of government by the whole population or all the eligible members of a state, typically through elected representatives	
republic	a state in which supreme power is held by elected representatives of the people and which has president rather than a monarch	

Figure 9.6. KIM Graphic Organizer.

Frayer Model The Frayer Model is another valuable tool for academic vocabulary instruction. This particular strategy works best with larger concepts because students must include a definition and facts/characteristics but also examples and nonexamples.

As with the KIM strategy, this can be adapted to be used within Google Docs or Slides. Students could collaborate on slides and present their information to the whole class to learn various concepts within a unit.

These strategies and many others are important to utilize in instruction to support all students in having access to the curriculum. Eric Jensen, shares, "Vocabulary instruction for adolescents shows not only increases in gray matter but that the increased density of gray matter was correlated with higher vocabulary test scores" (2016).

Teach Concepts Using Multiple Methods

For learning to be optimal, it must be layered with different access points to the content objectives. In lesson design, the instructor needs to consider the various ways to build understanding of new topics. Direct instruction certainly has a place and often is a great foundation for presenting new information; however, educators must consider what other points of entry need to be provided for students to have a deeper understanding of the information being taught. Would a video help to provide the visual that many students will need, including second language learners? Might students' learning be best supported by group collaboration, possibly using the jigsaw strategy? Can comic strips be brought in to teach the nuances of a topic? Could memes and gifs allow for engagement and humor as topics are discussed? The bottom line is

Culturally Responsive Teaching in a Virtual Classroom 193

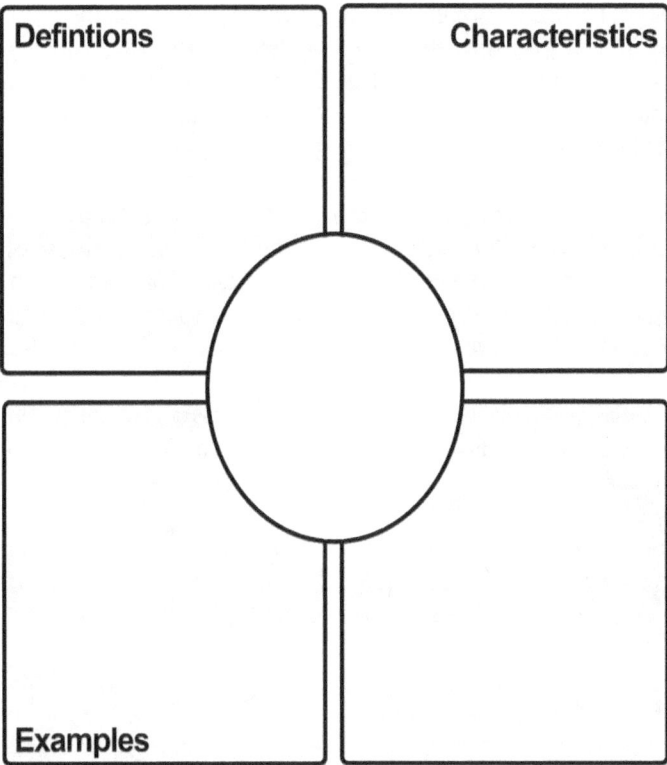

Figure 9.7. Frayer Model

that all educators must choose wisely and with intentionality the strategies and tools used to instruct. Teaching is both an art and a science. Educators should allow themselves the privilege of creating lessons that tap into both the art and science of teaching.

Engagement Strategies

Maintaining student engagement in an online setting takes diligent effort. Traditional learning settings provide plenty of challenges to engagement; however, the virtual student is at home with all of the distractions of family, friends, and the access to their own environment. Furthermore, distractions via technology are always present. Students can be present in the classroom, while playing video games, answering emails, texting, and browsing the internet. Instructors must do their best to hold students accountable and engaged despite all of these challenges.

Gestures   The use of gestures is still a viable option for the online classroom. If students are using their cameras, they can visually show you their hand gestures; however, they will also have the option of showing you a virtual thumbs up or an emoticon to interact with the content and questions posed by the instructor.

Scavenger Hunt   Incorporating activities that allow for movement within an online class keeps students alert. Even in adult classes, the use of a scavenger hunt can be incorporated for various purposes. For example, an instructor can place small groups of students in breakout rooms and task them with finding out what they have in common. Once they have decided on something they have in common, they must find an item in their house that symbolizes the commonality. This can be repeated with discussions on what characteristics are different within the group. These ideas can also be adapted to coincide with the course content.

Use of the Chat Feature   The chat feature allows for student interaction. Instructors can have students respond to a warm-up question, rate their level of agreement to various statements, and ask questions privately to the instructor.

Google Slides for Groups   Google Slides allow for small group and whole class collaboration. Students can be placed in breakout rooms to create Google Slides as directed by the instructor. The teacher can also create Google Slides and assign individuals specific slides to complete. Google Slides are a simple way to facilitate engagement and accountability within a lesson.

Technology Tools

Technology tools offer today's educators great options to support student engagement within virtual learning. While no one can be an expert in all of the tech options available, each educator can become adept at several that serve their context.

Mentimeter   This is a tool I began using during COVID. There are so many varieties of ways to engage students and gather information with this tool. Mentimeter can create word clouds based on student answers, create rankings and scales, as well as making use of the multiple choice and open-ended format.

What Else?   Other technology tools that are supportive of online learning include Kahoot, Edpuzzle, Jamboard, Quizziz, and Flipgrid. There are endless possibilities with more tools being developed daily. Educators should strive to master a few new tools every few months to continue to aid students in engagement and to increase the novelty of presentation and accountability methods.

Appropriate Assessments for Online Learning

Assessment in the online classroom is still vital for the instructor to make instructional decisions throughout the course. The following are ideas that extend beyond the traditional test and quiz.

Oral Presentations Think fast paced. Students present on a brief topic to the class in five minutes or fewer utilizing fifteen slides.

Digital One Pager Students create some type of visual presentation to share what they understand about the assigned topic. This could be a Google Slide, graphic organizer, word cloud, or other type of visual representation. Students could also do a one-page written reflection.

Recorded Small Group Sessions Students can be assigned to meet in small groups to collaborate and discuss assignments. These sessions can be recorded and sent to the instructor.

CONCLUSION

Virtual instruction necessitates the delivery of culturally responsive strategies. This pedagogy is responsive to student needs and affirming of student cultures. CRT also supports the motivation of students and supports critical thinking. The virtual culturally responsive teacher must be continually reflective of their practices and seek the feedback of their students in order to create meaningful learning experiences that hold the promise of rigor, strong collaborations, and the sharing of ideas. The virtual classroom holds the potential to be all of this and more with the intentionality of the instructor and the engagement of the student.

READER TAKEAWAYS

- Online modalities can offer meaningful opportunities to create a community of learners/
- CRT in an online modality takes intentionality, but is possible.

- Online teaching is not a less than experience. Online teaching holds potential for rigorous learning to take place.
- The success of online teaching requires strong organization from the instructor and within the learning management system.
- Online educators have a responsibility to incorporate instructional strategies that support engagement and interactivity between students and between the instructor and students.

REFERENCES

American Consortium for Equity in Education (2020, April 16). *Covid-19 facilitates the need for culturally competent educators*. Equity & Access Pre K–12 | The American Consortium for Equity in Education. Retrieved February 9, 2023, from https://www.ace-ed.org/covid-19-facilitates-the-need-for-culturally-competent-educators/.

AVID Open Access. (2022, August 11). *Create a culturally relevant classroom*. Retrieved February 19, 2023, from https://avidopenaccess.org/resource/create-a-culturally-relevant-classroom/.

California Department of Education, California Common Core State Standards (2013). Sacramento, California.

Cantor, P. (2020, July 30). The stress of this moment might be hurting kids' development. *Education Next*. Retrieved February 12, 2023, from https://www.educationnext.org/stress-of-coronavirus-might-be-hurting-kids-development-but-relationships-routines-resilience-can-help/.

Fink, L. D. (2016). Five high impact teaching practices: A list of possibilities. *Collected Essays on Learning and Teaching, 9*, 3–18.

Garrison, D. R., Anderson, T., and Archer, W. (2000). Critical inquiry in a text-based environment: Computer conferencing in higher education. *The Internet and Higher Education, 2*(2–3), 87–105. https://doi.org/10.1016/s1096-7516(00)00016-6.

Gay, G. (2010). *Culturally responsive teaching: Theory, research, and practice*. Second edition. Teachers College Press.

Hammon, Z. (2015). *Culturally responsive teaching and the brain*. Corwin.

Immordino-Yang, M. H., Christodoulou, J. A., and Singh, V. (2012). Rest is not idleness: Implications of the brain's default mode for human development and education. *Perspectives on Psychological Science, 7*(4), 352–64. https://doi.org/10.1177/1745691612447308.

Jensen, E. (2016). *Poor students, rich teaching: Mindsets for change*. Solution Tree Press.

Ladson-Billings, G. (1995). Toward a theory of culturally relevant pedagogy. *American Educational Research Journal, 32*(3), 465–91.

Montelongo, R. (2019). Less than/more than: Issues associated with high impact online teaching and learning. *Administrative Issues Journal Education Practice and Research, 9*(1). https://doi.org/10.5929/9.1.5.

Schmidt-Kassow, M., Deusser, M., Thiel, C., Otterbein, S., Montag, C., Reuter, M., Banzer, W., and Kaiser, J. (2013). Physical exercise during encoding improves vocabulary learning in young female adults: A neuroendocrinological study. *PloS ONE, 8*(5). https://doi.org/10.1371/journal.pone.0064172.

Vaughan, N. D., Cleveland-Innes, M., and Garrison, D. R. (2013). *Teaching in blended learning environments: Creating and sustaining communities of inquiry.* AU Press.

About the Authors

Dan Bryan, MA, has been teaching music in the public schools for nearly three decades in the Central Valley of California, focusing on students in grades 5 through 12. He currently serves as a Music Teacher/Lead for Stanislaus Union School District (Modesto, CA). Additionally, he serves as adjunct faculty in Teacher Education at California State University, Stanislaus.

Lindsay Bryan, MA, taught theatre for twenty years in a public high school in addition to being a teaching artist in the community for children in grades K–8. She is currently a theatre instructor at Modesto Junior College and is passionate about community building and making theatre accessible for all people.

Lauren E. Burrow, EdD, is a MotherScholar to three young adolescents. She taught a variety of grade levels (PK–12) as a primary classroom and theatre arts teacher for 10 years and has since spent the last decade in teacher education where she uses the fine arts and community-based Service-Learning to help prepare pre-service teachers to engage in meaningful partnerships to address social (in)justices in local communities.

Leona Calkins, PhD, has over a decade of secondary teaching experience having taught a variety of high school social studies classes before becoming a high school librarian. Dr. Calkins is currently an assistant professor of teacher education at California State University, Stanislaus. Dr. Calkins' current research interests focus on social studies education, teacher leadership, and preservice teacher burnout.

Heather Dean, PhD, has spent her career in education teaching English at the junior high and high school level. Currently, she is an associate professor of teacher education at California State University, Stanislaus with research interests in teacher retention, literacy education as well as understanding the best practices for training new teachers.

Dana Mayhall, PhD, is currently an assistant professor in teacher education at Abilene Christian University in Abilene, Texas. She has over twenty years of experience serving as teacher and administrator in elementary and secondary education, and over ten years of experience in teacher education. She works with teacher candidates in their school placements as well as providing instruction in educational foundations and methods, multicultural perspectives and culturally relevant pedagogy, and reframing learning at the graduate level.

Jon McFarland, EdD, has been an educator for over two decades and has worked at multiple levels in public and private education. He is currently an assistant professor of teacher education with research interests including the utilization of gamification in academic settings, issues of student motivation and engagement, effective uses of educational technology, and matters of equity and diversity in secondary schools.

Derek Riddle, PhD, has taught secondary English and has had experiences teaching at all grade levels (7–12), remedial to advanced students, and both in urban and rural areas for about 10 years. He currently is an assistant professor of teacher education at California State University, Stanislaus with research interests in teacher professional development, co-teaching, English education, literacy education, and teacher recruitment and retention.

Jennifer Rumsey, PhD, has been a public school educator for twenty five years. She has taught reading and English to students in grades 6–11, served as English Department Chair on two campuses, and is currently a middle school counselor. A mother of two children with ADHD, Jennifer has researched and read extensively about ADHD, and she works to inform educators about best practices in serving children with this disability.

Harleen Singh, PhD, is an assistant professor of education at California State University Stanislaus. She taught science at the secondary school level for seventeen years. Her research interest lies in teacher knowledge and teacher development. Specifically, her research centers on understanding the development of newly hired science teachers teaching out-of-field.

José M. Pavez, PhD, is an assistant professor of elementary and secondary science education at Western Illinois University. He is a former biology and science teacher who has extensive teaching experience, from elementary grades to the graduate level in culturally and linguistically diverse settings. Dr. Pavez has been involved in educational research since 2012. His research interest has been around science teacher education, nature of science, and science methods courses. He has collaborated with national and international research teams, and he is currently collaborating on an NSF grant studying resilience in newly hired science and math teachers.

Amber E. Wagnon, PhD, was a public school secondary educator for over a decade. She is currently an assistant professor of secondary education at Stephen F. Austin State University where her research interests include literacy education, experiential learning, and public school advocacy.

www.ingramcontent.com/pod-product-compliance
Lightning Source LLC
Chambersburg PA
CBHW030653230426
43665CB00011B/1067